THE BRETON LAYS IN MIDDLE ENGLISH

THE BRETON LAYS IN MIDDLE ENGLISH

EDITED BY THOMAS C. RUMBLE

WAYNE STATE UNIVERSITY PRESS
DETROIT

95 94 93 92 91 7 6 5 4 3

Library of Congress Catalog Card Number 65-11629

Thise olde gentil Britouns in hir dayes
of diverse aventures maden layes
rymeyed in hir firste Briton tonge,
whiche layes with hir instrumentz they songe
or elles redden hem for hir plesaunce,
and oon of hem have I in remembraunce . . .

Chaucer, *The Franklin's Prologue*

Preface

OF THE MANY LITERARY FORMS of medieval times few are more likely to appeal to the modern reader than the so-called Breton Lay. No doubt this is partly so because the lays were themselves composites of so much else of medieval literature, and lent themselves so readily to the imitation and popularization of all manner of "storial thyng." They were, above all, popular tales, designed to appeal to an audience less than learned, and one which had little time or taste for such forms as the longer, often intricately psychological courtly romances, or the overtly didactic and moralistic saints' lives. But more important, except that they were composed originally to be heard rather than read, the lays strove for many of the same effects as the modern short story. In length they had to be brief enough to be heard through on a single occasion and often by an itinerant audience, gathered either with some formality for an evening's entertainment in the hall of a manor house, or simply informally around the "maker" at some busy intersection of a town. In subject, though here the maker had a wide variety of lore to draw upon, they had to center upon some single character who must usually be brought through a series of critical situations to a happy end. In treatment they had to be dramatic, allowing the maker partly from memory, partly through improvisation, to pass quickly from one climactic scene or episode to the next, and to catch and hold his audience not only through his narration of the events themselves, but through the very spiritedness of his performance.

There are in Middle English eight tales that purport to be, or to be based upon, Breton Lays. Some of these have come down to us in single versions; others are extant in several manuscripts and early prints, the versions differing from each other largely in matters of length, dialect, and the degree of corruptness that is assumed to mark their distance from their originals in time and in the number of their copyings. All date from the fourteenth and fifteenth centuries, and all appear to derive ultimately from earlier and probably oral versions—with Chaucer's *Franklin's Tale* the most likely exception. Though all have been previously edited, they have never been brought together into a single volume; indeed most of them are only to be found either in separate editions that were prepared largely for scholarly audiences or in antiquarians' collections that are mostly quite old, quite poor, and quite difficult to obtain. Of the versions given here, the Rawlinson MS of *Sir Degaré* has not been edited except to give footnote citations of its variations from other manuscripts and early prints (see Bibliography, item 95); in a very poor manuscript, it is nevertheless one of the best remaining versions of that lay.

In this book, then, I have edited anew the eight Middle English Breton Lays and brought them together in the belief that a wider audience will find in them something of the same appeal and interest that students in my Middle English classes have found. They represent not only a remarkably wide range of the subjects and themes of medieval popular literature, but in a way the very wellsprings of English fiction. Though I have treated the manuscripts in most respects very conservatively, I have wanted the texts to accommodate, above all, the quickest reading possible by even the relatively inexperienced reader of Middle English: some of the force itself of the tales must have derived from the very rapidity of their pace. To this end I have expanded without indication the many abbreviations of the manuscripts, though I have tried always to make these expansions consistent with the unabbreviated forms written by each scribe. I have regularly converted *þ*'s and *ȝ*'s to their more modern equivalents in *th*, *g*, *gh*, and *y*; and have given always the modern form of such interchangeable pairs of letters as *i* and *y*, *u* and *v*. In a few of the manuscripts the letters *þ* and *d* are used with little consistency, in which case I have usually given the letter required by the modern form of the word except where a rhyme would be affected or where the scribe's preference is both clear and unobtrusive. This last change, as well as all others, I have indicated by giving the exact manuscript reading in footnotes. All capitalization and punctuation, of course, are mine, as is the paragraphing of the non-stanzaic lays.

In the further interest of aiding the reader who is unaccustomed to the vagaries of the Middle English vocabulary and its sometimes strange idiom and syntax, I have glossed on the same page those words and phrases that seem to me most likely to occasion difficulty and to require either explanation or a modern equivalent. In this respect I have no doubt far exceeded the need of anyone already familiar with Middle English and must beg forbearance; but I know all too well the frustration that results from interrupting the less experienced reader ten or twenty times per page by sending him to thumb a single glossary at the back of his book. For better or worse, I have also abandoned the brief head-notes that often precede each selection in a book of this kind. Such matters as language, dialect, meter, sources, authorship, date, literary relationships, paleographical descriptions—all these are very complex and, if they are to be gone into at all, deserve a great deal more attention than can be given them in short introductory notes; indeed they are subjects most appropriate either to classroom discussion or to the reader's independent study. I have included a fairly full bibliography which is designed to lead to the most essential information on all of these subjects.

My debts are many. I want especially to thank Professor R. M. Lumiansky for first kindling my interest in the inexhaustible wealth of medieval literature in general and Old and Middle English literature in particular. Miss Cecelia Pack of the Acquisitions Department of the Wayne State University Library was most helpful in obtaining photographs of the manuscripts here edited and placing them at my disposal. My wife is due no little credit for much of the typescript of this book, working in an unfamiliar language and from a hand, she claimed, often worse than that of the manuscript scribes. Finally, for permission to edit manuscripts in their keeping, I am grateful to the authorities of the National Library of Scotland, the Cambridge University Library, the Bodleian Library of Oxford, the British Museum, and the Huntington Library of California.

Thomas C. Rumble

1964

NOTE TO THE SECOND PRINTING:

I am most pleased that *The Breton Lays in Middle English* has proved useful enough to prompt a second and less expensive edition. In preparing this edition, I have taken the opportunity to correct a few obvious typographical errors, to revise a number of the footnote glosses, and to add a few recent items to the Bibliography.

T. C. Rumble
1967

Contents

Illustrations

Introduction

IN TWELFTH-CENTURY FRANCE and Norman England a story form called the "Breton Lay" was born and sprang to a remarkably quick and long-lived popularity. Its lineage is hard to trace in detail since, like so much of medieval story, it grew out of the oral tradition, and since even the earliest of its remaining written examples are already late and betray the embellishments of conscious literary hands. The designation *Breton* places its most important stage of development among those continental Armorican Celts whose skilled singers found in neighboring France and Normandy enthusiastic audiences for the tales they constructed with such fertile abandon from older lore. But the word *lai* points to a still earlier origin among the insular Celts of Wales and Ireland, in whose language it seems to have meant a short musical composition, or song, probably played on a harp-like instrument to accompany the telling of a tale.[1] Whether in this older oral tradition words and music followed a set melodic line in unison, whether they alternated in some conventional pattern,[2] or whether the instrument merely supplied a

[1] Other types of instruments are also often associated with the lays, especially the *viole*, and in fact two twelfth-century references imply that in some cases lays might have been performed on instruments alone: Wace speaks of "lays of viols, lays of rotes, lays of harps, lays of flutes" (*Roman de Brut*, ed. I. Arnold [SATF, 1938–40], 11. 10548–49); and Marie of France notes that the lay she tells of Guigemar is still to be heard played "on harp and on rote" (*Marie de France: Lais*, ed. A. Ewart [Oxford, 1952]; "Guigemar," 1. 885).

[2] This is the explanation accepted by A. J. Bliss (*Sir Launfal* [London, 1960], p. 17) on the basis of passages in the Anglo-Norman *Horn et Rimenhild* and Gottfried von Strassburg's *Tristan und Isold*; but both of these poems are

rhythmic accompaniment for the teller's tale, is now difficult to know. Of several early allusions, the one that seems most promising of a single answer to the question tantalizingly allows the possibility of all three: Thomas of Britain speaks of a lay made by Iseult in which "*la voiz acorde a l'estrument.*" He goes on to remark that Iseult's hands are fair upon the strings, the lay good, her voice sweet, the tone low;[3] but just where we might have hoped to hear something more specific about the relationship of voice and instrument, we are told only that the one "accords with" the other. Such enigmatic allusions suggest that by mid-twelfth century the oldest tradition of the lay may already have been so locked in the past that Thomas and other poets of his time knew only dimly the exact means of its original performance. They appear to have realized that it had earlier been a combined form, with song and tale equally important ingredients; but they imply, too, that that was a past or passing stage of its development, and their references to older tradition often seem calculated merely to enhance the archaic flavor of their own narratives, which were conventionally set in the long ago and far away.

Whatever its beginnings, the Breton Lay soon merged into that quickening stream of story called romance. Especially in Normandy, and thus in Norman England, among a newly landed people whose literary tastes had become softened and whose leisure and wealth easily indulged all manner of new diversions, the appetite for romances seems to have been insatiable; and the farther a teller might take his audience in time and place from the ennui of their own lives, the better apparently they were satisfied. It is sometimes difficult to look back upon what strikes us as the general turbulence of this time and think that its people could possibly have concerned themselves with much more than the constant local strife and political maneuverings of their age. But that is because we tend to telescope the events of so distant a past and fail to keep in mind how really slowly most of those events took shape and came about, and,

---

relatively late (13th c.) and may well reflect only a kind of rationalized conjecture.

[3] *Les fragments du Tristan de Thomas*, ed. B. H. Wind (Leiden, 1950); "Fragment Sneyd 1," ll. 791–94.

more important, how relatively isolated from them was the vast majority of the people they affected. The tenth and eleventh centuries had been tumultuous ones, of course—had seen the Normans wrest from the French the best and most fertile lands of what is now Normandy and Brittany, and from the Anglo-Saxons and their own Scandinavian cousins nearly all of present England. And the fourteenth and fifteenth centuries, marked first by the bitter social strife that gave rise finally to an important middle class in England, and later by the sporadic battles of England's Hundred Years' War against France, were to see the troubled emergence of a new and powerful nation. But the greater part of the twelfth and thirteenth centuries was really a time of comparative quiet, and often, apparently, even of tedium. Given so long a span of relatively peaceful conditions, and given as well an affluent feudal society, in which womankind had risen to a more important and respected station in life than ever before known in the western world, we should scarcely be surprised at the splendid flourishing of all manner of art and entertainment in these centuries—painting, sculpture, mosaic and tapestry making, music, dancing, tumbling, juggling, and especially the telling of tales. All this, in fact, together with the remarkably accelerated spread of learning under the auspices of the church, has prompted more than one historian to name the time a twelfth-century renaissance.

An appetite will always find its caterers. The great dining hall of many a twelfth- and thirteenth-century castle was designed specifically to accommodate the host of entertainers that wandered the countryside in troupes performing at feasts and fairs. From just above the main entrance of these rooms, opposite the dais where sat the lord and lady and their highest-ranking guests, jutted a balcony which, with its separate entrances and exits, served these wayfaring performers as a stage. Indeed, the wealthiest and most influential noblemen of the day often employed a permanent retinue of entertainers, and among these the position of court poet, or *trouvère*,[4]

[4] There is much confusion concerning the names given the makers and tellers of medieval tales. The words *minstrel* and *jongleur* are usually taken to designate those who chanted or recited tales, whether of their own composition or not. *Trouvère* seems to designate more specifically the composer of

appears to have been especially attractive and much competed for. Shortly after his occupation of England, William the Conqueror is said to have given over the rents of three Gloucestershire parishes to the support of his *joculator*, his "maker" of tales. A century later, though they were not so munificently rewarded as far as we know, such poets as Chrétien de Troyes, Wace, Benoît, and Alexandre de Bernay held roughly similar positions. These were the "resident poets" of the time. They lived on the periphery of nobility and enjoyed its liberal patronage, though every now and again we see in their verse some hint that the subjects set them by their patrons and patronesses may not always have been agreeable to their own taste.

Something of the avidity of their competition is reflected by their frequent references to other versions of the tales they tell and by their transparent efforts to attract attention and reputation through the assertion that their own version of this or that event or episode is the only true and right one. And something of their impatience with a public taste that had narrowed so confiningly to a steady diet of tales of courtly love is reflected by their occasional burlesquing of the very standardized, almost formulaic machinery of such tales. Chrétien's *Cligés* is quite probably such a parody, its mocking hyperbole poking fun especially at the very popular *Tristan* romance; and Andreas Capellanus' *De Amore* may well have been intended as a whimsically satiric codification of the whole intricate and sophisticated system of courtly love so steadily advocated in the romances.

But for every court poet whose works have come down to us, there appear to have been dozens, perhaps hundreds, of lesser makers and singers, those anonymous and itinerant minstrels who went about the country plying their trade of chanting tales, romances, and ballads at any town fair or manor feast where they might find an audience. The *trouvère*, in fact, occupied a unique position in the spread of popular story. He took much of his material from the oral tradition of the French-speaking Breton singers and through his ability as a poet refined it to suit the taste of his own more knowing courtly audience, overlaying it with subtler motivations, with longer

---

romances, who might pass them on to others for performance. Naturally, not all *trouvères* were "court poets."

and more ornate descriptions of the sight and sound of things, and often with lingering and labyrinthine analyses of the complex psychological dilemmas of love that he constructed for his characters. Thus consciously composed and written down, the court poet's version of a story came into the literary tradition, though its first presentation was still, no doubt, an oral one, the poet reading his work to an audience of fine ladies and gentlemen seated about him in a terrace garden to while away a long, soft, summer's afternoon. After this first presentation, however, the romance might come into public domain, as it were. The poet might allow it to circulate among those of his audience who read; and, if their interest in it were great enough to bear the expense, they could have it copied. In such a copy, or in one still further removed from the poet's original, many a *trouvère's* tale came again into the hands of a minstrel, who reworked it still again to suit it to the less sophisticated demands of his popular audiences, unraveling and discarding, paradoxically, exactly those courtly elements that the *trouvère* had taken such care to work into the rough weave of the material that he borrowed from the Breton singers.[5]

Often, too, while a story traced this circuitous route from popular to literary tradition and back again, it became even more firmly fixed in the literary tradition through conversion into greatly over-swollen and sometimes deadly dull prose romances. The authors of these latter versions are seldom known; where there is a name connected with them at all, it is usually a fictitious one. And to judge solely from the sheer bulk of their product, one might think that these *proseurs* must have sold their manuscripts by the pound, multiplying their poetic sources a hundredfold and more through the most mechanical and uningenious accretion of incident and episode.

But again, as with the first flourishing of the courtly poems, it was a widespread demand that prompted this development. By the end of the thirteenth century, when at least among the French and Norman upper classes the ability to read was no longer uncommon, and when lords and ladies had for the most part abandoned the clamorous entertainments of the dining hall in favor of the written

---

[5] I tried to show something of this pattern in an earlier essay, "The Middle English *Sir Tristrem*: Toward a Reappraisal," *Comp. Lit.*, XI (1959), 221–28.

word and the quiet of their chambers, the court poet's day was nearly done; and something of the ready market for the less-skilled prose writer's work is to be seen in the fact that in many instances for every few surviving manuscripts of a courtly poem there remain dozens of its later and longer versions in prose.

The material of these courtly romances — their themes, characters, poetic forms — came from all directions. In France their most immediate ancestors were the older, more heroic *chansons de geste,* which recounted sometimes the internecine strife of feudal barons among themselves, sometimes their combined revolt against the unjust rule of a tyrannical king, sometimes the struggles of Charlemagne and his Christian peers against the so-called Saracens. For poet and audience alike, the *chansons* were soon found entirely too confining. In the first place, their people and events were rooted all too firmly in pseudo-history. Tradition itself imposed limitations upon the material, however minimal these must seem to the reader acquainted with the real history of the times; and poets found it more and more difficult to overlay that material plausibly with the kind of elaborate embroidery increasingly demanded of them by the changing tastes of their audiences. Secondly, the *chansons* were steadily heroic in their spirit and concentrated so pervasively upon ideals of patriotism and deeds of war that they were better suited to the battlefield or victory celebration than to the manor court.[6] Only in the later *chansons d'aventure*, those transitional tales dealing mostly with the crusades, do we begin to see the introduction of romance elements — marvelous and supernatural events; the adventures of an errant knight in search of a reputation for courage and prowess; the dilemma of a beautiful pagan princess anxious to be brought into the true belief of Christianity, and as well, incidentally, into marriage with any true Christian knight minded to deliver her from the hateful bonds of heathendom. But the *chansons* were by no means the only older tales to be so modified and blended into this emerging tradition of chivalric romance. Earlier heroic tales of the English *scop*, the Scandinavian *skald*, the Welsh *bard*; epic eastern tales of

[6] The best known of these *chansons*, the *Chanson de Roland,* is said to have been sung by Taillefer, one of William's minstrel-warriors, as the Normans met the English in the Battle of Hastings.

Troy and Thèbes, and of Alexander the Great; tales from classical mythology—all were similarly adopted and adapted as they became known.

One of the factors most responsible for the changing tastes of courtly audiences and the new demands that these audiences made of their poets was the vastly improved position of women in French and Norman society. Thanks partly to the religious cult of the adoration of the Virgin Mary, and partly to the Provençal troubadours' exalted idealizations of women and the service of love, a cultured and refined wife had come to be counted one of the twelfth-century nobleman's most fashionable possessions. Increasingly it was the lady of the castle who arranged its social affairs and entertainments; and increasingly these entertainments celebrated the more "civilized" occasions of feudal life—engagements, marriages, coronations—where tales of chivalric love and adventure were far more appropriate than would have been the older *chansons de geste*. Noblewomen were by no means the merely passive recipients of this new and deferential homage accorded them. At least in the higher echelons of nobility the institution of marriage was more often based upon convenience and political expediency than upon love; and whereever two powerful houses were allied through such a marriage it was not uncommon for the lord and lady to live more apart than together, each overseeing the social and economic affairs of territories sometimes far distant from the other. It is little wonder that one of the prime ingredients of the increasingly popular literature of *amour courtois* became the open advocacy of extra-marital love, though evidence is lacking to conclude that this ingredient reflected, except perhaps vicariously, the courtly life in which it thrived. Whatever the case in this last respect, a good many noblewomen of the mid-twelfth century seem to have recognized clearly the opportunity further to improve their social position, and they fostered this new potential by the best means available to them—by attracting to their courts and sponsoring those poets who sang ever higher in praise of womankind and the ennobling service of love. The most influential of these women was Eleanor of Aquitaine, the wife first of King Louis VII of France, and then of Henry II, King of England and Duke of Normandy; a mere list of twelfth-century works written at her request, or dedicated to her, or containing flattering references to her beauty and liberal patronage, would be voluminous. Yet Eleanor's influence in the growth of courtly literature was even more important in the imitation it inspired. Throughout the length and breadth of England and France, and eventually in Flanders, Germany, Spain, and Italy, noblewomen took Eleanor as the paragon of all courtly grace and sophistication, and strove to emulate all that they had seen and heard of the magnificence of her courts at London, Angers, and Poitiers.

Eleanor's court at Poitiers was especially resplendent. Here had flourished for two generations already the tradition of the troubadours' love lyrics; and here Eleanor was joined for some time by her daughter, Marie of Champagne, who was, if anything, an even more avid devotee of courtly love and literature than Eleanor. Here was established, in effect, a "school" of *courtoisie*, seemingly dedicated to the conception that the noble classes might best be brought out of the old order of barbaric militancy through the refining influence of women and the service of love; and Marie was often, no doubt, the shaper of its curriculum, its *maitresse*. Here the year 'round gathered lords and ladies, artists, entertainers, courtiers, philosophers, and especially poets—all lending to the creation of an ethical code of behavior based upon love, courteous manners, noble decorum, in short everything that is summed up in the word so often used later by Chaucer, *gentilesse*. Here were probably composed many of the *jeux partis*, the "contentions," that both led to and sprang from the rapidly accumulating rules and conventions of courtly love that Andreas was shortly to codify at Marie's court in Troyes. Here, finally, in the spring of the year were held the most famous of the *cours amoureuses*, the "courts of love," where in imitation, perhaps in light parody, of the litigations of their husbands' baronial courts, ladies heard and judged "cases" of love. Andreas recorded twenty-one of these cases and the decisions handed down by various noblewomen whom they were brought before for adjudication. A young knight is required by the lady whose favor he seeks never to speak of her or praise her in any way. In a moment of anger he breaks this probationary condition one day by defending her against the slanderous remarks of some would-be detractors. Discovering his one lapse, and despite the circumstances, the lady renounces him. What is the justice of her action? Marie decided this case, judging that the lady's condition had been ill-considered because too difficult, and her punishment too harsh; she decreed that the lady must grant the knight her favor. Another young knight, fighting bravely in an honest battle, loses an eye or is otherwise disfigured, and because of this finds himself renounced by his love. In this case Ermengarde of Narbonne judged against the lady: since bravery in battle is a quality that most inspires a woman's love and most merits her favor, why should a disfigurement gained through bravery cost the lover his love? The lady must reinstate her knight. Still another knight, not having frequent occasion to see his lady, and wishing to observe the secrecy imposed by the code of courtly love, discreetly appointed a go-between to convey his sentiments. The go-between, however, promptly abandoned the lover's cause, sought the lady's favor for himself, and was not long in finding it granted. The knight brought his double betrayal before the court, and Marie, with the consultation of sixty other ladies, judged that the disloyal go-between and the easy lady deserved each other — that both should henceforth be deprived of any other love and banished from all gatherings of knights and ladies. Were such cases the thinly veiled synopses of actual affairs? Probably not. More likely they were abstracts of the love dilemmas posed in the *tensons* and courtly romances — *demandes d'amour* which provided the court entertaining opportunities to debate in mock seriousness and in highly sophisticated dialectic the various merits of all sides of the questions that the poets were so fond of putting. In Poitiers or Troyes the question posed at the end of Chaucer's *Franklin's Tale* (p. 259) would no doubt have been debated long and enthusiastically, though surely there it would have been seen immediately that the Franklin's *demande* excludes the one person best qualified to be judged "mooste fre."

The court at Poitiers was by no means the only noble household to sponsor these courts of love, though we may well suppose that in this, as in many another aspect of courtly life, it was the one most widely imitated. They flourished first in southern France; but by the latter part of the twelfth century they had spread north, too, and especially into the courts of noblewomen who were either related to Eleanor or closely linked with her political fortunes. Historians have viewed these courts of love as little more than the parlor games of the idle and indulgent rich, and have accorded them but little significance in the course of national and world events to which we sometimes limit ourselves too severely in studying history. But anyone concerned with literary history or the history of ideas can only wish that we might know more about them than we do; for it is clear that they both shaped and reflected conventions of chivalry and courtship that were to persist in literature and in social customs down to our own times. Today's young student who, smitten by the beauty of the new girl in class, yet too awed to approach her directly, arranges for a mutual acquaintance to speak on his behalf, and then plies her with little gifts and attributes to her inspiration his best efforts on, say, the football field—this young man scarcely knows how conditioned are his emotions and behavior by ideals first promulgated in the twelfth-century romances and courts of love. And if the young lady is standoffish, and only after the boy's long and anguished persuasion consents to "go steady" with him, that, too, is part of the pattern of our twelfth-century legacy. It is all very easy to smile at now, as indeed it was even by Chaucer's time. Few who have read *The Knight's Tale* will forget Duke Theseus' long speech on the pains so willingly suffered by those who serve love. Two sworn brothers, Arcite and Palamon, see the beautiful Emily from the window of their cell in Theseus' prison, and each vows to serve her faithfully the remaining days of his life. Arcite is freed from prison and Palamon escapes and, meeting later, they so far renounce their sworn brotherhood that they begin a battle to the death to see which will have the clear way in wooing the lady. Theseus happens upon the scene, stops the bloody battle, learns its cause, and after his first ire, smiling tolerantly, "spak thise same wordes al on highte":

"The god of love, a, *benedicite*!
How myghty and how greet a lord is he!
Ayeyns his myght ther gayneth none obstacles.
He may be cleped a god for his myracles;
For he kan maken, at his owene gyse,
Of everich herte as that hym list divyse.
Lo heere this Arcite and this Palamoun,
That quitly weren out of my prisoun,
And myghte han lyved in Thebes roially,
And witen I am hir mortal enemy,

And that hir deth lith in my myght also;
And yet hath love, maugree hir eyen two,
Broght hem hyder bothe for to dye.
Now looketh, is nat that an heigh folye?
Who may been a fool, but if he love?
Bihoold, for Goddes sake that sit above,
Se how they blede! be they noght wel arrayed?
Thus hath hir lord, the god of love, ypayed
Hir wages and hir fees for hir servyse!
And yet they wenen for to been ful wyse
That serven love, for aught that may bifalle.
But this is yet the beste game of alle,
That she for whom they han this jolitee
Kan hem therfore as muche thank as me.
She woot namoore of al this hoote fare,
By God, than woot a cokkow or an hare!
But all moot ben assayed, hoot and coold;
A man moot ben a fool, or yong or oold,—
I woot it by myself ful yore agon,
For in my tyme a servant was I oon.
And therfore, syn I knowe of loves peyne,
And woot hou soore it kan a man distreyne,
As he that hath ben caught ofte in his laas,
I yow foryeve al hoolly this trespaas. . . ."[7]

If Chaucer saw how sympathetically and tolerantly one smiles at the earnest passion that prompts such "hoote fare" over a lady who scarcely even knows of her young wooers' existence, he also saw how readily the exaggerated artificialities of courtly love lend themselves to high comedy through the simple rhetorical expedient of *reductio ad absurdum*. It is a cardinal rule of courtly love—occasionally stated, everywhere implied—that the less than aristocratically born have neither the leisure to conduct a proper courtship nor the fine sensitivity of feeling to appreciate the ennobling emotional depths of the passion of true *amour*. Once bring so syn-

[7] Lines A 1785–1818. F. N. Robinson, ed., *The Works of Geoffrey Chaucer*, 2nd. ed. (Boston, 1957).

thetic a code of behavior out of its high environment of nobility, once set it into the realistic context of a work-a-day world, peopled by carpenters, clerks, village dandies, and willing young wives, and it quickly lapses into the ridiculous and even, sometimes, into sheer bawdy. Nowhere is this tension clearer than in the close juxtaposition of Chaucer's Knight's and Miller's tales; and nowhere is its principle clearer than in Harry Bailly's rebuking the middle-class Franklin with how ill it befits a man of his station to speak of *gentilesse*. It is the subtlest kind of comedy that the Franklin pretends acquiescently to understand the breach of propriety implied by the Host's rebuke, yet goes on to tell a highly sophisticated Breton Lay of courtly love.[8]

Little more than two centuries separate the courts of love and *The Canterbury Tales*; yet the tongue in Chaucer's cheek as he speaks of romance and courtly love allows us to glimpse occasionally something of the near end of the whole tradition—and something, as well, of the literary extravagances that helped bring about its gradual decline. No doubt Chaucer's cavalier attitude had been influenced to some extent by his travels in Italy, where from the beginning poets had scoffed at what they regarded as the flimsy and jogging meters of the romances. But even in France and Normandy, and by a hundred years before Chaucer's time, audiences had begun to tire of the romances; apparently they had fed upon passion and adventure to the point of complete satiety. Possibly, too, there are political implications that need to be considered, though these are hard to weigh. In the century following Chrétien and Marie de France, courtly poets had turned increasingly to the Arthurian legend for material; and in view of the steadily worsening relations between France and England during that time, it is hardly surprising to find among the French a gradually slaking appetite for tales that centered so often around a British king and court. Of course, Arthur had never been considered, strictly speaking, an *English* hero; but he was at least a hero of English soil, and by the late thirteenth century the combined Normans and Anglo-Saxons had begun to see themselves more and more a single English people and eagerly claimed Arthur

---

[8] See R. M. Lumiansky, *Of Sondry Folk* (Austin, Texas; 1955), pp. 184–86.

as their own, diminishing wherever possible his pseudo-historical role as Britain's most effective defender against the Saxons, and emphasizing his romantic role as conqueror of most of western Europe, France and Rome included.

For whatever additional reasons, it was an already dying tradition that the English poets and minstrels inherited almost a full century before Chaucer's day, and in fact the English minstrels are often given the dubious credit of having finished it off. Apart from what must have been the natural appeal of the Arthurian portion of their inheritance, just why they adopted it so enthusiastically is sometimes difficult to see. An aristocratic genre, existing in a language that the average Englishman did not know and that apparently often troubled even the minstrel-translators, involving a synthetic love relationship that minstrel and audience alike seldom seem to have understood or cared for — surely everything would appear to have been against its rise to a second and prolonged popularity. But we have seen often enough since medieval times how little unusual it is for a conquered people, after the first waves of oppression and resistance, to adapt themselves and strive to imitate the tastes and customs of their conquerors. By the late thirteenth century the middle and lower-class English imitation of all things French *because* they were French had become so pronounced as to be well termed a kind of Gallomania;[9] and in their exotic remoteness from the everyday world and their reflection of near-contemporary French courtly manners and chivalric ideals, the romances again fell on eager ears. There is another important consideration, too. The time was one when few works were composed that did not rely upon the authority of at least a long tradition, and usually a written source; and since for nearly two centuries English had been reduced to an insignificant and largely spoken language, poets and minstrels had little alternative but to garner their tales from the great store of French narrative that had accumulated in England during the long span of Norman-French rule. Well over ninety percent of the thirteenth- and fourteenth-century English romances thus stem from French originals; those that cannot be traced to specific French

---

[9] G. P. Krapp, *Modern English: Its Growth and Present Use* (New York, 1909), p. 31.

sources can be shown through analogues and other evidence to fit the general pattern. A few of them, *Libeaus Desconus* and the lay of *Sir Degaré*, for example, give evidence of being rather late composites of earlier French material, but these can hardly be considered exceptions to the rule. In short, to account for the decline of romance in French and its new flourishing in English, we need most to remember that in the early fourteenth century the English audience was still an aural audience, which the French had ceased to be, and that here, in French, lay a whole body of traditional and originally oral story, ready to the minstrel's hand and wanting only translation and the kind of adaptation that would suit it again to oral delivery and to the humbler and less sophisticated tastes of an uncourtly listening audience.

The devices that the minstrels used in translating and adapting their French sources are mostly those which Chaucer ridiculed through wholesale exaggeration in his *Tale of Sir Thopas*. That fragment is a hilarious burlesque, and perfectly suited to its purpose in the *Canterbury Tales*; but its unfortunate side-effect has been to cast the whole object of its parody into long and undue critical neglect. In fact, it may well be doubted whether anything of a really valid critical appraisal of the English romances is possible at this late date; for again—and it can hardly be too often stressed—we find ourselves in the difficult position of having to judge from the printed page what was probably never intended for the printed page. True, the romances come down to us in written form, but their manuscripts are mostly later than the oral versions we suppose them based upon, and often so carelessly written, and on such inexpensive materials, that we cannot believe the romances in them were at all the more prized for being written down. Marred by everything from strike-overs to ink blots, some of these manuscripts are to all appearances the practice work of apprentice scribes; none of them remotely approaches the elaborate care of script and illumination of, say, the Ellesmere *Canterbury Tales*. More important, internal evidence suggests that most of the romances were composed exclusively for recital, probably to an unlettered audience and probably by minstrels who were highly skilled at satisfying the expectations of that audience. Occasionally a minstrel refers to clerics' versions of his tale, or alludes vaguely and no doubt often fraudulently to some source in parchment or in book; but almost never is there the slightest suggestion that the romance is primarily to be read. "Ladies and gentlemen," he begins, "if you will stop a while, hark and dwell, I shall say, talk, tell a tale, sing in song . . ."; any one of these or a whole host of other such stock phrases is ever to be found in his opening advertisement, and he usually closes with a benediction that asks God's blessing on all who have heard him through.

Many a critic has regarded the English romances with the attitude that God's blessing would have been all too slight reward for having had to hear one through. In this we are reminded of Harry Bailly's reaction to the "verray lewednesse" and "drasty speche" of the *Sir Thopas*: "this may wel be rym dogerel," he grumbles, and demands something in a longer line, "in geeste," or prose, "in which ther be som murthe or some doctryne." Harry's enthusiastic satisfaction with the *Tale of Melibee*, that long, dull "litel thyng in prose" that follows, bespeaks all that needs saying about his acumen as critic. Difficult as it may now be to do, anyone who wants the fullest understanding of the English romances must first attempt to reconstruct the setting and circumstances of their performance. They began to fall into general disrepute, of course, when gradually their audience became a reading audience, just as had their French counterparts before: on manuscript or printed page what is left of them is exactly what Chaucer so easily exaggerated. Yet even so, whoever read the fourteenth- and early fifteenth-century manuscripts probably read the romances in them as much with ear as eye. That first few generations of readers must have scanned their rough rhythms with a very certain mind's-eye view of the typical scene of their performance—a crowded street corner, or tavern, or manor yard after some festivity; and must have read, as well, with a very sure aural and visual sense of all the possibilities of mimetic cadence and histrionic gesture available to the skilled minstrel in their delivery. Perhaps such a reader even heard, or imagined that he heard, behind the stiff and wooden lines before his eyes a rhythmic beat of harp that accentuated those cadences and gestures.

If as modern readers we are struck, then, by what some have thought the monotony of the English metrical romances, their general sameness of theme, diction, meter, rhyme, characterization, incident, and episode, that may well be because we read them so entirely out of their intended context, and fail to keep steadily in mind that their original appeal must have been precisely in the great variety of effects that the expert performer could achieve in their telling. Moreover, anyone interested in these romances today will read more of them in a week than the Middle-Englishman probably had opportunity to hear in years; and whatever are their infelicities, through sheer concentration these could not help but be apparent to the reader in a way that they never would have been to the audience they were intended for.[10] To an audience which heard these stories but seldom, and whose attention must have been fixed as much on teller as on tale, what would it have mattered that the minstrel fell into every formula? "I say no lie," the minstrel interjects in a dozen different ways, and where there is no reason to suspect him of anything less honest than needing a quick metrical "filler" ending with a rhyme. Even so simple a formula as this would probably have had a whole range of additional psychological effects that are lost on the printed page. Quite beyond its easy informality, used by a teller who had to be constantly concerned with his audience's "willing suspension of disbelief," it would have asserted, however mechanically, the veracity of his tale. It would have interrupted, however momentarily, the all too relentless forward movement of a story which for the sake of brevity had to be reduced to the bare skeleton of its plot. It would have provided, however fleeting, an instant of opportunity for the teller's dramatic gesture or quick variation of tonality and pace. In short, to the ear the effects of such a formula were probably exactly the opposite of what they are to the eye, and the same is true for a whole multitude of similar set-phrases. Again, what would it have mattered to the listening audience that some of the minstrels—the northern ones mostly—made constant use of the ballad-like "tail rhyme" stanza whose meters look so awkward on the printed page[11] and whose regularity is so

[10] This would seem the main reason why many an 18th- and 19th-century antiquarian brought the English romances into print more for their illustration of the "usages and customs of a bygone day" than for any intrinsic narrative or poetic merit of their own.

[11] Four of the eight Breton Lays of this volume are in the tail-rhyme stanza. It consists usually of six or twelve lines, the first two lines of each triplet being four-stress lines and rhyming with each other, the third being a three-

exaggerated in *Sir Thopas* that the real humor of Harry Bailly's complaint lies in his suspecting that Chaucer's verse *may be* "rym dogerel"? Much of the monotony of this stanza would probably have gone unnoticed in the variety of the minstrel's tone and pace and gesture, and all the more so if he sang or recited to the skillful accompaniment of a harp. What, finally, would it have mattered to such an audience that the minstrel left little in his tale of explicit and detailed character description? It was a simple and credulous audience, expecting only that every hero be "a stout wyght and a strong," and every lady so "bright of blee," so "fair of flesh and bone," that "no man might ever fully tell her fairness." The rest could be inferred, and the minstrel had better get straight to his story if in a single hearing his audience was to learn what mattered to them most — that is, what *happened* to the knight and lady: they were not likely to cast their shillings at his feet if he were so long-winded that they had to leave when he was but halfway through his tale.

The subject of the origin and development of medieval romance is an intricate one, whose full discussion would require far more than the limited space available here. In these introductory remarks I have wished only to sketch what seem to me the more important aspects of the subject, hoping that the books and articles in the bibliography at the end of this book will point the main directions for its further exploration.

As for the general characteristics of the genre, especially as reflected in the English romances, I have purposely said little of these, feeling that they are far better illustrated in the Middle English Breton Lays of this volume than could possibly be accomplished in any brief introductory analysis. On the whole, these lays comprise a remarkably representative cross-section of the themes and motifs

---

stress line (a short, or "bobbed," line) and rhyming with that of the other triplets; thus *aab*, *ccb*, or *aab*, *ccb*, *ddb*, *eeb*. Most editors indent the "bob-lines" of these stanzas and thus accentuate their jingling look on the page. So far as I know there is little manuscript authority for this practice; and I have set all the lines flush, as they are written in the manuscripts. Some of the manuscripts show a paragraph symbol — indeed, some of them a hand with pointed finger — before the first line of each stanza; I have abandoned this device in favor of the more modern practice of spacing stanzas on the printed page.

of the romances,[12] and more than one commentator has pointed out that they provide an excellent introduction to the whole subject.[13] For all their similarities, however, and despite the fact that they are almost always considered together, it must not be supposed that the lays and romances are one and the same thing. Indeed, the differences between the two go a long way towards mitigating in the lays just those aspects of the romances that have been most often criticized. Though interfused with romance elements, the Breton Lays were from the beginning less ornate than the romances — shorter, simpler, less diffuse in their effects, more reliant upon pure folklore motifs and faery lore; and while love was frequently one of their central interests, they were less concerned with the elaborately embroidered subtleties of *courtly* love than were the romances. More important, these qualities survive their English adaptations well. Already concentrated, the lays tended to be more dramatic than the romances, and the minstrel therefore had no pressing need to abridge them so severely or to pare away their love interest so rigorously. Even the English lays that are perhaps lays only because their composers call them so (*The Erle of Tolous* and possibly *Sir Degaré*) reflect these qualities; and we must conclude that the distinction, however fine, was both observed and observable by the minstrel and his audience.

All that here remains unsaid, then, I leave to those professional and semi-professional Middle English "makers," and to what seems to me their very sure touch with an especially rich vein of medieval "storial thyng."

---

12 On this subject see esp. G. V. Smithers, "Story-Patterns in Some Breton Lays," *Med. AEv.*, XXII (1953), 61–92.

13 See, for example, G. K. Anderson, *Old and Middle English Literature from the Beginnings to 1485* (New York, 1962), pp. 84 and 136.

Launfal miles

Be doughty Artours dawes
Þat held Engelond yn good lawes
Þer fell a wondyr cas
Of a ley þat was ysette
Þat hyȝt Launval & hatte ȝette
Now herkeneþ how hyt was

Doughty Artour som whyle
Soiournede yn Kardevyle
Wyth ioye & greet solas
And knyȝtes þat wer profitable
Wyth Artour of þe rounde table
Never noon better þer nas

Sere Persevall & Syr Gawayn
Syr Gyheries & Syr Agrafrayn
And Launcelet du Lake
Syr Kay and Syr Ewayn
Þat well couþe fyȝte yn playn
Bateles for to take

Kyng Ban Booȝt & Kyng Bos
Of ham þer was a greet los
Men sawe þo nowher her make
Syr Galafre & Syr Launfale
Wherof a noble tale
Among us schall awake

With Artour þer was a bacheler
And hadde ybe well many a ȝer
Launfal forsoþ he hyȝt
He gaf gyftys largelyche
Gold & sylver & cloþes ryche
To squyer & to knyȝt

For hys largesse & hys bounte
Þe kynges stuward made was he
Ten yer y you plyȝt
Of alle þe knyȝtes of þe table rounde
So large þer nas noon yfounde
Be dayes ne be nyȝt

So hyt befyll yn þe tenþe ȝer
Marlyn was Artours counsalere
He radde hym for to wende
To kyng Ryon of Irlond ryȝt
And fette hym þer a lady bryȝt
Gwennere hys douȝtyr hende

So he dede & hom her brouȝt
But Syr Launfal lykede her noȝt
Ne oþer knyȝtes þat wer hende
For þe lady bar los of swych word
Þat sche hadde lemmannys under her lord
So fele þer nas noon ende

Þey wer ywedded as y you say
Upon a Wytsonday
Before princes of moch pryde
No man ne may telle yn tale
What folk þer was at þat bredale
Of countreys fer & wyde

No noþer man was yn halle ysette
But he wer prelat oþer baronette
In herte ys naȝt to hyde
Yf þey satte noȝt alle ylyke
Har servyse was good & ryche
Certeyn yn ech a syde

And whan þe lordes hadde ete yn þe halle
And þe cloþes wer drawen alle
As ye mowe her & lyþe
Þe botelers sentyn wyn
To alle þe lordes þat wer þeryn
Wyth chere boþe glad & blyþe

Þe quene yaf yftes for þe nones
Gold & selver & precyous stonys
Her curtasye to kyþe
Everych knyȝt sche ȝaf broche oþer ryng
But Syr Launfal sche ȝaf noþyng
Þat grevede hym many a syþe

Sir Launfal

Be [1] doughty Artours dawes [2]
That held Engelond yn good lawes
Ther fell a wondyr cas
Of a ley that was ysette [3]
That hyght [4] Launval, and hatte yette; [5]
Now herkeneth how hyt was.

Doughty Artour somwhyle
Sojournede yn Kardeuyle [6]
Wyth joye and greet solas
And knyghtes that wer profitable; [7]
Wyth Artour of the Rounde Table
Never noon better ther nas:

Sere Persevall and Syr Gawayn,
Syr Gyheryes and Syr Agrafrayn,
And Launcelet du Lake;
Syr Kay and Syr Ewayn,
That well couthe [8] fyghte yn playn,
Bateles for to take;

Kyng Banbooght and Kyn Bos [9]

---

[1] by, in [2] days [3] composed [4] was named
[5] and has yet that name [6] Carlisle [7] of good service
[8] knew how to
[9] Ban and Bors, brothers; the first was King of Benwick and father of Lancelot

(Of ham [10] ther was a greet los,[11]
Men sawe tho [12] nowher her [13] make[14]);
Syr Galafre and Syr Launfale,
Whereof a noble tale
Among us schall awake.

With Artour ther was a bacheler,[15]
And hadde ybe [16] well many a yer;
Launfal forsoth he hyght;
He gaf gyftys largelyche, [17]
Gold and sylver, and clothes [18] ryche,
To squyer and to knyght.

For hys largesse and hys bounté,
The kynges stuward made was he
Ten yer, Y you plyght;
Of alle the knyghtes of the Table Rounde
So large ther nas noon yfounde,
Be dayes ne be nyght.

So hyt befyll yn the tenthe yer
Marlyn was Artours counsalere;
He radde [19] hym for to wende
To Kyng Ryon of Irlond ryght,
And fette hym ther a lady bryght,
Gwennere, hys doughtyr hende.[20]

So he dede, and hom her brought,
But Syr Launfal lykede her noght,
Ne other knyghtes that wer hende;
For the lady bar los of swych word

---

[10] them [11] praise, fame [12] then [13] their [14] match
[15] a young knight or one aspiring to knighthood [16] been
[17] largely, generously [18] ms. *clodes* [19] advised [20] noble

That sche hadde lemannys under [21] her lord
So fele ther nas noon ende.[22]

They wer ywedded, as Y you say,
Upon a Wytsonday
Before princes of moch pryde;
No man ne may telle yn tale
What folk ther was at that bredale
Of countreys fer and wyde.

No nother man was yn halle ysette
But he wer prelat other [23] baronette.
In herte ys naght to hyde: [24]
Yf [25] they satte noght alle ylyke,
Har servyse was good and ryche,
Certeyn yn ech a syde.

And whan the lordes hadde ete yn the halle,
And the clothes wer drawen [26] alle—
As ye mowe her and lythe [27] —
The botelers sentyn wyn
To alle the lordes that wer theryn,
Wyth chere bothe glad and blythe.

The quene yaf gyftes [28] for the nones,[29]
Gold and selver and precyous stonys,
Her curtasye to kythe; [30]
Everych knyght sche yaf broche other ryng,
But Syr Launfal sche yaf no thyng:
That grevede hym many a sythe. [31]

---

[21] ms. *unþer*
[22] *i.e.* she was reputed to have so many lovers other than her lord that there was no end [23] or
[24] I shall keep back nothing of the story [25] though
[26] tablecloths were removed [27] as you may listen and hear
[28] ms. *yſtes* [29] occasion [30] show [31] time; ms. *syde*

And whan the bredale was at ende,
Launfal tok hys leve to wende
At Artour the kyng,
And seyde a lettere was to hym come
That deth hadde hys fadyr ynome:[32]
He most to hys beryynge.

Tho[33] seyde Kyng Artour, that was hende,
"Launfal, yf thou wylt fro me wende,
Tak wyth the greet spendyng;
And my suster sones two,
Bothe they schull wyth the go,
At hom the for to bryng."

Launfal tok leve, wythoute fable,[34]
Wyth knyghtes of the Rounde Table,
And wente forth yn hys journé
Tyl he com to Karlyoun,
To the Meyrys[35] hous of the toune,
Hys servaunt that hadde ybe.[36]

The Meyr stod, as ye may here,
And sawe hym come ryde up anblere[37]
Wyth two knyghtes and other mayné;[38]
Agayns hym he hath wey ynome,[39]
And seyde, "Syr, thou art wellcome;
How faryth our kyng, tel me?"

Launfal answerede and seyde than:
"He faryth as well as any man,
And elles greet ruthe[40] hyt wore.

---

[32] taken [33] then [34] without lie [35] Mayor's
[36] who had been Launfal's servant [37] at an ambling pace
[38] retinue [39] has come out to meet Launfal [40] pity

But, Syr Meyr, wythout lesyng, [41]
I am departyd [42] fram the kyng,
And that rewyth me sore;

Nether thar [43] no man, benethe ne above.
For the Kyng Artours love,
Onowre [44] me nevermore.
But, Syr Meyr, Y pray the, par amour,
May Y take wyth the sojour?
Somtyme we knewe us yore." [45]

The Meyr stod and bethought hym there
What myght be hys answere,
And to hym than gan he sayn:
"Syr, seven knyghtes han her har in ynom[e],[46]
And ever Y wayte whan they wyl come,
That arn of Lytyll Bretayne." [47]

Launfal turnede hymself and lowgh,[48]
Thereof he hadde scorn inowgh,
And seyde to hys knyghtes tweyne:
"Now may ye se, swych ys service
Under [49] a lord of lytyll pryse—
How he may therof be fayn!" [50]

Launfal awayward gan to ryde;
The Meyr bad he schuld abyde,
And seyde yn thys manere:
"Syr, yn a chamber by my orchard-syd[e],

[41] without lie [42] ms. *þepartyþ* [43] need [44] honor
[45] we have long known each other
[46] have here their lodging taken [47] Brittany [48] laughed
[49] ms. *unþer*
[50] see what it is to be a lord of little power, and how anxious your former servants are to please you!

Ther may ye dwelle wyth joye and pryde,
Yyf hyt your wyll were."

Launfal anoon ryghtes,
He and hys two knytes,
Sojournede ther yn fere;
So savagelych hys good he besette [51]
That he ward [52] yn greet dette,
Ryght yn the ferst yere.

So hyt befell at Pentecost—
Swych tyme as the Holy Gost
Among mankend gan lyght—
That Syr Huwe and Syr Jon
Tok her leve for to gon
At [53] Syr Launfal the knyght.

They seyd, "Syr, our robes beth torent,[54]
And your tresour [55] ys all yspent,
And we goth ewyll ydyght." [56]
Thanne seyde Syr Launfal to the knyghtes fr[e]:
"Tellyth [57] no man of my poverté,
For the love of God almyght!"

The knyghtes answerede and seyde tho
That they nolde [58] hym wreye [59] never mo,
All thys world to wynne.
Wyth that word they wente hym fro
To Glastynbery, bothe two,
Ther Kyng Artour was inne.

The kyng sawe the knyghtes hende,
And agens [60] ham he gan wende,

---

[51] so freely did he spend his wealth [52] became [53] from
[54] all torn, worn out [55] ms. *tosour* [56] poorly clothed
[57] ms. *Tellyd* [58] would not [59] betray [60] against, toward

For they wer of hys kenne; [61]
Noon other robes they ne hadde
Than they owt with ham ladde,[62]
And tho were totore and thynne.

Than seyde Quene Gwenore, that was fel: [63]
"How faryth the prowde knyght, Launfal?
May he hys armes welde?"
"Ye, madame," sayde the knytes than;
"He faryth as well as any man,
And ellys God hyt schelde!" [64]

Moche worchyp and greet honour
To Gonnore the quene and Kyng Artour
Of Syr Launfal they telde,
And seyde, "He lovede us so
That he wold us evermo
At wyll have yhelde;

But upon a rayny day hyt befel
An huntynge wente Syr Launfel,
To chasy yn holtes hore;
In our old robes we yede that day,
And thus we beth ywent away
As we before hym wore." [65]

Glad was Artour the kyng
That Launfal was yn good lykyng; [66]
The quene hyt rew well sore,
For sche wold [67] wyth all her myght

[61] kin
[62] than those they had ridden away in a year before
[63] evil, spiteful [64] may God not allow it otherwise!
[65] we left Launfal dressed just as we were
[66] *i.e.* was doing well
[67] wished

That he hadde be, bothe day and nyght,
In paynys more and more.[68]

Upon a day of the Trinité,
A feste of greet solempnité
In Carlyoun was holde;
Erles and barones of that countré,
Ladyes and boriaes[69] of that cité,
Thyder come bothe yongh and old.

But Launfal, for hys poverté,
Was not bede to that semblé:
Lyte men of hym tolde.[70]
The Meyr to the feste was ofsent;[71]
The Meyrys doughter to Launfal went,
And axede yf he wolde

In halle dyne wyth her that day.
"Damesele," he sayde, "nay;
To dyne have Y no herte.
Thre days ther ben agon,
Mete ne drynke eet Y noon,
And all was for povert.[72]

Today to cherche Y wolde have gon,
But me fawtede[73] hosyn and schon,[74]
Clenly brech[75] and scherte;
And for defawte of clothynge[76]
Ne myghte Y yn wyth the peple thrynge;
No wonder[77] though[78] me smerte![79]

---

[68] ever in greater pain, disrepute [69] townspeople
[70] he was of little repute [71] invited [72] poverty [73] lacked
[74] hose and shoes [75] clean breeches [76] ms. *clodynge*
[77] ms. *wonþer* [78] ms. *douȝ*
[79] no wonder I am ashamed!

But o thyng, damesele, Y pray the,
Sadel and brydel lene[80] thou me
A whyle for to ryde,
That Y myght confortede be
By a launde [81] under [82] thys cyté
Al yn thys undern-tyde." [83]

Launfal dyghte [84] hys courser
Wythoute knave other squyer;
He rood wyth lytyll pryde;
Hys horse slod and fel yn the fen,[85]
Wherefore hym scorned many men
Abowte hym fer and wyde.

Poverly [86] the knyght to hors gan sprynge;
For to dryve away lokynge [87]
He rood toward the west.
The wether was hot, the undern-tyde;
He lyghte adoun and gan abyde,
Under [88] a fayr forest.

And for hete of the wedere,
Hys mantell he feld togydere,
And sette hym doun to reste.
Thus sat the knyght yn symplyté
In the schadwe under [89] a tre
Ther that hym lykede best.

As he sat yn sorow and sore,
He sawe come out of holtes hore
Gentyll maydenes two;

---

[80] lend [81] meadow [82] nearby; ms. *vnþer* [83] morning-time
[84] readied, harnessed [85] mire [86] ashamedly
[87] *i.e.* to escape the ridicule of onlookers
[88] near [89] ms. *vnþer*

Har kerteles [90] wer of Inde-sandel, [91]
Ilased smalle, jolyf, and well;
Ther myght noon gayer go.

Har manteles wer of grene felwet, [92]
Ybordured wyth gold, ryght well ysette,
Ipelvred wyth grys and gro; [93]
Har heddys wer dyght well wythalle:
Everych hadde oon a jolyf coronall [94]
Wyth syxty gemmys and mo.

Har faces wer whyt as snow on downe;
Har rode [95] was red, her eyn wer browne:
I sawe never non swyche!
That oon bar of gold a basyn;
That other a towayle whyt and fyn,
Of selk that was good and ryche.

Har kercheves wer well schyre, [96]
Arayd wyth ryche gold wyre; [97]
Launfal began to syche. [98]
They com to hym over the hoth; [99]
He was curteys and agens hem goth [100]
And greette hem myldelyche.

"Damesels," he seyde, "God yow se!"
"Syr Knyght," they seyde, "well the be!
Our lady, Dame Tryamour,
Bad thou schuldest com speke wyth here,

---

[90] vest-like garments worn under an outer mantle [91] blue silk
[92] velvet
[93] trimmed with the pelts of gray and gray-white squirrels
[94] crown
[95] usually "complexion"; here probably more specifically the color of their cheeks [96] sheer [97] embroidered with gold thread
[98] sigh [99] heath [100] went to meet them

Yyf hyt wer thy wylle, sere,
258 Wythoute more sojour."[101]

Launfal hem grauntede curteyslyche,
And wente wyth hem myldelyche;
They wheryn[102] whyt as flour;
And when they come in the forest an hygh,
A pavyloun[103] yteld[104] he sygh,
264 Wyth merthe and mochell honour.

The pavyloun was wrouth,[105] for sothe, ywys,
All of werk of Sarsynys:[106]
The pomelles[107] of crystall;
Upon the toppe an ern[108] ther stod
Of bournede[109] gold, ryche and good,
270 Iflorysched[110] wyth ryche amall;[111]

Hys eyn wer carbonkeles[112] bryght—
As the mone they[113] schon a-nyght,
That spreteth out ovyr all;
Alysaundre the Conquerour,
Ne Kyng Artour, yn hys most honour,
276 Ne hadde noon scwych juell.

He fond yn the pavyloun
The kynges doughter of Olyroun,
Dame Tryamour that hyghte;
Her fadyr was kyng of fayrye,
Of occient,[114] fer and nyghe,
282 A man of mochell myghte.

---

[101] delay [102] were [103] tent [104] pitched
[105] wrought [106] saracens [107] tent-pole tips
[108] eagle [109] burnished [110] trimmed, decorated
[111] enamel [112] rubies [113] ms. *the*
[114] occident, the west

In the pavyloun he fond a bed of prys,
Yheled wyth purpur bys,[115]
That semylé was of syghte;
Therinne lay that lady gent
That after Syr Launfal hedde ysent—
That lefsom lemede[116] bryght.

For hete her clothes down sche dede
Almest to her gerdyl-stede,[117]
Than lay sche uncovert;
Sche was as whyt as lylye yn May,
Or sno that sneweth yn wynterys day;
He seygh never non so pert.[118]

The rede rose, whan sche ys newe,
Agens her rode nes naught of hewe,[119]
I dar well say, yn sert;[120]
Her here schon as gold wyre;
May no man rede[121] here atyre,
Ne naught well thenke yn hert.

Sche seyde, "Launfal, my lemman[122] swete,
Al my joye for the Y lete,[123]
Swetyng[124] paramour!
Ther nys no man yn Cristenté
That Y love so moche as the,
Kyng neyther empourer!"

Launfal beheld that swete wyghth[125]
(All hys love yn her was lyghth),

---

[115] covered with a purple linen spread [116] lovely one shone
[117] waist, girdle-place [118] beautiful
[119] the new red rose is nothing compared to her color
[120] certainly [121] tell of [122] lover [123] forsake [124] sweet
[125] creature

And keste that swete flour,
And sat adoun her bysyde,
And seyde, "Swetyng, what so betyde,
I am to thyn honour." [126]

She seyde, "Syr knyght, gentyl and hende,
I wot thy stat, ord and ende; [127]
Be naught aschamed of me;[128]
Yf thou wylt truly to me take,
And alle wemen for me forsake,
Ryche I wyll make the.

I wyll the geve an alner [129]
Imad of sylk and of gold cler,
Wyth fayre ymages thre;
As oft thou puttest the hond therinne,
A mark of gold thou schalt wynne,
In wat place that thou be.

Also," sche seyde, "Syr Launfal,
I geve the Blaunchard, my stede lel,[130]
And Gyfre, my owen knave;
And of my armes oo pensel [131]
Wyth thre ermyns ypeynted well,
Also thou schalt have.

In werre ne yn turnement
Ne schall the greve [132] no knyghtes dent [133]
So well Y schall the save."
Than answarede the gantyl knyght,

---

[126] at your service
[127] I know your state from beginning to end
[128] in my presence
[129] purse, wallet [130] loyal [131] a pennant, banner [132] harm
[133] blow, stroke

And seyde, "Gramarcy, my swete wyght,
No bettere klepte [134] Y have."

The damesell gan her up sette,
And bad her maydenes her fette
To hyr hondys watyr clere;
Hyt was ydo wythout lette:
The cloth was spred, the bord was sette,
They wente to hare sopere.

Mete and drynk they hadde afyn,[135]
Pyement, clare,[136] and Reynysch [137] wyn,
And elles greet wondyr hyt wer;
Whan they had sowped,[138] and the day was gon,
They wente to bedde, and that anoon,
Launfal and sche yn fere.[139]

For play lytyll they sclepte that nyght,
Tyll on morn hyt was daylyght;
She badd hym aryse anoon.
Hy [140] seyde to hym, "Syr gantyl knyght,
And [141] thou wylt speke wyth me any wyght,[142]
To a derne stede [143] thou gon;

Well privyly [144] I woll come to the
(No man alyve ne schall me se)
As stylle as any ston."
Tho was Launfal glad and blythe;
He cowde no man hys joye kythe,[145]
And keste her well good won.[146]

---

[134] ms. *kepte*; I have emended conjecturally to derive the word from O.E. *clyppan*, to embrace [135] aplenty [136] spiced wines [137] Rhine [138] ms. *sowpeþ* [139] together [140] she [141] if [142] whit, time [143] secluded place [144] secretly [145] tell, express [146] again and again

"But of o thyng, Syr Knyght, I warne the,
That thou make no bost of me
For no kennes mede; [147]
And yf thou doost, Y warny the before:
All my love thou hast forlore!"
366 And thus to hym sche seyde.

Launfal tok hys leve to wende;
Gyfre kedde [148] that he was hende,
And brought Launfal hys stede;
Launfal lepte ynto the arsoun [149]
And rood hom to Karlyoun
372 In hys pover wede.[150]

Tho was the knyght yn herte at wylle; [151]
In hys chanber he hyld hym stylle [152]
All that undern-tyde;
Than come ther thorwgh the cyté ten
Well yharneysyd [153] men
378 Upon ten somers ryde; [154]

Some wyth sylver, some wyth gold—
All to Syr Launfal hyt schold.[155]
To presente hym wyth pryde
Wyth ryche clothes and armure bryght,
They axede after Launfal the knyght,
384 Whar he gan abyde.

The yong men wer clothed [156] yn ynde; [157]
Gyfre, he rood all behynde
Up [158] Blaunchard, whyt as flour.
Tho seyde a boy that yn the market stod:

---

[147] for any reason, or any kind of gain [148] showed [149] saddle
[150] poor clothes [151] at ease, happy [152] remained
[153] ms. *yharneysyþ* [154] upon ten pack-horses riding
[155] should go, be given [156] ms. *clodeþ* [157] blue [158] upon

"How fer schall[159] all thys good?
Tell us, par amour!"

Tho seyde Gyfre, "Hyt ys ysent
To Syr Launfal, yn present,
That hath leved yn greet dolour."
Than seyde the boy, "Nys he but a wrecche![160]
What thar[161] any man of hym recce?[162]
At the Meyrys hous he taketh sojour."

At the Merys hous they gon alyght,
And presented the noble knyghte
Wyth swych good as hym was sent;
And whan the Meyr seygh that rychesse,
And Syr Launfals noblenesse,
He held hymself foule yschent.[163]

Tho seyde the Meyr, "Syr, par charyté,
In halle today that thou wylt ete wyth me.
Yesterday Y hadde yment
At the feste we wold han be yn same[164]
And yhadde solas and game;
And erst thou were ywent."[165]

"Syr Meyr, God foryelde[166] the!
Whyles Y was yn my poverté,
Thou bede me never dyne;
Now Y have more gold and fe,[167]
That myne frendes han sent me,
Than thou and alle thyne!"[168]

[159] where shall go [160] he is but a wretch! [161] need
[162] reckon, care [163] ashamed [164] together
[165] but before I could speak of it, you were gone
[166] forgive
[167] goods
[168] ms. *dyne*

The Meyr for schame away yede;[169]
Launfal yn purpure gan hym schrede,[170]
Ipelvred[171] wyth whyt ermyne.
All that Launfal had borwyd[172] before,
Gyfre, be tayle[173] and be score,
420 Yald[174] hyt well and fyne.

Launfal helde ryche festes:
Fyfty fedde povere gestes
That yn myschef wer;
Fyfty boughte stronge stedes;
Fyfty yaf ryche wedes
426 To knyghtes and squyere;

Fyfty rewardede relygyons;
Fyfty delyverede povere prisouns,
And made ham quyt and schere;[175]
Fyfty clothede[176] gestours[177]—
To many men he dede honours
432 In countreys fer and nere.

Alle the lordes of Karlyoun
Lette crye a turnement yn the toun,
For love of Syr Launfal,
And for Blaunchard, hys good stede,
To wyte[178] how hym wold spede
438 That was ymade so well.

And whan the day was ycome
That the justes were yn ynome,[179]
They ryde out al so snell;[180]

---

[169] went [170] dress [171] furred [172] ms. *borwyþ* [173] by tally
[174] repaid [175] free and clear of their debts [176] ms. *cloded*
[177] minstrels [178] know [179] that jousts were undertaken
[180] quickly, eagerly

Trompours gon har bemes [181] blowe;
The lordes ryden out a-rowe [182]
That were yn that castell.

Ther began the turnement,
And ech knyght leyd on other good dent [183]
Wyth mases [184] and wyth swerdes bothe;
Me myghte yse [185] some, therefore,
Stedes ywonne, and some ylore, [186]
And knyghtes wonder wroth. [187]

Syth the Rounde Table was,
A bettere turnement ther nas,
I dar well say, for sothe.
Many a lorde of Karlyoun
That day were ybore adoun,
Certayn, wythouten othe.

Of Karlyoun the ryche constable
Rod to Launfal, wythout fable;
He nolde no lengere abyde;
He smot to Launfal, and he to hym;
Well sterne strokes, and well grym,
There wer yn eche a syde. [188]

Launfal was of hym yware; [189]
Out of hys sadell he hym bar
To grounde that ylke tyde; [190]
And whan the constable was bore adoun,
Gyfre lepte ynto the arsoun,
And awey he gan to ryde.

---

[181] long horns [182] in a row [183] blow [184] maces
[185] one might see [186] lost [187] ms. *kyȝtes wonþer wroȝth*
[188] on each side [189] wary, cautious
[190] that very time

The Erl of Chestere therof segh;
For wrethe [191] yn herte he was wod negh,[192]
And rood to Syr Launfale,
And smot hym yn the helm on hegh
That the crest adoun flegh —
Thus seyd the Frenssch tale;

Launfal was mochel of myght;
Of hys stede he dede hym lyght,[193]
And bar hym doun yn the dale.
Than come ther Syr Launfal abowte
Of Walssche knyghtes a greet rowte,
The number Y not how fale.[194]

Than myghte me se [195] scheldes ryve,[196]
Speres to-breste and to-dryve,[197]
Behynde and ek before; [198]
Thorugh Launfal and hys stedes dent,
Many a knyght, verement,
To ground was ibore.

So the prys of that turnay
Was delyvered to Launfal that day,
Wythout oath yswore.[199]
Launfal rod to Karl[youn]
To the Meyrys hous [of] the toun,[200]
And many a lorde hym before.

And than the noble knyght Launfal
Held a feste, ryche and ryall,

---

[191] ms. *wreþþe* [192] nearly mad [193] caused him to fall
[194] I know not how many [195] one might see
[196] riven, pierced [197] splintered and shattered
[198] everywhere [199] without any doubt
[200] an ink blot in the ms. obscures the bracketed letters of these two lines, but see ll. 88-89

That leste fourtenyght;
Erles and barouns fale[201]
Semely wer sette yn sale,[202]
And ryaly were adyght.[203]

And every day Dame Triamour,
Sche com to Syr Launfal bour
Aday[204] whan hyt was nyght;
Of all that ever wer ther tho,
Segh[205] her[206] non but they two—
Gyfre and Launfal the knyght.

A knyght there was yn Lumbardye;
To Syr Launfal hadde he greet envye;
Syr Valentyne he hyghte.
He herde speke of Syr Launfal
That he couth justy well
And was a man of mochel myghte.

Syr Valentyne was wonder[207] strong;
Fyftene feet he was longe:
Hym thoughte he brente bryghte
But he myghte[208] wyth Launfal pleye
In the feld, betwene ham tweye
To justy, other to fyghte.

Syr Valentyne sat yn hys halle;
Hys massengere he let ycalle,[209]
And seyde he moste wende
To Syr Launfal the noble knyght,

---

[201] many [202] hall [203] provided for [204] at that time of day
[205] saw [206] ms. *he* [207] ms. *wonþer*
[208] *i.e.* he thought his "envye" would consume him unless he might . . .
[209] caused to be called

That was yholde [210] so mychel of myght:
To Bretayne he wolde hym sende;

"And sey hym, for the love of hys lemman [211] —
Yf sche be any gantyle woman,
Courteys, fre, other hende —
That he come wyth me to juste
To kepe hys harneys [212] from the ruste,
And elles hys manhod schende." [213]

The messenger ys forth ywent
To do [214] hys lordys commaundement;
He hadde wynde at wylle.[215]
Whan he was over the water ycome,
The way to Syr Launfal he hath ynome,[216]
And grette hym wyth wordes stylle,

And seyd, "Syr, my lord, Syr Valentyne,
A noble werrour, and queynte of gynne,[217]
Hath me sent the tylle,
And prayth the, for thy lemmanes sake,
Thou schuldest wyth hym justes take."
Tho lough [218] Launfal full stylle,

And seyde, as he was gentyl knyght,
Thylke [219] day a fourtenyght
He wold wyth hym play.
He yaf the messenger, for that tydyng,
A noble courser [220] and a ryng,
And a robe of ray.[221]

---

[210] held, reputed [211] lady [212] armor, equipment
[213] disgrace [214] ms. *þo*
[215] a willing wind; a wind to his liking
[216] taken [217] clever at the tricks of his trade [218] laughed
[219] that same [220] war horse, charger [221] striped cloth

Launfal tok leve at Triamour,
That was the bryght berde[222] yn bour,
And keste that swete may.[223]
Thanne seyde that swete wyght:
"Dreed the nothyng, Syr gentyl knyght,
Thou schalt hym sle that day."

Launfal nolde nothyng wyth hym have
But Blaunchard hys stede and Gyfre hys kna[ve],
Of all hys fayr mayné.
He schypede and hadde wynd well good,
And wente over the salte flod
Into Lumbardye.

Whan he was over the water ycome,
Ther[224] the justes schulde be nome,[225]
In the cité of Atalye,
Syr Valentyne hadde a greet ost,
And Syr Launfal abatede her bost
Wyth lytyll companye.[226]

And whan Syr Launfal was ydyght[227]
Upon Blaunchard, hys stede lyght,
Wyth helm and spere and schelde,
All that sawe hym yn armes bryght
Seyde they sawe never swych a knyght,
That hym wyth eyen beheld.

Tho ryde togydere thes knyghtes two,
That har schaftes to-broste bo,[228]
And to-scyverede yn the felde;

---

[222] lady [223] maid [224] where [225] held, taken
[226] *i.e.* gave them nothing to boast of since he came with so little company [227] ready for battle
[228] . . . (so hard) that both of their spears broke to pieces

Another cours togedere they rod,
That Syr Launfal helm of glod[229] —
In tale as hyt ys telde.

Syr Valentyn logh and hadde good game;
Hadde Launfal never so moche schame
Beforhond yn no fyght.
Gyfre kedde[230] he was good at nede,
And lepte upon hys maystrys stede
(No man ne segh wyth syght);[231]

And er than they togedere mette,
Hys lordes helm he on sette
Fayre and well adyght.
Tho was Launfal glad and blythe,
And thonkede[232] Gyfre many sythe[233]
For hys dede so mochel of myght.

Syr Valentyne smot Launfal soo
That hys scheld fel hym fro,
Anoon ryght yn that stounde;[234]
And Gyfre the scheld up hente[235]
And broughte hyt hys lord to presente
Er hyt cam doune[236] to grounde.

Tho was Launfal glad and blythe,
And rode ayen the thridde sythe,[237]
As a knyght of mochell mounde;[238]
Syr Valentyne he smot so there
That hors and man bothe deed were,
Gronyng wyth grysly wounde.

---

[229] . . . (so hard) that Launfal's helmet flew off
[230] showed
[231] Gyfre is not seen because, like Triamor, he is invisible
[232] ms. *donkede* [233] times; ms. *syde* [234] place [235] caught
[236] ms. *þoune* [237] ms. *syde* [238] prowess, courage

Alle the lords of Atalye
To Syr Launfal hadde greet envye [239]
That Valentyne was yslawe,
And swore that he schold dye
Er he wente out of Lumbardye,
606 And be hongede and todrawe.[240]

Syr Launfal brayde out hys fachon,[241]
And as lyght as dew he leyde hem doune
In a lytyll drawe; [242]
And whan he hadde the lordes sclayn,
He wente ayen ynto Bretayn
612 Wyth solas and wyth plawe.[243]

The tydyng com to Artour the kyng
Anoon, wythout lesyng,
Of Syr Launfales noblesse;
Anoon a let to hym sende [244]
That Launfale schuld to hym wende
618 At Seynt Jonnys Masse;

For Kyng Artour wold a feste holde
Of erles and of barouns bolde,
Of lordynges more and lesse;
Syr Launfal schud be stuward [245] of halle
For to agye [246] hys gestes alle,
624 For cowthe of largesse.

Launfal toke leve at Tryamour,
For to wende to Kyng Artour
Hys feste for to agye;

---

[239] rancor, malice [240] drawn [241] drew his sword
[242] short while [243] joy
[244] he caused a message to be sent him [245] ms. *stward*
[246] guide, manage

Ther he fond merthe and moch honour,
Ladyes that wer well bryght yn bour,
630 Of knyghtes greet companye.

Fourty dayes leste the feste,
Ryche, ryall, and honeste —
What help hyt for to lye?
And at the fourty dayes ende
The lordes toke har leve to wende,
636 Everych yn hys partye.[247]

And aftyr mete Syr Gaweyn,
Syr Gyeryes, and Agrafayn,
And Syr Launfal also,
Wente to daunce upon the grene
Under[248] the tour ther[249] lay the quene
642 Wyth syxty ladyes and mo.

To lede the daunce Launfal was set;[250]
For hys largesse he was lovede the bet,
Sertayn, of alle tho.
The quene lay out and beheld hem alle;
"I se," sche seyde, "daunce large Launfalle;
648 To hym than wyll Y go.

Of alle the knyghtes that Y se there,
He ys the fayreste bachelere;
He ne hadde never no wyf.
Tyde[251] me good other ylle,
I wyll go and wyte[252] hys wylle;
654 Y love hym as my lyf!"

---

[247] each to his own land [248] ms. *unþer*
[249] where [250] appointed, chosen [251] befall
[252] know

Sche tok wyth her a companye,
The fayrest that sch[e] myghte aspye—
Syxty ladyes and fyf—
And wente hem doun anoon ryghtes,
Ham to pley [253] among the knyghtes
660 Well stylle, wythouten stryf.

The quene yede to the formeste [254] ende,
Betwene Launfal and Gauweyn the hende,
And after, her ladyes bryght
To daunce they wente alle yn same—
To se hem play, hyt was fayr game,[255]
666 A lady and a knyght.[256]

They hadde menstrales of moch honours,
Fydelers, sytolyrs,[257] and trompours,
And elles hyt were unryght; [258]
Ther they playde, for sothe to say,
After mete the somerys day
672 All-what [259] hyt was neygh nyght.

And whanne the daunce began to slake,
The quene gan Launfal to counsell take,
And seyde yn thys manere: [260]
"Sertaynlyche, Syr Knyght,
I have the lovyd wyth all my myght
678 More than thys seven yere.

But that [261] thou lovye me,
Sertes Y dye for love of the,

---

[253] to entertain themselves
[254] formost, or ranking position in the dance group
[255] very pleasant
[256] *i.e.* one after another, knights and ladies alternating
[257] citole players (zither-like stringed instruments)
[258] ms. *vn Rryȝt* [259] until [260] ms. *marnere,* possibly *mainere*
[261] unless

Launfal, my lemman dere!"
Thanne answerede the gentyll knyght:
"I nell[262] be traytour, day[263] ne nyght,
Be God that all may stere!"[264]

Sche seyde, "Fy on the, thou coward!
An-honged worth thou,[265] hye and hard!
That thou ever were ybore,
That thou lyvest, hyt ys pyté!
Thou lovyst no woman, ne no woman the;
Thou wer worthy forlore!"[266]

The knyght was sore aschamed[267] tho;
To speke ne myght he forgo,
And seyde the quene before:
"I have loved a fayryr woman
Than thou ever leydest thyn ey upon
Thys seven yer and more.

Hyr lothlokste[268] mayde, wythoute wene,[269]
Myght bet be a quene
Than thou, yn all thy lyve!"
Therfore the quene was swythe wroth;[270]
Sche taketh hyr maydenes and forth hy go[th]
Into her tour al so blyve;[271]

And anon sche ley doun yn her bedde;
For wreth syk sche hyr bredde[272]
And swore, so moste sche thryve,[273]
Sche wold of Launfal be so awreke[274]

---

262 will not 263 ms. *þay* 264 guide
265 may you be hanged! ms. *An hongeþ*
266 you might as well be dead! 267 enraged, angered
268 loathliest 269 doubt 270 ms. *wroȝt* 271 quickly
272 she made herself sick in her anger 273 as she hoped to thrive
274 avenged

That all the lond shuld of hym speke
Wythinne the dayes fyfe.

Kyng Artour com fro huntynge;
Blythe and glad yn all thyng,
To hys chamber than wente he;
Anoon the quene on hym gan crye:
"But Y be awreke, Y schall dye!
Myn herte wyll breke a-thre!

I spak to Launfal yn my game,
And he besofte [275] me, of schame,
My lemman for to be;
And of a lemman hys yelp [276] he made,
That the lothlokest [277] mayde that sche hadde
Myght be a quene above me!"

Kyng Artour was well wroth,[278]
And be God he swor hys oth
That Launfal schuld be sclawe;
He wente aftyr doghty knyghtes
To brynge Launfal anoon ryghtes
To be honged [279] and to-drawe.

The knyghtes softe [280] hym anoon,
But Launfal was to hys chaumber gon
To han hadde solas and plawe; [281]
He softe hys leef,[282] but sche was lore,[283]
As sche hadde warnede hym before:
Tho was Launfal unfawe! [284]

---

[275] besought [276] boast [277] ms. *lodlokest*
[278] ms. *worþ* [279] ms. *hongeþ* [280] sought [281] amusement
[282] love, beloved [283] gone
[284] distraught, joyless

He lokede yn hys alner,[285]
That fond hym spendyng all plener [286]
Whan that he hadde nede,
And ther nas noon, for soth to say,
And Gyfre was yryde away
Up Blaunchard, hys stede.

All that he hadde before ywonne,
Hyt malt [287] as snow agens the sunne —
In romaunce as we rede;
Hys armur, that was whyt as flour,
Hyt becom of blak colour,
And thus than Launfal seyde:

"Alas!" he seyde, "My creature,
How schall I from the endure,
Swetyng Tryamour?
All my joye I have forlore,
And the, that me ys worst fore,[288]
Thou blysfull berde yn bour!"

He bet hys body and hys hedde ek,
And cursede the mouth that he wyth spek;
Wyth care and greet dolour,
And for sorow yn that stounde,
Anoon he fell aswowe [289] to grounde.
Wyth that come knyghtes four,

And bond hym and ladde hym tho —
Tho was the knyghte yn doble wo! —
Before Artour the kyng.

---

[285] purse [286] that supplied him spending money plenteously
[287] melted [288] and you, whose loss I am the worse for
[289] swooning

Than seyde Kyng Artour:
"Fyle ataynte traytour! [290]
Why madest thou swyche yelpyng?

That thy lemmanes lothlokest [291] mayde
Was fayrer than my wyf, thou seyde;
That was a fowll lesynge! [292]
And thou besoftest her befor than
That sche schold be thy lemman:
That was mysprowd lykynge!" [293]

The knyght answerede with egre mode, [294]
Before the kyng ther he stode,
The quene on hym gan lye: [295]
"Sethe that Y ever was yborn,
I besofte her here beforn
Never of no folye!

But sche seyde Y nas no man,
Ne that me lovede [296] no woman,
Ne no womannes companye;
And I answerede her and sayde
That my lemmannes lothlokest [297] mayde
To be a quene was better worthye. [298]

Sertes, lordynges, hyt ys so;
I am aredy for to do [299]
All that the court wyll loke." [300]
To say the sothe, wythout les,

---

[290] vile, tainted traitor! [291] ms. *lodlokest* [292] lie
[293] an overweening goal [294] eagerly
[295] (that) the queen lied about him [296] nor was pleasing to me
[297] ms. *lodlokest* [298] ms *wordye*
[299] ms. *þo*
[300] command, require

All togedere how hyt was,
Twelve knyght[es] wer dryve to bok.[301]

All they seyde ham betwene,
That knewe the maners[302] of the quene,
And the queste toke:[303]
The quene bar los of swych a word[304]
That sche lovede lemmannes wythout[305] her lord;
Har never on hyt forsoke.[306]

Therfor they seyden alle
Hyt was long on the quene,[307] and not on Launfal;
Therof[308] they gonne hym skere.[309]
And yf he myghte hys lemman brynge,
That he made of swych yelpynge,
Other the maydens, were[310]

Bryghter than the quene of hewe,
Launfal schuld[311] be holde trewe[312]
Of that yn all manere;
And yf he myghte not brynge hys lef,
He schud be hongede, as a thef,
They seyden all yn fere.

Alle yn fere they made proferynge[313]
That Launfal schuld hys lemman brynge;
Hys heed he gan to laye.[314]
Than seyde the quene, wythout lesynge:

---

[301] brought to the book (Bible); *i.e.* sworn in as jurors [302] ways
[303] the inquest undertake
[304] (that) the queen's reputation was such [305] other than
[306] not one denied it of her
[307] (that) the blame belonged to the queen
[308] of that, the first charge [309] acquit [310] (who) were
[311] ms. seems to read *sclud* [312] acquitted [313] they proposed
[314] he laid his head in pledge to bring his lady

"Yyf he bryngeth a fayrer thynge,
Put out my eeyn [315] gray!"

Whan that wajowr [316] was take on honde,[317]
Launfal therto two borwes [318] fonde,
Noble knyghtes twayn;
Syr Percevall and Syr Gawayn,
They wer hys borwes, soth to sayn,
Tyll a certayn day.

The certayn day, I yow plyght,
Was twelve moneth and fourtenyght,
That he schuld hys lemman brynge;
Syr Launfal, that noble knyght,
Greet sorow and care yn hym was lyght:
Hys hondys he gan wrynge.

So greet sorowe hym was upan,
Gladlyche hys lyf he wold a forgon; [319]
In care and in marnynge,
Gladlyche he wold hys hed forgo;
Everych man therfore was wo
That wyste of that tydynge.[320]

The certayn day was nyghyng;
Hys borowes hym broght befor the kyng.
The kyng recordede [321] tho,
And bad hym bryng hys lef [322] yn syght.

---

[315] eyes [316] wager [317] was set

[318] hostages, who, in effect, wagered their own lives guaranteeing not only the appearance of the accused on the appointed day, but also his innocence [319] would have given up

[320] ms. *tydynde*

[321] *i.e.* rehearsed the charges and judgment of Launfal's trial

[322] beloved

Syr Launfal seyde that he ne myght;
Therfore hym was well wo.

The kyng commaundede the barouns alle
To yeve jugement on Launfal,
And dampny hym to sclo.[323]
Than sayde the Erl of Cornewayle,
That was wyth ham at that counceyle:
"We wyllyth [324] naght do so;

Greet schame hyt wer us alle upon
For to dampny that gantylman,
That hath be [325] hende and fre;
Therfor, lordynges, doth be my reed; [326]
Our kyng we wyllyth another wey lede:
Out of lond Launfal schall fle." [327]

And as they stod thus spekynge,
The barouns sawe come rydynge
Ten maydenes, bryght of ble;
Ham thoghte they wer so bryght and schene
That the lothlokest,[328] wythout wene,[329]
Har quene than myghte be.

Tho seyde Gawayne, that corteys knyght:
"Launfal, brothyr,[330] drede the no wyght; [331]
Her cometh thy lemman hende!"
Launfal answerede and seyde, "Ywys,
Non of ham my lemman nys,
Gawayn, my lefly frende!"

---

[323] and damn (condemn) him to be slain [324] ms. *wyllyd*
[325] been [326] do according to my advice [327] be exiled
[328] ms. *lodlokest* [329] doubt [330] ms. *brodyr*
[331] whit; *i.e.* not in the least

To that castell they wente ryght;
At the gate they gonne alyght;
Befor Kyng Artour gonne they wende,
And bede hym make aredy hastyly
A fayr chamber for her lady,
That was come of kynges kende.[332]

"Ho ys your lady?" Artour seyde;
"Ye schull ywyte," seyde the mayde,
"For sche cometh ryde."[333]
The kyng commaundede, for her sake,
The fayryst chaunber for to take
In hys palys that tyde;

And anon to hys barouns he sente
For to yeve jugemente
Upon that traytour full of pryde;
The barouns answerede anoon ryght:
"Have we seyn[334] the maydenes bryght,
Whe[335] schull not longe abyde."

A newe tale they gonne tho,[336]
Some of wele and some of wo,
Har lord the kyng to queme.[337]
Some dampnede Launfal there,
And some made hym quyt and skere;
Har tales wer well breme.[338]

Tho saw they other ten maydenes bryght,
Fayryr than the other ten of syght,
As they gone hym deme;[339]

---

[332] lineage [333] riding [334] since we have seen [335] we
[336] then they began their argument anew; or, then they took a new ballot (tally) [337] please [338] their arguments were heated
[339] as they were reaching a decision, judgment

They ryd upon joly moyles[340] of Spayne,
Wyth sadell and brydell of Champayne;
Har lorayns lyght gonne leme.[341]

They wer yclothed[342] yn samyt tyre;[343]
Ech man hadde greet desyre
To se har clothynge;[344]
Tho seyde Gaweyn, that curtayse knyght:
"Launfal, her cometh thy swete wyght,
That may thy bote[345] brynge."

Launfal answerede wyth drery thoght,[346]
And seyde, "Alas, Y knowe hem noght,
Ne non of all the ofsprynge."[347]
Forth they wente to that palys
And lyghte at the hye deys[348]
Before Artour the kynge,

And grette the kyng and quene ek,
And oo[349] mayde thys wordes spak
To the kyng, Artour:
"Thyn halle agraythe[350] and hele[351] the walles
Wyth clothes[352] and wyth ryche palles,[353]
Agens[354] my lady Tryamour!"

---

[340] mules
[341] their reins shone brightly (probably because gem-studded)
[342] ms. *yclodeþ* [343] clothes of silk [344] ms. *clodynge* [345] help
[346] ms. *doȝt*
[347] a confusing and probably corrupt line; the sense required of the passage would seem to be, "I know them not, nor is my love one of them" (11. 892-897 are paralleled very closely by 11. 357-362 of *Sir Landevale*, the last line of which reads: "My leman of hem ther non is.")
[348] high dais [349] one [350] make ready; ms. *agrayde*
[351] cover, drape [352] drapes; ms. *clodes*
[353] tapestries
[354] against, in preparation for; ms. *A ȝens*

The kyng answerede bedene:
"Wellcome, ye maydenes schene,
Be our Lord, the Savyour!"
He commaundede Launcelot du Lake to brynge hem yn Efere
In the chamber ther har felawes were,
Wyth merth and moche honoure.

Anoon the quene supposed[355] gyle—
That Launfal schulld yn a whyle
Be ymade quyt and skere
Thorugh hys lemman that was commynge.
Anon sche seyde to Artour the kyng:
"Syre, curtays yf thou were,[356]

Or yf thou lovedest thyn honour,
I schuld be awreke of that traytour
That doth me changy chere;[357]
To Launfal thou schuldest not spare—
Thy barouns dryveth the to bysmare;[358]
He ys hem lef and dere."

And as the quene spak to the kyng,
The barouns seygh come rydynge
A damesele alone
Upoon a whyt comely palfrey;
They saw never non so gay
Upon the grounde gone:

Gentyll, jolyf as bryd on bowe,
In all manere fayr inowe
To wonye yn wordly wone.[359]

---

[355] ms. *suppose* [356] ms. omits *thou*
[357] who causes me so much anguish of mind [358] scorn, mockery
[359] to live in wordly dwelling; *i.e.* to be human

The lady was bryght as blosme on brere,
Wyth eyen gray, wyth lovelych chere;
Her leyre [360] lyght schoone.

As rose on rys [361] her rode was red;
The her schon upon her hed
As gold wyre that schynyth bryght;
Sche hadde a crounne upon here molde [362]
Of ryche stones and of golde,
That lofsom lemede [363] lyght.

The lady was clad yn purpere palle,[364]
Wyth gentyll body and myddyll small,
That semely was of syght;
Her mantyll was furryd [365] wyth whyt ermyn,
Ireversyd jolyf and fyn:
No rychere be ne myght.

Her sadell was semyly set;
The sambus [366] wer grene felvet,
Ipaynted wyth ymagerye;
The bordure was of belles
Of ryche gold, and nothyng elles,
That any man myghte aspye.

In the arsouns,[367] before and behynde,
Were twey stones of Ynde,
Gay for the maystrye;
The paytrelle [368] of her palfraye
Was worth an erldome, stoute and gay,
The best yn Lumbardye.

---

[360] visage [361] stem [362] head [363] gleamed [364] rich cloth
[365] ms. *furryþ* [366] saddle-blankets [367] saddle-bows
[368] usually breast armour, but here probably a jewel-studded leather breast-plate for ornament

A gerfawcon [369] sche bar on her hond,
A softe pas [370] her palfray fond,
That men her schuld beholde;
Thorugh Karlyon rood that lady;
Twey whyte grehoundys ronne hyr by;
Har colers were of golde.

And whan Launfal sawe that lady,
To alle the folk he gon crye an hy,
Bothe to yonge and olde:
"Here," he seyde, "comyth my lemman swete!
Sche myghte me of my balys bete,[371]
Yef that lady wolde!"

Forth sche wente ynto the halle,
Ther was the quene and the ladyes alle,
And also Kyng Artour;
Her maydenes come ayens her ryght,
To take her styrop whan sche lyght,
Of the lady, Dame Tryamour.

Sche dede of her mantyll on the flet [372]
That men schuld her beholde the bet,[373]
Wythoute a more sojour; [374]
Kyng Artour gan her fayre grete,
And sche hym agayn wyth wordes swete,
That were of greet valour.

Up stod the quene and ladyes stoute,[375]
Her for to beholde all aboute,
How evene sche stod upryght; [376]
Than wer they wyth her al so donne

---

[369] hunting falcon [370] an easy pace
[371] *i.e.* she might set right my troubles [372] floor [373] better
[374] delay [375] tall, graceful [376] how stately was her bearing

As ys the mone ayen the sonne,
A-day whan hyt ys lyght.[377]

Than seyde sche to Artour the kyng:
"Syr, hydyr I com for swych a thyng,
To skere[378] Launfal the knyght—
That he never, yn no folye,
Besofte the quene of no drurye,[379]
By dayes ne be nyght.

Therfor, Syr Kyng, good kepe thou nyme:[380]
He bad naght her, but sche bad hym
Here lemman for to be;
And he answerede her and seyde
That hys lemmannes lothlokest mayde
Was fayryr than was sche."

Kyng Artour seyde, wythouten othe,
"Ech man may yse that ys sothe,
Bryghtere that ye be!"[381]
Wyth that, Dame Tryamour to the quene geth,
And blew on her swych a breth
That never eft[382] myght sche se.[383]

The lady lep an hyr palfray,
And bad hem alle have good day;
Sche nolde no lengere abyde.
Wyth that com Gyfre all so prest,[384]
Wyth Launfalys stede out of the forest,
And stode Launfal besyde.

---

[377] compared with her, they were as pale as the moon against the sun in daylight [378] to prove the innocence of [379] adultery
[380] ms. *myne*; I have emended to derive the word from O.E. *nimman*, "to take"; thus "take good keep," an idiom still heard
[381] everyone can see that it is the truth: you are the fairer
[382] again, after [383] see 11. 809-810 [384] quickly

The knyght to horse began to sprynge,
Anoon, wythout any lettynge,
Wyth hys lemman away to ryde.
The lady tok her maydenys achon,[385]
And wente the way that sche hadde er gon,
1020 Wyth solas and wyth pryde.

The lady rod thorugh[386] Cardeuyle,
Fer ynto a jolyf ile,
Olyroun that hyghte;[387]
Every yer,[388] upon a certayne day,
Me may here[389] Launfales stede nay,
1026 And hym se wyth syght.

Ho[390] that wyll ther axsy justus,[391]
To kepe hys armes fro the rustus,
In turnement other fyght,
Dar[392] he never forther gon:
Ther he may fynde justes anoon
1032 Wyth Syr Launfal the knyght.

Thus Launfal, wythouten fable,
That noble knyght of the Rounde Table,
Was take ynto fayrye;[393]
Sethe[394] saw hym yn thys lond no man,
Ne no more of hym telle Y, ne can,
1038 For sothe, wythoute lye.

Thomas Chestre made thys tale
Of the noble knyght, Syr Launfale,
Good of chyvalrye;

[385] each one [386] ms. *dorȝ* [387] was named [388] ms. *er*
[389] one may hear [390] whoever [391] ask to joust [392] need
[393] the land of faery [394] afterward; ms. *seþþe*

Jhesus, that ys Hevene-Kyng,
Yeve us alle Hys blessyng,
And Hys Modyr Marye!

Amen
Explicit Launfal

And certys thyng that wolde ye not say
Therfor, Lord, I bed thy selfe aske me
What thyng that ys best for the
For I have lovyd the wyth all thyn ...
Whyle thou made my modyr messyng
And all my ... in that degre
For to pray me for the

The kyng ye to love me on all thyng
Than be thou sekyr at thyn endyng
That thou shalt have more to be
More than any man may have or se
On that thyng or tunge tell
Sythen that thou not to dyde the peyne of hell
Thys was sayd to hym than the Gode
Went on hye that to the ... stod.
The kyng was full of sorowe ...
... any thyng love me ...
That ye erthely more than me
Well be ... and dyed for thee

Lordynges, lyst ye wyll here of dyvers
Of noble men that were ... full
Of knyghtes that were in Englond
... wondyrs for they wold fonde
... aventurs bothe day and nyght
How they myght theyr strength assay
So dyd a knyght, Syr Degare
Lyst ye here what was hys ...
Somtyme in Englond was a kyng
A gret power on all thyng
Stalworth ... and ... stalworth
... in batayle ... forthe

There was no man nor servaunt
That myght wyth hym in turnament
Whether of these two thyng hys sete
So strong was he in body and blode
The kyng had chyld none
Son ne ... but on
A mayden, she loved as hys own lyff
The modyr was dede, the kynges wyff
In travayle of chyld she her lyff lore
But when that mayd of age was
Kynges sonys spake to her tho
Emperours and dukys also
To have that mayd in maryage
For the love of her gret herytage
Than the kyng thys answerd on
That none schuld her have non
But that he myght wyth strength ryde
The kyng owte off hys sadyll to ryde
And doe hym to kysse ... the
Many on asayd they myght yt not doe
Every yere the ... kyng word
A noble feste than ... to holde
For hys quene ... twelve monthys day
That was gravyn in an abbay
Tyll on a day the kyng wold ryde
Un to the abbay wyth mykyll pryde
To doe dyrige and masse bothe
The pore to fede, the nakyd clothe
Hys doghter wyth hym yode
And in a forest she abode
She callyd her chamburlayn her to
And other damysels many mo also
And seyd that she most alyght
Nede her clothys for to dyght
Adown they lyght at a tre
Her damysell and so dyd she

Sir Degaré

Lordynges, yf ye wyll herk and dwell,
Of noblemen Y wole yow tell,
Of knyghtys somtyme in Englond —
How wondyr far [1] they wold fonde [2]
To seke aventyr both nyght and day [3]
How they myght theyr strength asay,
So dydd a knyght, Syr Degaré;
Wyll ye here what man was he?
Somtyme in Englond was a kyng
In grett power over all thyng,
Stowtt in armys unther scheld,
And mekyl thowtyd [4] in battayle and felde.
Ther was no maner man, verament,
That myght wyth hym werr in turnement,
Owt of hys styrop bryng hys fote,
So strong was he in body and blode.
The kyng hadd chyld never non,
Son nor thowtter,[5] butt on:
A mayd-chyld, he lovyd as hys own lyff.
The mother was dede, the kyngys own wyff;
In travayll of chylde sche hur lyfe lees.[6]
Butte whan the mayd of age was,

---

[1] ms. *for* [2] go, fare [3] ms. *day* & *ny3tt* [4] doubted, feared
[5] daughter [6] lost

Kynggys sones spake to hur tho,
Emperoures and dukes, also,
To have that mayd in maryage
For the love of hur gret herytage.
Then the kyng theym answerd ever
That no man schuld hur have never
Butt that he myght wyth stowtt rydyng
This kyng owtt of hys sadyl bryng
And doe[7] hym to lesse[8] hys styroppys two.
Many-on asayd; they myght yt nat doe.
Every yere thys rych kyng wold
A noble feste have and holde[9]
For hys queneys twelve-monthys day,
That was gravyn[10] in a abbay.
Tyll on a day the kyng wold ryde
Unto that abbay wyth mykyl pryde
To doe dyrge and masses both —
The powr[11] to fede, the nakyd cloth.
Hys own thowtter wyth hym rode,
And in a forest sche abode;
Sche callyd hur chamburleyn hur too,
And other damysels many moe also,
And seyd that sche most alyghtte,
Bett[12] hur clothys for to dyghtte.
Adown they lyght at a tre,
Hur damyselss, and so dyd sche.
A well good stownd[13] ther they abode,[14]
Tyll all the folk fro theym rode;
They lokyd up and aftyr they wolde,[15]
Butt they cowth[16] naughtt the ryght wey hold;
The wodd was rowh[17] and thykke, ywys,
And they toke theyr wey amys:

---

[7] cause [8] lose [9] ms. *to holde* [10] buried [11] poor [12] better
[13] time [14] ms. *aboth* [15] would go, follow [16] could [17] rough

They schold have goo south; they went west,
Into the thykke of the forest.
Ynto a laund than they comyn;
Than had they ryght well [18] undyrnomyn [19]
That amys they hadd to for [20] gon.
Adown they lyghtt, everychon,
And callyd and cryed all in fere,[21]
But no man myght ther them here.
The wethyr was hote byfore the non;
They wyst not [22] what was best to don,
Butte leyd theym down on the grene
Unther a hawthorn tre, Y wene.
They fyl asclepe, everylkon,
All butt the kynggys thowtter alon;
Sche went abowt and gaderyd flowrys
And herd the song of somer fowlys.
  So long sche went in that laund, ywys,
That sche ne wyst wher sche was;
To hur damysels sche wold anon,
Butt sche ne wyst how for to gon.
Than sche cryyd evermore,
Wepte and wrong hur handys sore,
And sayd, "Alas, that Y was born!
For well Y wot Y am forlorn!
Wyld bestys schall me gryndyn [23]
That never creature schal me fyndyn!"
  Than wythall sche saw a swet syghtt;
To hur com prikand [24] a joly knyght —
Gentyl, hur thoght, and a joly man —
And ryche robys he had on,
Wel feyr fete and hond;

---

[18] ms. *than had the ryght wey* [19] understanding [20] too far
[21] all together; this line is missing from the ms. and is supplied from *C* [22] ms. *wystyd* [23] tear to pieces [24] riding

Ther was no swilk [25] in the kyngys lond,
So stowtt a man was he.
And seyd, "Madame, God the see; [26]
Be noughtt adrad, thou swete wyght,
Y am com to the as a knyght;
My kynd ys [27] armys for to bere,
On horss to ryde wyth scheld and spere.
Be dradd of me ryght noughtt—
Y have no armys [28] wyth me brought.
I have lovyd the many a yere,
And now Y have found the here;
Ye schalt be my lemman [29] or that ye goe,
Whethyr the lyke wel nor noe!"
No more doe [30] than cowd sche,
Butt weptte and cryed and wold fle.
Anon he bygan hur to hold,[31]
And dydd wyth hur whatso he wold,
And rafte hur of hyr maydynhod.
And seth [32] byfore the lady he stod,
And seyd, "Madame, gentyl and fre,
Wyth chyld Y wot thou schall be;
Wel Y wot yt schall be a knave,[33]
Therfor my swerd thou schallt have.
My swerd ys good and avenauntt; [34]
Therwith I sclew a stowt geauntt.[35]
Y brak the poynt in hys hed;
In the feld ther Y hym leved.
Take yt up; loke yt here;
Thow spekyst not wyth me many a yere,

---

[25] such [26] save
[27] this word is omitted in the ms.; it is given in both *A* and *C*, and since the sense requires it ("my business is to bear arms . . . ."), I have supplied it [28] ms. *harnys* [29] lover, mistress
[30] ms. *to doe*
[31] ms. *take*; "holde" is the word given in *A* and required for the rhyme [32] then [33] boy [34] hardy, comely [35] giant

Yytt paraventure [36] the tyme may com
That Y may speke wyth my son,
And by thys swerd may hym kenne." [37]
He kyst hys lemman and wentt thenne —
The knyghtt passyd forth as he cam.
Well sore wepyng, the swerd sche name; [38]
Sche went away well sore wepyng,
And fande her maydnys all sclepyng.
Sche hydd the swerd as sche myght,
And callyd theym up [39] anon ryght;
And toke theyr horss [40] everylkon
And bygan to ryd forth [41] anon.
Than ther cam, at the last,
Many sqyers prekand fast;
Fro the kyng they were ysentt
To wytte how and were [42] they wentt,
And broughtt hur into the ryght wey,
And wentt forth to that abbey,
And dydd servyse and all theyr thyngys
Wyth many masses and rych offryngys.
Whan the servyse was all ydone,
And gan to passe the hye none,
The kyng to hys palyss gan ryde
Wyth mykyll meyne [43] by hys syde.
Whan every man was glad and blyth,
The mayd syghed and sorowyd swyth; [44]
Hur wombe wexyd and gretyd [45] more;
Sche wepte and wrong her handes sore.
Upon a day as sche sore wepte,
A mayd to hur toke good kepe,
And seyd, "Madam, for charyté,

---

[36] perhaps [37] know [38] took [39] wakened them [40] horses
[41] this word is repeated in the ms., the scribe apparently so hurried that he failed to strike through one of the two, as would be usual [42] where [43] company [44] greatly [45] grew

Why that thow wepyst[46] tell yt me."
"Gentyl mayd, I tell the byfore,
But that thow me help, Y am forlore;[47]
Y have be[48] meke and mylde,
And certys now Y am wyth chyld.
Yf any man yt wytte,
What wold men sey be wey and stret? —
That my father on me yt wan,
For Y ne lovyd never non other man!
And yf my father may yt wytte,
Swych sorow wold to hys hert smytte
That glad schold he never be,
For all hys joye he leyd on me."
Sche told hur all together there
How that chyld was getyn, and where.
"Gentyll mayd, care ye ryght noughtt,
For prevely fro the yt schal be broughtt,
That no man schall yt wytt, sekyrly
Madame, butt thyselff and Y."
  Tyme cam sche was unbounde,
A knave chyld was ther ybore.
Gladd was that lady therfore;
The mayd servyd hur all at hyr wyll,
And delyvyred hole and sounde:
And putt yt in clothys ful styll,
And leyd yt in the cradyll alone,
And was wel redy therwythall to gone.
Yytt the mother bygan yt hold,
And gaff hym twenty pounds[49] of gold
And ten pounds[50] of sylver also;
Unther hys hed sche can yt for to doe —
Mykyll ys that a chyld behovys.[51]
The lady toke a peyr of glovys

[46] ms. *wepyts* [47] lost [48] been [49] ms. *xx £s* [50] ms. *x £s*
[51] needs

Hur lemman to hur for to sonde [52] —
They wold [53] on no womannes hond,
Chyld ne womanys, neyther they nold,
Butt on the mothers hond wel they wold —
And badd that he schold wedd no wyff in lond
Butt yf the glovys wold on hur hond;
For they wold, neyther for [54] nor ner,
But on the modyrs hond that hym bere.
A letter wyth the chyld sche wrote,
The glovys unthyr hys hed sche broughtt;
Sche knytt the letter wyth a threde
Abowt hys nekke, wel good spede.
Then was yt in the letter ywretyn,
Who that hym fyndd schall yt wetyn:
"For Godys love, yf any good man
Thys helples chyld fynd can,
Doe [55] hym to be crystyn off prestys [56] hond,
And help hym to leve in lond
Wyth the tresoure that ye here see
Ten wyntyr old tyll that he be;
And kepe hym wyth hys owen good,
For he ys ycom off gentyll blode."
When that they thus hadd ydone,
The mayd toke the chyld ful sone,
And the cradyll, wyth all these thyng,
And stale awey ryght in the evenyng.
Sche went forth over wyld heth;
Throwgh thykke and thyn, forth sche goth
All the wyntyr-long nyghtt.
The wedyr was feyyr, the mone bryght;
Then wass sche ware anone
Off a hermytage in a stone; [57]
A holy man had ther hys dwellyng.

[52] that her lover sent to her from far away [53] would fit [54] far
[55] let, cause [56] priest's [57] made of stone

Thethyr sche went, wythowt lesyng,
And sette the cradyll at the dore,
Ne durste sche no longer dwell there,
Butt turnyd agayn anon ryght,
And com agayn on the other nyght.[58]
The hermytte ros amorow tho,
And hys man dede also:
"A, Lord, Y cry the mercy!
For now Y here a chyld cry!"
The holy man hys dore undede,
And fond a cradyll in that stede;
He lyffte up the clowtte [59] anon,
And lokyd upon the lytyl grome.[60]
He held that body in hys hond,
And thankyd God of Hys sond.[61]
He bare hym to hys chapel,
And for joy he rang his bel;
He leyd up the glovys and the tresowr,
And crystyn hym wyth mych honowre
In the name off the Trynité.
He callyd the chyld Degaré:
"Degaré" no more than ys
Butt a thyng that ny forlorn ys [62] —
As a thyng that was almost ygo,[63]
Therfor the holy man callyd hym so.
The hermyte was a holy man of lyve;
He hadd a syster that was a wyve.
He sent hur that chyld full rath [64]
Wyth mykyl sylver by hys knave,[65]

---

[58] came home again by the next night [59] cover, blanket [60] boy
[61] mercy
[62] *i.e.* "Degaré" means only something "almost lost"; the French *d'égaré* is no doubt intended, but this may well be a false, or "rationalized" etymology [63] gone, lost
[64] soon, quickly [65] servant

And badd sche schold take good hede
That chyld to noryssh and to fede.
The lytyll chyld, Degaré,
Was born into that cyté;
The good man and hys wyff, in fere,[66]
Keptte hym as theyr own were[67]
Tyll that he was ten yere old—
A well fayr chyld, and a bold,
Well noryschyd, good and hende;[68]
To the ermyte then was he sentt.
The ermyt was gladd hym to see,
So fayr a chyld he was and fre;
And taughtte hym on clerkys lore
Othyr[69] ten yere and more.
When he was a man of twenty yere,
He was a man of gret power;
Ther was no man in all that land
That myght hym grettly[70] wythstand.
Whan that the ermyte saw that case—
That he a man hymselff was,
A stalworth[71] man in every werke,
And off hys tyme[72] a wel good clerke—
He tok hym this gold, wyth hys glovys,
That the ermyte had kepte tyl hys behovys;[73]
Butt this ten pownd off sterlyng
Was spent abowtt hys upbrynggyng.
He tok eke a letter for to rede;
He[74] lokyd in that ylk dede:
"Syr," he seyd, "for charyté,
Was thys letter mad by me?"[75]
"Ye, son, by Hym that me deme shall,
All thys Y found!" and told hym all.

---

[66] together [67] as if he were their own child [68] courteous
[69] another [70] long [71] stalwart [72] for his age
[73] until he should need them [74] Degaré [75] about me; ms. *by be*

He sette hym down al belyve,[76]
And thangyd [77] God wel fele syth,[78]
And seyde he wolde stynt no stownde [79]
Or he had hys kynne founde.[80]
  Halff this gold he gaff the ermytte,
And that other partt up he dydd.[81]
He toke hys leve and wold goe;
The ermyte seyd nay, he schold not so:
"To seke thy kyn thou may not dry [82]
Wythowtt horss and armory." [83]
"Nay, syr," he seyd, "by hevyn kyng!
I woll [84] non other thyng."
Butt a batt,[85] grett and grym,
He bere [86] in hys hond with hym,
A well good staff of a oke;
Whoso he sett therwyth a stroke—
Wher [87] ever he so good a man,
Ne so good armyre had hym uppon—
He schold hym fel to the grounde
Wyth hys batte in a lytyl stounde.
He kessyd the ermytte tho,
And toke hys leve forevermoe.
  Degaré went forth on hys wey
Throwh a forest halff a day;
Man he ne herd, ne no man syghe,
Tyll yt was passyd the non hye;
Than herd he mych noyse wythall,
And grett strokys herd he fall.
Thether fayn wold he
To wytt what that strokys myght be.

---

[76] quickly [77] thanked [78] full many a time [79] abide no time
[80] this couplet I have supplied from *C* since its sense is garbled in *R*: Tyll that he hadd ferder mor found, / He seyd he wold not mykyl syt nor stond [81] he wrapped up [82] endure
[83] armor and weapons [84] wish [85] a stout stick
[86] he bore; ms. *To bere* [87] were

There was an erle, both stout and gaye;
He was come thyther the same day [88]
For to huntt a dere or two,
Butt all hys houndys were went hym fro.
Then was there a dragown, gret and grym,
Full of attyr [89] and venym,
Wyth throtte wyde and tuskys grete;
Upon that knyght faste gan he bete.[90]
As a lyon, he hadd fete; [91]
Hys tayll was grete and unmete; [92]
Bytwyxtt hys hed and hys tayll
Was thirty fete, saun fayle; [93]
Hys body was as wytte wython [94]
As whan that [95] bryght schynnyth the son;
Hys sydys were bryghter than the glass,
Hys wynggys harder than any brass;
He was ymanyd as a sted,[96]
And bare hys hed wyth mykyl prede;
The reke [97] owt of hys mouth gan blow
As yt had be [98] a ferys [99] glow;
He was on to loke,[100] as Y the tell,

---

[88] this couplet is supplied from *U*, which is closest to *R* throughout this whole episode; in *R* the first of the two lines is missing and the second obscure (unless the last word is meant to be "foresters," who are, in any case, never mentioned again): He was comyn thether wyth many fosters [89] poison

[90] this line is supplied from *U* since it seems corrupt in *R*: And wyth the fyght the knyght fast can bete

[91] he had feet like a lion's; ms. *lyn*

[92] huge terrifying; the next 32 lines in *R* are much scrambled, with some groups ordered most illogically; I have reordered them after *U* [93] without fail

[94] as white without (*i.e.* on the outside); the last word is abbreviated and scribbled, but *wython* seems the only possibility in view of the rhyme needed, and it may be a forced and unusual contraction of *wythouten*

[95] ms. *þe*

[96] maned as a horse; ms. *And was . . .* [97] foul breath [98] been

[99] fire's [100] to look on

As yt hadd be the fend off hell;
Many a man hadd he ischentt,[101]
And many horss all torentt.[102]
That erle he hard asayl [103] began,
And he defendyd hym as a man;
Stowttly he smott hym wyth hys swerd,
And grett strokys to hym he gertt.[104]
Off hys strokys ne gaff he non; [105]
Hys skyn was harder than the ston.
  Whan this erle saw Degaré,
He seyd, "Help, syr! For charyté!"
Whan the dragoun saw Degaré cam,
He left the knyght, and to hym nam.[106]
Than the chyld, that was so strong,
Toke hys batt, that was so long,
And smote the dragown on the crown
That in that sted [107] he fyl adown;
And thys byfell at none ryght.
He wrappyd hys tayle wyth swylk a myght
Ryght upon Syr Degaré syde,
Adown he fyll that ylk tyde.[108]
Butt he stert up anon ryght,
And defended hym thoe aplyght,[109]
And wyth hys staff, grett and long,
He brake both fett and hond,
And so he dydd bak and bone,
That the dragon lay styl as ston.
This Degaré was ful strong,
And wyth hys batte, gret and long,
He smott hym on the crown on hye,
That hys hedd all to-flyghe.[110]

---

[101] destroyed [102] torn to pieces [103] ms. *asaly* [104] struck
[105] he gave no heed [106] took [107] place
[108] immediately
[109] fiercely [110] flew all to pieces

Than was the erle gladd and blyth,
And thankyd hym fele syth,[111]
And preyed he shold wyth hym go hom
Tyll hys palyss sone anon.
Thoe answerd Degaré,
"Blythly," he seyd, "so mot Y the!" [112]
There a knyght he gan hym make,
And proferryd hym halff hys [113] good a [114] hadd—
Rentys, tresoure, and halff hys land,
For to sease [115] into hys hand.
Than seyd Syr Degaré:
"Do [116] cum here byfor me
All thy ladys bold—
Wyvys, wedowss, yong and olde,
And also thy dameselss eke;
Yf my glovys be theym mete [117]
To any off all hur honde,
Y wyll fayn take thy londe;
And yf my glovys wyl nat soe,
Be God, Y take my leve and wyl goe!"
All the women were forth ybrought
In all the londd that myght be sought;
All dydd asay [118] the glovys thanne,
Butt wold not [119] serve to no woman.[120]
Syr Degaré hys glovys up-dyde,
And toke hys leve in that stede.
The erle was a man of gentyl blode;
He gaff hym a sted, that full goode,
And also harneyss [121] good and fyn,
Whan that he wold justyn in;

[111] many times [112] as I hope to thrive [113] ms. *ys* [114] he
[115] hold [116] let [117] *i.e.* if they will fit [118] try [119] ms. *no*
[120] but they would not fit any woman
[121] "armor" is apparently meant, and is the word given in the other mss.

And a hakney [122] to ryd upon,
And a knave to be hys man.
Syr Degaré was gladd and [123] blyth,
And thankyd hym fele syth,
And lepet [124] upon hys hakeney,
And went hym forward on hys wey.
Upon a day gret folk he mett;
He hovyd styll and wyth theym lett,[125]
Asked a gentylman, "What tydyng?
Fro whens commyth all this folk rydyng?"
The gentylman answerd, "Verament,
They come fro a parlament;
A counsel the kyng dyd make,
For nedys that he to done hadd;
Butt whan the parlament was most plener,[126]
He dyd do cry,[127] both fer and nere,
Yff ony man was so bold
That wyth the kyng juste wold,
He schold have hys thowtter in maryage,
Hys lond and all hys erytage.
Yt ys a lond both good and fayyr,
And our kyng hath non ayre; [128]
Butt certys, no man dar grauntt therto;
Many man hath yt prevyd,[129] ne they myght do.
For every man that to hym rydd,
Off hym they take grett despyte;
Sume thorowe the body he glytte,[130]
And sume so venously [131] he hytte

---

[122] a riding horse, as opposed to a jousting "steed" [123] ms. *an*
[124] leaped [125] stopped [126] *i.e.* when all had come
[127] caused to be announced [128] heir
[129] attempted; the other mss. give "assayed"; the following word, *ne,* is a mere blurred scribble above the line, and I have supplied it conjecturally because the sense requires it
[130] strikes
[131] vehemently

That no man may doe hym no thyng,
For suche a grace hath our kyng!"
Syr Degaré stod and thought hym upon:
"Y wene Y am a myghty man,
And Y am in my yong blode,
And Y have harneyss rych and good;
And on a welle good stede
Y wyll asay yf that Y may spede.[132]
Yf that Y may bere the kyng adown,
Y may be a man of gret renown;
And yf that he me fel can,
No man wot never what that Y am;
Deth or lyve, whatso me betyde,
I wyl asay yf that Y can ryde."
In that cyté hys in [133] he takys;
He restys [134] hym and mery hym makys.
Upon the morne [135] the kyng he mett;
He knelyd down, and fayyr hym grett,[136]
And sayd, "Syr Kyng, of mykyl myght,
My lord hath sent to the now ryght:
Y warne yow, yt shall be
My lord wyl com and just wyth the;
To juste wyth the he hath ynom." [137]
"Parde," seyd the kyng, "bee hym [138] welcomyn;
Be he baron, be he erle,
Be he gentylman, or cherle,[139]
Man alyve I wyl non forsake;
Whoso all may wyn, all take!"
Upon the morow the day was sett;
The kyng avysyd hym well the bett.[140]

---

[132] succeed [133] inn, lodgings [134] ms. *rest* [135] one morning
[136] greeted [137] undertaken
[138] these two words appear to have been partially rubbed out and written over, and are supplied conjecturally; much of the last eight lines of col. a, fol. 14r is blurred and indistinct
[139] common man, serf [140] considered himself much the better

There was no lyvyng man
That Degaré trystyd mykyl upon;
Butt to the chyrch ryght went he,
And herd a mass off the Trynyté.
To the Father he offryd a floryn,
And to the Son on [141] al so fyne,
And to the Holy Gost the thryde;
The prest for hym wel fast gan bydd.[142]
Whan that the servyse was ydon,
To hys in he went ful sone;
He gan hym arme well and fyne
In ryght good armyr to just in;
Hys good sted he gan to stryde,
And toke a shafft, and bygan to ryde.
Hys knave toke another spere,
And besyde yt bere;
In the feld the kyng he abyde bygan.[143]
The kyng cam rydyng wyth many a man;
Many came thyther redelye,[144]
For they wold the justyng see.
All men that in the feld were,
They seydyn and swore, all in fere,
That they never ne syghe [145]
So fayyr a man wyth theyr ye [146]
As was thoutty [147] Degaré;
But no man wyst what man was he.
But they bygan to ryde up [148] anon,
And Degaré cowd butt lytyl theron; [149]
The kyng had wel the gretter schafte,
And cowd ryght wel hys craffte;

---

[141] one [142] pray [143] he awaited the king
[144] this line is supplied from *U* and *P*; in *R* it reads: Many a man to the feld cam [145] saw [146] eye [147] doughty, strong
[148] to ride toward each other on the jousting course
[149] knew little of jousting

To dassh hym down hadd he yment,
And in hys scheld he sett a dentt
That hys good schafft all tobrast.[150]
Butt Syr Degaré was strong and sate fast;
The kyng seyd then, "Alas, Alas!
Me byfyll never sylk [151] a cas
A man that Y onys [152] myght hytt
That my stroke myght ever sytt.[153]
Thys ys a man, for the nonys,
For he ys a man of strong bonys!"
The kyng toke a gretter tre,[154]
And he swore, "So mutt Y the,[155]
Yyff hys nykke wyll natt two,[156]
Hys bak shall, or that Y goe!"
The kyng rod to hym with tresoun,
And thowght to dassh hym down;
He hyt Syr Degaré anon
Ryght byfore the bryst bon,
That hys sted tofore was reryd on hyghe,
And Syr Degaré was fellyd nye.
Syr Degaré sett hys cowrss owtt ryght,[157]
And he was grevyd [158] owt of hys wyt,
And sayd, "Alas, and wel-a-woe yytt!
The kyng hath me now twyes [159] hytt!
And [160] Y onys wyth hym mete,
By God, Y shalt avyse me bett!"
They rydyn togeders wyth mykyl myght,
In myddys the scheld theyre schafftys pyght,[161]
That theyr good schafftys al torevyn,[162]

---

[150] splintered [151] such [152] once
[153] the last two words here are my conjecture, though they agree with the other versions; the ms. seems to read *we seutt* or *we sentt* [154] a larger shaft [155] as I hope to thrive
[156] break in two [157] rode out the rest of his course [158] angered
[159] twice [160] if [161] thrust [162] broke to pieces

And up to theyr hondys all to-drevyn.[163]
Than the kyng stouttly gan speke:
"Tak [164] me a schafft that wyl nat breke;
He schall down, all and som,[165]
Thow he be as strong [166] as Samson!
And he be the devyl of hel,
He shall down, as Y the tell!"
The kyng tok a schafft of regard; [167]
And Sir Degaré toke another, also hard,
And stowttly to the kyng he rydyd;
The kyng faylyth, and Sir Degaré hym hytt.[168]
Syr Degaré full well he lett
Off the kynggys sted he reryd the forfett; [169]
And boldly he rod up than,
Mawgre woe grucche bygan,[170]
And the kyng owt of hys sadyl he raught—
Horss and man to ground he caughtt.[171]
Than was there mych noyse and crye;
The kyng was sore aschamyd forthye; [172]
And all hys barons to hym cam
To comfort hym, and up hym nam.
Than the kynggys thowtter forthy,
Well Y wott,[173] sche was sory;
For than wel wyst sche
That sche shuld ymaryd be,
And lede hur lyff wyth swych a man
That sche nyst [174] never fro whens he cam.
The kyng seyd to Syr Degaré:
"Come her, son, byfor me.

---

[163] shattered right up to their hands [164] bring, give
[165] he shall be struck down completely [166] ms. *astrong*
[167] strong, worthy of regard
[168] the words *kyng* and *hym* are omitted in *R* and supplied from the other versions
[169] *i.e.* Sir Degaré caused the king's horse to rear up his forefeet
[170] despite whosoever (*woe*) did begrudge it [171] cast
[172] for that defeat [173] know [174] knew not

And [175] thou were al so gentyl a man
As thou semyst to loke upon,
And kowdyst wysdom doe
As thow art thowtty [176] therto,
Y hold my land well ysett.
Be thou wyrss, be thow bett,[177]
Forward [178] Y must me nedys hold.
Here byfore my baronss bold
Y take [179] the here my thoutter by the honde,
And sease [180] the wyth all my lond,
To be my eyyre [181] aftyr me;
And good God maynteyn the!"
Gret purvyauns [182] ther was ywrought;
To chyrch-dur [183] they were broght,
And were yweddyd, verament,
Unther the holy sacrament.
Butt loke what foly and balaunce [184]
Befallyth many man throghe chaunce
That [185] com togedyrss wyth gay rede
To take a wyff for any mede! [186]
For he knew nat off hur kyn,
Ne sche ne knew ryght [187] nought off hym;
And were ordeyn together for to lybbe,[188]
Yytt paraventure they myght be sybbe.[189]
So dyd Syr Degaré the bold:
He weddyd hys mother, to have and hold.

---

[175] if [176] doughty
[177] whether you are worse or better, *i.e.* poor or rich, low-born or noble [178] promise, agreement [179] give [180] seize, cede to
[181] heir [182] preparation
[183] church door, the place of the marriage ceremony
[184] probably "bale-ance," sorrow [185] who; ms. *They*
[186] reason, reward; the sense of these lines is somewhat garbled and is clearer in *A*: See what sorrow befalls a man who comes into an unknown land and takes a wife, for whatever reason, without knowing who she is or of what kin [187] ms. *rygh*
[188] live [189] relatives

God wot all, and that ye may both se and here:
He wold not that they synnyd in fere.[190]
   It passyd over the hye non,
And the day was nyghe done;
To bed schuld [191] he and sche
Wyth grett solempnyté.
Syr Degaré stod and thoughtt hym upon,
Off the ermyte, that holy man:
That he schuld, for no wele,
Wedde no damysele
Butt sche myght the glovys two
Lyghtly [192] on hur handys doe.
"Alas!" seyd Syr Degaré,
"What fortune fallyth to me?
Wykkyd man that Y am,
Me were lever than all this kyndom
That ys ysesyd into my hond
That Y were fare owtt of this lond!"
   The kyng those wordys herd thoe,
And seyd, "Syr Degaré, why seyst thou soe?
Ys ther aught [193] ageyns thy wyll
Evyll ydon or seyd yll?
Aughtt ageyns the mysdone?
Tell yt me; yt schall be amendeyd sone!"
"Nay, lord," he seyd, and spak:
"Butt Y wyll never, for no wedloke,
Wyle [194] Y am alyve, wyth no woman dele —
Wyff, wedow, nor no damysele —
But sche myght these glovys twoe
Lyghtly [195] on hur handys doe."
The lady thoe [196] thus gan here;
Anon sche schaungyd all hur chere,

---

[190] together   [191] should go   [192] ms. *lyȝthly*
[193] anything; ms. *auȝth*   [194] while   [195] ms. *lyghly*
[196] ms. *doe*

All anon chaungyd here mode:
Here vysage waxed as red as the blod;
Sche knew the glovys that were hur.[197]
"Tak me the glovys, swete sur."
Sche toke the glovys in that sted,
And lyghtly on hur handys sche dyd.
Sche fyll down and bygan to crye:
"Lord," sche seyd, "Y cry the mercy!
Y am the mother which [198] the bare,
And thou artt my sone here!"
Syr Degaré well swyth thoe [199]
Toke hur in hys armys two—
They were both gladd and blyth—
And kyst hure mowth [200] and many a syth.
Than the kyng grett mervayle hadd
Off the noyse [201] which [202] that they maad,
And was ferefull [203] of theyr wepyng,
And seyd, "Dame, what ys thys thyng?"
"Syr," sche seyd, "Y wyll that ye here:
Ye wend that Y a maydyn were;
Nay, by God; Y am none,
For yt ys twenty wyntyr gone
That mi maidenhed I les
In a forest as I wes; [204]
Thys ys my sone, God yt wot wele,
And by these glovys full well Y the telle."
And told hym altogedere
How that chyld was getyn, and where.
Than spake Syr Degaré:
"Swete madame, thou sey me,

---

[197] hers [198] ms. *wich* [199] ms. *doe* [200] ms. *owt*
[201] sorrowing [202] ms. *wich*
[203] concerned
[204] this couplet is supplied from *A*; in *R* its first line reads "That Y my maydynhod dyd bere"; its second line is omitted

Were [205] ys my fadyrss wonnyng?
Whan herd ye of hym any tydyng?"
"Nay, son," sche seyd, "by hevyn Kyng,
Y the of hym kan tell no tydyng.
Butt whan thy father fro me raughtt,[206]
A poyntles swerd he me betaughtt,[207]
And bad me take yt the forthan
Yyff that thou levyst and were a man."
Sche fet [208] hym the swerd anon ryght,
And Syr Degaré yt up plyghtt.[209]
Long and brod, Y wot, yt was;
In all the lond no swych swerd ther nas.
"Certys," seyd Syr Degaré forthan,
"Whosoe thys owyth,[210] he was a man!
Now Y have all that Y kepe; [211]
Nyght nor day wyl Y slepe
Untyl the tyme Y my father see,
In Crystyndom yf that he be!"
He made hym mery that ylk nyght;
Amorow, when yt was daylyghtt,
He went to chyrch and herd mass,
And was all redy for to pass.[212]
Than seyd the kyng, "My leve frend,
Take of my knyghtys wyth the to wende."
Syr Degaré seyd, "Gramercy thenne,
For Y wyll non of all thy menne,
Butt my man to take good hede
To my harneys and to my stede."
He lept upon hys hakney,
And hym dyghtt forward on hys wey;

---

[205] where [206] left [207] gave [208] fetched [209] took up
[210] owns
[211] the sense seems to be "Now I have all that I care about"
[212] go

Many a myle and many gret jorney
He rode forth on his palfrey.[213]
Evermore he rode ryght west
Into the thyke of a forest;
Wyld bestys went hym by,
And bryddys song[214] so many and hyghe.
So long he rod, yt fyl to nyght;
The son went doune that was so bryght.
Tyl a town then wold he ryde,
Butt he wyst in no syde.[215]
Theraftyr long he saw a castel clere[216] —
A mayd, forsoth, dwellyd there —
A fayr castell off lyme and stone;
In the farest[217] was town none.
Syr Degaré seyd to hys man that tyde:
"Unto that castell we wyll ryde,
And abyde wyll we
To aske harborow[218] for charyté."
The brygge[219] was down thoe,
And the yatys[220] were opyn also;
Into that castel he cam full good spede.
And fyrst he stabelyd his sted,
And tyyed up hys hakney;
Ynowth[221] he fond of corn and hey.
He went abowtt and bygan to call,
Both in bour and eke in hall;
Neyther for lowth,[222] neyther for awe,
Lyvys[223] man he ne herd nother saw.
In the myddys ryght of the hall flore

[213] this line is missing in *R* and supplied from *U* and *P*
[214] birds sang
[215] *i.e.* but he knew of none in any direction
[216] the last word of this line is missing in *R* and supplied from *U* and *P* [217] forest [218] lodging [219] drawbridge [220] gates
[221] enough [222] fear [223] living

Ther was a fyyr, gret and stowr:
"Parmafay!" [224] seyd thys syre,
"Whoso made thys ylk fyre,
He wyll com agayn this ylk nyght;
Y schall abyd, as Y am knyght."
He sett hym down on the deyse,[225]
And warmyd hym at hys ese.
Than was he ware off on [226]
That in at the dore com
Four maydynys, fayr and fre,
That were trussyd [227] to the kne;
Tweyn [228] of theym bowys bere,
And tweyn of theym chargyd [229] were
Wyth venyson, both rych and good.
And Syr Degaré thoe up stod,
And blyssyd hym [230] anon ryght;
And they answerd not thys knyghtt,
Butt went into the chambre everylkon,
And speryd [231] the dore son anon.
Theraftyr well long wythall
Ther come a dwerff into that hall;
Foure fote of length was in hym;
Hys vysage was gret and grym,
But hys berd and eke hys face
Was as yelow as any wax.
He seyd neyther bow ne be,[232]
Butt ryght stowttly lokyd he.
He hadd on a sorkett hovertt [233]

---

[224] by my faith [225] dais, a raised table in the hall
[226] possibly "on ware of" (aware of) awkwardly inverted for the sake of the rhyme [227] bound, as with hunters' leather thongs
[228] two [229] burdened
[230] greeted them with a blessing, as "God save you!"
[231] sparred; barred and latched
[232] this line seems to be corrupt; if not, it may mean "He said nothing, nor bowed, nor bent" [233] an outer coat open at the front

Wyth menyver furryd apert.[234]
He was clodyd and well dyghtt; [235]
Hys schone were copyd as a knyght; [236]
He was mykyl of fote and hond
As the most [237] man of a land.
Syr Degaré lokyd on hym and lowth,[238]
And gretyd hym wel and fayr ynowth;
And he agayn [239] spak no word,
But was redy to sett a bord,[240]
And leyd both cloth and bred,
Wyn, both whyte and red;
Torchys in the hall he lyghtte,
And redy to soper they were dyghtte.
Theraftyr long, wyth mykyl honoure
Ther com a lady owtt of hur boure;
With hur ther com maydnys ten,
Sum in skarlett, sum in grene.
Syr Degaré blyssyd hym anon ryght,
And they answerd nat thys knyght,
Butt to the table they went, everylkone,
And fast to soper they can togone.[241]
The lady was wel fayr and bryght;
Sche sett hur amyddys the deyse ryght,
Be every syd [242] maydnys fyve;
The dwerff theym servyd al so blyve.[243]
"Be God!" seyd Syr Degaré,
"I have yow blyssyd, and ye naughtt me!
Butt ye [244] be dumbe, by and by
Y schall doe [245] yow speke tonyghtt, so the!"

---

[234] appropriately trimmed with a fine grey fur
[235] well clothed and arrayed
[236] the leather of his shoes was cut away in designs, as a knight's shoes [237] largest [238] bowed [239] in return [240] table
[241] did go, went [242] on each side [243] well, quickly
[244] ms. *sche* [245] cause

Syr Degaré cowth of curtesy;
He toke a chayr and set tofore [246] the lady,
And hymselff therin he sett,
And toke a knyve and kut hys met.
Lytyl met at soper ete he
For lokyng of that lady so fre;
Sche was the fayryst woman one [247]
That ever wyth eyyen [248] he lokyd hone; [249]
All hys hertt and all hys thowtt
Was only on that lady broughtt.
Whan they had sopyd ynowth,
The dwerff com and the cloth drowth; [250]
And tho they rose, everychone,
And to the chamber gan they gone.
"Be God!" seyd Sir Degaré, "After Y wyll,[251]
To loke on the lady ther my fyll.
Whoso me warn, Y wyll be by,[252]
Or doe hym make [253] a sory cry!"
Up at the gres [254] hys wey he nam,
And sone into that chamber he cam.
The lady was both fayr and bryght;
Sche set hur amyddys the bed ryght;
Sche harpyd the notys good and fyn;
A mayd fyllyd the pese [255] wyth wyn.
And Syr Degaré set hym down
To here of the harpys sown;
Thorow the notys that sche harpyd schryll,
He fyl down and sclept hys fyll.
The lady wyth all hur myght
Kevertyd [256] hym anon ryght;

---

[246] before [247] one of the fairest women [248] eyes; ms. *eyȝen*
[249] on, upon [250] withdrew [251] will go, follow
[252] whoever tries to stop me, I will get by him
[253] cause him to make
[254] grace; probably the sign of the cross made at the end of the meal [255] piece, wine glass [256] covered

Clothys [257] unther hys hed sche dydd,
And went to bed in another sted.
Upon the morow, when yt was day,
The lady rose and went hur wey;
Into hur chamber the wey can tak,
And seyd, "Syr Knyght, awake!"
The lady seyd, upon hur game,[258]
"Ye were worthy to have blame!
As a best all nyght ye sclepyth,
And of my maydnys naughtt ye kepyth!" [259]
Than answerd Syr Degaré,
"Mercy, madame, forgyf [260] yt me;
The notys of thy harp yt mad,
Other ells the good wyn that Y hadd.
But tell me now, my lady hend [261] —
Owtt of thy chamber or [262] Y wend —
Who ys lord of thys lond,
Who hath thys castell in hys hond,
Whethyr that ye be mayd or wyff,
In what maner ye led yowr lyff,
And why be here thus fele women
Alone here, wythowttyn men."
"Syr, blythly woll Y yow tell wythall,
Yf me the better myght befall: [263]
My father was a bold baronne,
And hadd both towr and towne;
He had no chyld butt me.
And Y am hys eyre in thys cuntré;
I held men and many a knyght,
And many squyer wel ydyghtte,
And many men of maystre [264]

---

[257] pillows [258] in jest
[259] probably "guard"; but possibly (in keeping with the lady's "game") "pay attention to," "care about" [260] ms. *for yf*
[261] kind, fair [262] before [263] if I may fare any better
[264] of mastery, *i.e.* serfdom

To serve me, both fer and ner.
Than hovyth her bysyde [265]
A stowtt geaunt,[266] knowyn wyde;
He hath me lovyd many a yere,
And Y may love hym never the more.
He ys abowt be maystré [267]
For to doe me a vylony,
And all my men hath sclayn echone —
All-but [268] my dwerff, he levyd me none."
As they stod sche fyl to ground,
And swonnyd ther upon stounde; [269]
All hur damysels to hur com
To comfort hur, and up hur nam.
The lady lokyd on Degaré;
"Leve madam," tho seyd he,
"Be glad now that Y am here;
Y wyll the help wyth my power."
"Syr," sche seyd, "all [270] my lond
Y wyll sease into [271] yowr hand,
And all my good Y wyl the geve,
And my body, whyle that Y leve,
For to be at yowr wyll,
Erly and latte, lowd and styll,[272]
And thy lemman redyly,
To help me of [273] my enmye."
Than was Syr Degaré glad to fyghtt,
And full fayn yf that he myght —
Yf he myght scle that other knyght
To wynne thys damysel that ys so bryght.
As they stodyn and spak in fere,
A mayd cam cryand wyth hevy chere,

---

[265] came here nearby [266] giant [267] by force [268] except
[269] in that place; ms. *ther up and . . .* [270] ms. *with all*
[271] ms. *on to* [272] at any time, in all respects
[273] if you will help me against

And bad, "Draw the brigg and spar the yate;
Our enemy [274] comyth fast therat!
Or ells he wyl us scle ylkon!"
Syr Degaré stert up anon;
Owtt at a wyndow he hym syghe,[275]
And armyd was on horss hyghe;
So stowtt a man as he was one
In armys saw Degaré never none.

Syr Degaré armyd hym as blyve; [276]
Upon a stede he can owtt dryve,
And rod the geaunt agayn;
And they strok together wyth mykyl mayn,[277]
That both theyr good schafftys al tobrast.[278]
But Syr Degaré was strong, and sat fast;
Butt his stedys bak all tobarst a-two,
And Syr Degaré fyll to ground thoe.
Syr Degaré stertt up and lowghe,[279]
And his good swerd owtt drowgh,
And seyd to the geauntt anon,
"On fote we [280]schull togethyr gon!"
Swych a strong stroke gaff hym Syr Degaré
That ryght to the grownd than fyll he.
"Thou hast ysclayn my good stede,
And Y schall quyte the thy mede; [281]
Scle thy stede naughtt Y ne kepe,[282]
Butt on fote wyth the to fyghtt."
Then faughtt they on fote in fere
Wyth styff strokys on helmys clere;
The geaunt gaff Syr Degaré
Good strokys gret plenté,

---

[274] this word is omitted in *R* and supplied from *U* and *P* [275] saw
[276] quickly [277] force [278] ms. *to barst* [279] laughed
[280] ms. *whe* [281] pay you your reward
[282] I do not care to; it will be seen that the rhyme of this couplet is imperfect, but the other versions do not offer good possibilities for reconstruction and I have let it stand

And Syr Degaré dyd hym also,
Tyll helm and hauberk brak a-two.
The geaunt was grevyd sore
That hys armyr brokyn were;
Syr Degaré smot sore a-plyghtt,
That swych a stroke he gaf that other knyght —
Upon hys crown he hym hytt
Throw hed, helm, and basynet,
And at the brygerdyl[283] the swerd stent[284] —
He fyll to the ground, verament.[285]
The lady sat[286] in that castell,
And byheld that batayll, everydell[287] —
How the geaunt was a-sclaw,[288]
And broughtt owt of hys lyve-daw.[289]
Sche was fayn off that syghtt
As ys the fowle of hys flyghtt.
Syr Degaré com to that castell;
Agaynss hym[290] com the damysell;
Sche thangyd[291] hym mykyl of his good dede,
And into chamber sche gan hym lede.
Sche sett hym on hyr bed ryght,
And unarmyd this gentyl knyght;
Sche toke hym in hyr armys blyve,
And kyssyd hym a hundred syth:
"Now all my good Y wyll yow gyve,
And my body, whyl that Y leve,
For to be at yowr wyll,
Erly and late, lowd and styll."
"Grammercy, damysel," seyd he,
"Of that profer ye bydd me;

[283] collarbone [284] stopped
[285] in the ms. the order of these two lines is reversed
[286] this word is omitted in *R* and supplied from *U*
[287] every bit [288] slain [289] life's days [290] to meet him
[291] thanked

Butt Y must [292] into other londe
Mor aventure for to fond.[293]
But or this twelmonth be agoe,[294]
Damysel, Y com agayn the to."
Sche gaff hym sylver, gold, and rych armyr,
And other thingys wer good and dere.
He tok hys leve in all thyng,
And betaughtt [295] hur to hevyn Kyng;
The lady mad mykyll mornyng,
And wepte ryght sore at hys departyng.
  Syr Degaré went forth in hys way
Many a myle and many jorney;
Evermore he rod ryght west
Into a lawnd of a forest.
  To hym com prekand a joly knyghtt
Upon a sted both good and lyghtt,
In armys both good and dere.
Hys scheld was poyntyd wyth asure; [296]
Three borys hedys were [297] therin
That were ymad of gold ful fyn.
Wele feyyr blyssyd [298] he that other knyghtt;
And he hym answerd anon ryght,
And he seyd, "Velaine,[299] what dost thou here
In my forest to stroy [300] my dere?"
Syr Degaré seyd wyth wordys meke,
"Syr, of thy dere Y ne kepe;
Y am aventurss knyght,
For to seke were [301] and fyghtt."
The knyght answerd, and seyde, "Sauns [302] fayle,

---

[292] must go [293] seek [294] gone [295] blessed
[296] painted, or possibly pointed (trimmed), with azure
[297] this word is omitted in *R* and supplied from *U* and *P*
[298] greeted
[299] the ms. reads *belamy* (good friend), which would be inconsistent with the tone of the address; the other versions give *villain* [300] destroy [301] war [302] ms. *saunȝ*

Yf that thou be com to seke batayle,
Doe arme the in a stound,
For now thou hast thy pere [303] yfound!"
Syr Degaré and hys squyer
Dede arme theym in rych atyr; [304]
A well good helm, for the nonys—
Yt was full of precyus stonys—
The lady hyt hadd gyve hym, san fayle,
That he had won in batayle.
He cast a scheld abowt hys swere; [305]
Yt was of armys [306] good and dere;
His good sted he bygan to stryde,
And toke a schafft and bygan to ryde.
Hys squyer toke another spere,
And by his syde he gan ytt bere.
(But, lo, what foly bygan [307] that tyde!
The sone agayn the father gan ryde,
Butt neyther knew other a-ryght!)
  And thus bygan the ferst fyghtt:
Syr Degaré [308] had well the gretter schaft,
And cowd well hys craft;
To dassh hym down had he mentt,[309]
And in hys scheld he set a dentt
That hys good schafft all tobrast.[310]
Butt the knyght was strong and sat fast.
Another courss then had they tak: [311]
The father for the sonys sake
[Tok] a sschaft that was gret and long,

[303] better; no doubt the pun on French *pere* (father) is intended
[304] attire; ms. *artyr* [305] neck
[306] *i.e.* it bore a heraldic device; ms. *amys*
[307] befell
[308] *Degaré* is omitted in *R* and supplied from *A* and *U*
[309] mind, intent [310] ms. *to barst* [311] ms. *takyn*

And he another, al so strong;[312]
So hard they smytte together, forsoth,
That theyr stedys bakkys tobrak both;
Then faughtt they on fote in fere
Wyth steff strokys on helmys clere.
But the knyght amerveyld[313] ys
Of Degaré ys swerd,[314] that was poyntles,[315]
And seyd than, anon ryght,
"Abyde awhyle, thou gentyll knyght;[316]
Wher was thou born, and in what land?"
"In Yngland, Syr, Y undyrstand;
Y am the kynggys thowtter sone,[317] ywys,
But Y ne wott who my father ys."
"What ys thy name?" seyd he.
"Syr, Y hyghtt[318] Syr Degaré."
"Syr Degaré, thow art welcome,
For, redely,[319] thow artt my sun!
By thys swerd Y knew the here;
The poyntt ys in my pawtever."[320]
He toke the poynt and set thertyl,[321]
And yt joyned, all at wyll.[322]
So long[323] they dydd the batayl togedyr,
Both the sun and eke the father,
There they were full well at one—
The father wyth the sun alone.
Syr Degaré and hys father dere,
Into Ynglond they went in fere.

---

[312] this couplet is missing in both *R* and *U*; since it is required to complete the sense of the previous line, I have supplied it from *A* [313] astonished [314] of Degaré's sword
[315] ms. *poynles*
[316] this line is missing in *R* and supplied from *U* and *P*
[317] the king's daughter's son [318] I am called [319] truly
[320] pocket, purse [321] *i.e.* set it to the end of Degaré's sword
[322] easily [323] *i.e.* after so long

They were armyd and well dyghtt;
As sone as the lady saw that knyght,
Wonther wel sche knew the knyght;
Anon sche chaungyd hur colowr aryght,
And seyd, "My dere [324] sun, Degaré,
Now thou hast broughtt thy father wyth the!"
"Ye, madame, sekyr thow be; [325]
Now well Y wot that yt ys he."
"I thank, by God," seyd the kyng,
"Now Y wot, wythowtt lesyng,[326]
Who Syr Degaré his [327] father was!"
The lady swounyd in that plass.
Then afterward, now sykyrly,
The knyghtt weddyd the lady;
Sche and hur sun were [328] partyd a-twynn,
For they were to nyghe off kyn.
Now went forth Syr Degaré;
He toke wyth hym the kyng and his meyné,[329]
His father and his mother dere.
Hom into that castel they went in fere
Wher that wonnyd that lady bryght
That he hadd wonne in gret fyght,
And weddyd hur wyth gret solempnité
Byfor all the lordis in that cuntré.
Thus cam the knyght outt of his care;
God gyff [330] us grace well to fare.

Amen

The lyff of Syr Degaré
Both curteys and fre.

---

[324] *my dere* is omitted in *R* and supplied from *U* and *P*
[325] you are right [326] without doubt [327] Sir Degaré's
[328] ms. *we* [329] retinue [330] ms. *yff*

Lay le Freine.

We redeþ oft & findeþ y write
As þis clerkes wele it wite
Layes þat ben in harping
Ben y founde of ferli þing.
Sum beþe of wer & sum of wo
& sum of ioie & mirþe al so
& sum of trecherie & of gile
Of old auentours þat fel while
& sum of bourdes & ribaudy
& mani þer beþ of fairy.
Of al þinges þat men seþ
Mest o loue for soþe þai beþ.
In bretayne bi hold time
þis layes were wrouȝt so seiþ þis rime.
When kinges miȝt our y here
Of ani meruailes þat þer were
Þai token an harp in gle & game
& maked a lay & ȝaf it name.
Now of þis auentours þat weren y falle
Y can tel sum ac nouȝt alle.
Ac herkneþ lordinges soþe to sain
Ichil ȝou telle lay le frayn.
Bifel a cas in bretayne
Wher of was made lay le frain.
In ingliche for to tellen y wis
Of an asche for soþe it is.
On ensaumple fair wiþ alle
Þat sum time was bi falle.
In þe west cuntre woned tvay kniȝtes
& loued hem wele in al riȝtes
Riche men in her best liif
& aiþer of hem hadde wedded wiif.
Þat o kniȝt made his leuedi milde
Þat sche was wonder gret wiþ childe.
& when hir time was comen þo
Sche was delyuerd out of wo.
Þe kniȝt þonked god almiȝt
& cleped his messanger an hiȝt.
Go he seyd to mi neiȝebour swiþe
& say y gret him fele siþe
& pray him þat he com to me
& say he schal mi gossibbe be.
Þe messanger goþ & hab nouȝt forȝete
& fint þe kniȝt at his mete
& fair he gret in þe halle
Þe lord þe leuedi þe meyne alle
& seþþen on knes doun him sett
& þe lord ful fair he grett.
He bad þat þou schust to him te
& for loue his gossibbe be.
Is his leuedi deliuerd wiþ sounde
Ȝa sir y þonked be god þe stounde.
& wheþer a maidenchild oþer a knaue
Tvay sones sir god hem saue.
Þe kniȝt þer of was glad & bliþe
& þonked godes sond swiþe
& graunted his erand in al þing
& ȝaf him a palfray for his tiding.
Þan was þe leuedi of þe hous
A proude dame & an enuious
Hokerfulliche missegging
Squeymous & eke scorning.
To ich woman sche hadde envie
Sche spac þis wordes of felonie.
Ich haue wonder þou messanger
Who was þi lordes conseiler
To teche him about to sende
& telle schame in ich an ende
Þat his wiif haþ to childer y bore.
Wele may ich man wite þer fore
Þat tvay men hir hadde bi
& þat is hir boþe deshonour.
Þe messanger was sore aschamed.
Þe kniȝt him self was sore agramed
& rebouked his leuedy
To speke ani woman vilaynie.

Lay Le Freine

We redeth oft, and findeth ywrite,
And this clerkes wele it wite,[1]
Layes that ben in harping,
Ben yfounde of ferli[2] thing:
Sum bethe of wer and sum of wo,
And sum of joie and mirthe also,
And sum of trecherie and of gile,
Of old aventours that fel while;[3]
And sum of bourdes and ribaudy,[4]
And many ther beth of fairy;[5]
Of al thinges[6] that men seth,[7]
Mest o love, forsothe, thai beth.
In Breteyne, bi hold time,[8]
This layes were wrought, so seith this rime.
When kinges might our[9] yhere
Of ani mervailes that ther were,
Thai token an harp in gle and game,
And maked a lay and gaf it name.
Now, of this aventours that weren yfalle
Y can tel sum, ac[10] nought alle.
Ac herkneth, lordinges, sothe to sain;
Ichil[11] you telle "Lay le Frayn."

---

[1] know [2] wondrous [3] adventures that happened long ago
[4] coarse jokes and ribaldry [5] fairyland [6] ms. *þingeþ*
[7] tell of [8] in olden times [9] anywhere [10] but [11] I will

Bifel a cas [12] in Breteyne,
Wherof was made "Lay le Frain";
In Ingliche for to tellen, ywis,
Of an asche [13] forsothe it is
On ensaumple, fair withalle,
That sumtime was bifalle.
In the west-cuntré woned tvay knightes,[14]
And loved hem wele in al rightes —
Riche men, in her best liif,
And aither of hem hadde wedded wiif.
That o [15] knight made his levedi [16] milde
That sche was wonder gret with childe;
And when hir time was comen tho,[17]
Sche was deliverd out of wo.
The knight thonked God Almight,
And cleped [18] his messanger an hight:[19]
"Go," he seyd, "to mi neighebour swithe,[20]
And say Y gret him fele sithe,[21]
And pray him that he com to me,
And say he schal mi gossibbe [22] be."
The messanger goth and hath nought forgete,
And fint the knight at his mete;
And fair he gret in the halle
The lord, the levedi, the meyne [23] alle.
And sethen [24] on knes doun him sett,
And the lord ful fair he gret:
"He bad that thou schult to him té,[25]
And for love his gossibbe be."
"Is his levedi deliverd with sounde?" [26]
"Ya, sir, ythonked be God the stounde!" [27]
"And whether,[28] a maidenchild other a knave?" [29]

---

[12] case, event [13] ash-tree [14] lived two knights; ms. *kni3te*
[15] one [16] lady [17] then [18] called [19] on high, there
[20] quickly [21] many times [22] godparent
[23] company, household [24] then; ms. *seþþen* [25] come
[26] soundly, safely [27] for the time [28] which [29] boy

"Tvay sones, sir, God hem save!"
The knight therof was glad and blithe,
And thonked Godes sond[30] swithe,
And graunted his erand in al thing,
And gaf him a palfray for his tiding.
Than was the levedi of the hous
A proude dame and an envieous —
Hokerfulliche missegging,[31]
Squeymous[32] and eke scorning.
To ich woman sche hadde envie;
Sche spak this wordes of felonie:
"Ich have wonder, thou messanger,
Who was thi lordis conseiler,
To teche him about to sende
And telle schame, in ich an ende,[33]
That his wiif hath to[34] childer ybore
Wele may ich man wite[35] therfore
That tvay men hir han hadde in bour;
That is hir bothe deshonour!"
The messanger was sore aschamed;
The knight himself was sore agramed,[36]
And rebouked his levedy,
To speke ani woman vilaynie.
And ich woman therof might here,
Curssed hir alle yfere,[37]
And bisought God in heven,
For His holy name seven,
That yif hye[38] ever ani child schuld abide,
A wers aventour hir schuld bitide.
Sone therafter bifel a cas
That hirself with child was.
When God wild, sche was unbounde,

---

[30] mercy [31] slanderously missaying, lying [32] disdainful
[33] all around, everywhere [34] two [35] know [36] angered
[37] together [38] she

And deliverd al with sounde:
To[39] maidenchilder sche hadde ybore.
When hye it wist, wo hir was therfore;
"Allas," sche seyd, "that this hap come;
Ich have ygoven[40] min owen dome![41]
Forboden bite[42] ich woman
To speken ani other harm upon!
Falsliche another Y gan deme:[43]
The selve happe[44] is on me sene.
"Allas," sche seyd, "that Y was born!
Withouten ende Ich am forlorn!
Or Ich mot siggen, sikerly,[45]
That tvay men han yly me by,
Or Ich mot sigge in al mi liif
That Y bileighe[46] mi neghbours wiif;
Or Ich mot—that God it schilde![47]—
Help to sle min owhen child.
On of this thre thinges Ich mot nede
Sigge, other don[48] in dede.
Yyf Ich say Ich hadde a bi-leman,[49]
Than Ich leighe[50] meselve opon,
And eke thai wil, that me se,
Held me wers than comoun be;
And yyf Ich knawelethe[51] to ich man
That Ich leighe the levedi opon,
Than Ich wold[52] of old and yong
Be hold leighster,[53] and fals of tong.
Yete me is best take mi chaunce,
And sle mi childe and do penaunce."
Hir midwiif hye cleped hir to:
"Anon," sche seyd, "this child fordo,[54]

---

[39] two [40] given, brought about [41] doom, judgment [42] be it
[43] judge [44] same thing [45] either I must say, surely, . . .
[46] lied about, wronged [47] prevent [48] do
[49] second lover, paramour [50] lie [51] acknowledge
[52] ms. *worþ* (become) [53] liar [54] slay

And ever say thou, wher thou go,
That Ich have o child and na mo."
The midwiif answerd thurchout al [55]
That hye nil,[56] no hye ne schal.
[The levedi hadde a maiden fre
Who ther ynurtured hade ybe
And fostered fair ful mony a yere;
Sche saw her kepe this sori chere,
And wepe, and syke,[57] and crye, "Alas!"
And thoghte to helpen her in this cas.
And thus sche spake, this maiden ying,
"So nolde [58] Y wepen for no kind thing:
But this o child wol I of-bare
And in a covent [59] leve it yare.
Ne schalt thou be aschamed at al;
And whoso findeth this childe smal,
By Mary, blissful quene above,] [60]
May help it for Godes love!"
The levedi graunted anon therto,
And wold wele that it were ydo.[61]
Sche toke a riche baudekine [62]
That hir lord brought fram Costentine,
And lapped the litel maiden therin,
And toke a ring of gold fin,
And on hir right arm it knitt,
With a lace of silke therin plit.[63]
And whoso hir founde schulde have in mende [64]
That it were comen of riche kende.[65]
The maide toke the childe hir mide,[66]

---

[55] to all of this [56] will not [57] sigh [58] would not
[59] convent
[60] the thirteen lines here bracketed are missing from the ms.; the reconstruction is Weber's, who followed closely 11. 99-115 of Marie de Francé's *Lai le Fresne* [61] done
[62] embroidered cloth [63] pleated, enfolded; ms. *pilt*
[64] mind, *i.e.* should recognize [65] kind, kin [66] with

And stale oway in an eventide,
And passed over a wild heth;
Thurch feld and thurch wode hye geth
Al the winterlong night.
The weder was clere, the mone was light;
So that [67] hye com bi a forest side,
Sche wax al weri and gan abide.
Sone after sche gan herk [68]
Cokkes crowe and houndes berk.
Sche arose and thider wold; [69]
Ner and nere [70] sche gan bihold.
Walles and hous fele [71] hye seighe,
A chirche with stepel fair and heighe;
Than nas ther noither strete no toun,
But an hous of religioun,
An order of nonnes, wele ydight [72]
To servy God bothe day and night.
The maiden abod no lengore,
Bot yede hir [73] to the chirche dore,
And on knes sche sat adoun,
And seyd, wepeand,[74] her orisoun: [75]
"O Lord," hye [76] seyd, "Jhesu Crist,
That sinful man bedes herst,[77]
Underfong [78] this present,
And help this seli [79] innocent
That it mot [80] ycristned be,
For Marie love, thi moder fre!"
Hye loked up, and bi hir seighe
An asche bi hir, fair and heighe,
Wele ybowed,[81] of michel priis; [82]
The bodi was holow, as mani on is.

---

[67] when [68] hear [69] would go [70] nearer and nearer
[71] many [72] prepared, dedicated [73] went, took herself
[74] weeping [75] prayer [76] ms. *he* [77] sinful man's prayers hears
[78] receive [79] poor, wretched [80] may [81] branched [82] worth

Therin sche leyd the child for cold,
In the pel [83] as it was bifold,
And blisced [84] it with al hir might.
With that it gan to dawe [85] light;
The foules up and song on bough,
And acre-men yede to the plough.
The maiden turned ogain anon,
And toke the waye hye [86] hadde er gon.
The porter of the abbay aros,
And dede his ofice in the clos,[87]
Rong the belles and taperes light,
Leyd forth bokes and al redi dight.
The chirche dore he undede,[88]
And seigh anon in the stede
The pel liggen [89] in the tre,
And thought wele that it might be
That theves hadde yrobbed sumwhare
And gon therforth and lete it thare.
Therto he yede and it unwond,
And the maiden child therin he fond.
He tok it up bituen his hond
And thonked Jhesu Cristes sond,
And hom to his hous he it brought,
And tok it his douhter, and hir bisought
That hye schuld kepe it as sche can,
For sche was melche [90] and couthe theran.
Sche bad it souke, and it nold,
For it was neighe ded for cold.
Anon fer [91] sche alight,
And warmed it wele aplight; [92]
Sche gaf it souke opon hir barm,[93]
And sethen [94] laid it to slepe warm.

---

[83] swaddling blanket, pallet [84] blessed [85] dawn [86] ms. *he*
[87] closet, vestry [88] unlatched [89] lying [90] nursing [91] fire
[92] wrapped in its blanket [93] breast [94] then; ms. *seþþen*

And when the masse was ydon,
The porter to the abbesse com ful son:
"Madame, what rede [95] ye of this thing?
Today, right in the morning,
Sone after the first stounde,[96]
A litel maiden child Ich founde
In the holwe assche therout;
And a pel her [97] about.
A ring of gold also was there;
Hou it com thider, Y not nere." [98]
The abbesse was awonderd of this thing:
"Go," hye seyd, "on heighing,[99]
And feche it hider, Y pray the;
It is welcom to God and to me.
Ichil it help as Y can,
And sigge [100] it is mi kinswoman."
The porter anon it gan forth bring,
With the pal and with the ring.
The abbesse lete clepe a prest anon,
And let it cristin [101] in funston.[102]
And, for it was in an asche yfounde,
Sche cleped it Frain in that stounde;
The Freyns [103] of the asche is a *freyn*
After the language of Breteyn;
Forthi [104] "le Frein" men clepeth this lay
More than "Asche" in ich cuntray.
This Frein thrived fram yer to yer;
The abbesse nece men wend it were.
The abbesse hir gan teche and beld,[105]
Bi that [106] hye was of twelve winter eld;
In al Inglond ther nas non [107]

---

[95] advise [96] canonical hour [97] ms. *him* [98] I know not at all
[99] in haste [100] say [101] be christened [102] at the baptismal font
[103] French [104] therefor [105] rear, bring up
[106] until
[107] there was not at all

A fairer maiden than hye was on.
And when hye couthe ought of manhed,[108]
Hye bad the abbesse hir wis and rede [109]
Whiche wer her kin, on or other,
Fader or moder, soster or brother.
The abbesse hir in conseyl toke;
To tellen hir hye nought forsoke,
Hou hye was founden, in al thing,
And tok hir the cloth and the ring,
And bad hir kepe it in that stede,
And therwhiles sche lived, so sche dede.
  Than was ther in that cuntré
A riche knight of lond and fe,[110]
Proud, and yong, and jolive,[111]
And had nought yete ywedded wive.
He was stout, of gret renoun,
And was ycleped Sir Guroun.
He herd praise that maiden fre,
And seyd he wald hir se.
He dight him in the way anon,
And joliflich thider he come,
And bad his man sigge verrament [112]
He schuld [113] toward a turnament.
  The abbesse and the nones alle
Fair him gret in the gest-halle;
And damisel Frein, so hende [114] of mouthe,
Gret him faire, as hye wele couthe.
And swithe [115] wele he gan devise [116]
Her semblaunt and hir gentrise,[117]
Her lovesum eiyen,[118] her rode [119] so bright,
And comenced [120] to love hir anon right,

---

[108] *i.e.* when she was old enough to be curious about her parentage [109] inform and advise [110] income [111] jolly
[112] say truly [113] should go [114] courteous [115] ms. *swhe*
[116] take notice of [117] semblance and gentility [118] eyes
[119] complexion [120] ms. *comced*

And thought hou he might take on [121]
To have hir to his leman.[122]
He thought, "Yyf Ich com hir to
More than Ich have [123] ydo,
The abbesse wil souchy gile,[124]
And voide [125] hir in a litel while."
He compast [126] another enchesoun: [127]
To be brother of that religioun.
"Madame," he seyd to the abbesse,
"Y lovi wele [128] in al godenisse:
Ichil give on and other,
Londes and rentes,[129] to bicom your brother,
That ye schul ever fare the bet [130]
When Y com to have recet." [131]
At [132] fewe wordes thai ben at on; [133]
He graythes [134] him and forth is gon.
Oft he come bi day and night
To speke with that maiden bright;
So that, with his fair bihest,[135]
And with his gloseing,[136] atte lest
Hye graunted him to don his wille
When he wil, loude and stille.[137]
"Leman," he seyd, "thou most lat be
The abbesse, thi nece,[138] and go with me,
For Ich am riche, of swithe pouwere;
The finde bet [139] than thou hast here."
The maiden grant, and to him trist,[140]
And stale oway, that no man wist.
With hir toke hye no thing
Bot hir pel and hir ring.

---

[121] conduct himself [122] mistress, paramour [123] ms. *ichave*
[124] suspect guile [125] remove [126] devised [127] reason, strategy
[128] joy [129] income [130] better [131] reception [132] with
[133] agreed [134] makes ready [135] promise [136] flattery
[137] in all respects [138] kinswoman [139] you will find better
[140] placed her trust in him

When the abbesse gan aspie
That hye was with the knight owy,[141]
Sche made morning in hir thought,
And hir biment,[142] and gained nought.
So long sche was in his castel
That al his meyne [143] loved hir wel;
To riche and poure sche gan hir dresse [144]
That al hir loved, more and lesse.
And thus sche lad with him hir liif,
Right as sche hadde ben his wedded wiif.
His knightes com and to him speke,
And holy chirche comandeth eke,
Sum lordes douhter for to take,
And his leman al forsake;
And seyd him wer wel more feir [145]
In wedlok to geten him an air [146]
Than lede his liif with swiche on
Of was [147] kin he knewe non; [148]
And seyd, "Her bisides [149] is a knight
That hath a douhter fair and bright,
That schal bere his hiritage; [150]
Taketh hir in mariage."
Loth him was that dede to do,
Ac atte last he graunt therto.
The forward [151] was ymaked aright,
And were at on [152] and treuthe plight.
Allas! that he no hadde ywite
Er the forward were ysmite [153]
That hye and his leman also
Sostren [154] were, and tvinnes to;

---

[141] away, gone [142] lamented [143] household
[144] conducted herself [145] *i.e.* it would be better for him [146] heir
[147] whose [148] nothing [149] nearby [150] inheritance
[151] contract [152] they were agreed [153] struck, made
[154] sisters

Of o fader bigeten thai were,
Of o moder born yfere —
That hye so ware, nist non,
Forsothe Y say, bot God alon!
The newe bride was grayd[155] withalle,
And brought hom to the lordes halle.
Hir fader com with hir also,
The levedi, hir moder, and other mo.[156]
The bischop of the lond, withoute fail,
Com to do the spusseayl.[157]
[That maiden bird, in bour bright,
Le Codre[158] sche was yhight;[159]
And ther the guests had gamen and gle,
And sayd to Sir Guroun joyfully:
"Fairer maiden n'as never seen,
Better than ash is hazle Y ween!"
(For in romaunce[160] *Le Frain* ash is,
And *Le Codre* hazle, y-wis.)
A gret fest than gan they hold
With gle and pleasaunce manifold;
And mo than al servauntes, the maid
Y-hight Le Frain as servant sped;
Albe[161] her herte wel nigh to-broke,
No word of pride ne grame[162] she spoke.
The levedi[163] marked her simple chere,
And gan to love her, wonder dere.
Scant could sche feel more pine or reuth
War it hir owen childe in sooth.
Than to the bour the damsel sped,
Whar graithed was the spousaile bed;

---

[155] made ready [156] more
[157] espousal, marriage; the remainder of the story is missing in the ms.; the following bracketed lines are Weber's reconstruction, which follows closely 11. 365-518 of Marie de France's *Lai le Fresne* [158] *i.e.* the hazel tree [159] called [160] French
[161] although [162] anger [163] *i.e.* the mother

Sche demed it was ful foully dight,
And yll besemed a may [164] so bright;
So to her coffer quick she cam,
And her riche baudekyn out-nam,[165]
Which from the abbess sche had got;
Fayrer mantel n'as ther not;
And deftly on the bed it layd;
Her lord woulde thus be well apayd.
Le Codre and her mother, thare,
Ynsame [166] unto the bour gan fare,
But whan the levedi that mantyll seighe
Sche wel neighe swoned oway.
The chamberleynt [167] sche cleped tho,
But he ne wist of it no mo.
Then came that hendi [168] maid Le Frain,
And the levedi gan to her sain,
And asked whose mantyll it ware.
Then answered that maiden fair:
"It is mine without lesing; [169]
Y had it together with this ringe.
Myne aunte tolde me a ferli cas,[170]
Hou in this mantyll i-fold I was,
And hadde upon mine arm this ring
Whanne I was y-sent to norysching."
Then was the levedi astonied [171] sore:
"Fair child! my doughter! Y thé bore!"
Sche swoned and was wel neighe ded,
And lay sikeand [172] on that bed.
Her husbond was fet [173] tho,
And sche told him al her wo,
Hou of her neighbour sche had missayn,
For sche was delyvered of childre twain;

[164] maid [165] took out [166] together [167] chamberlain
[168] courteous [169] lying [170] a wondrous event [171] astonished
[172] sighing [173] fetched

And hou to children herself sche bore; —
"And that o child I of-sent thore,
In a covent y-fostered to be;
And this is sche, our doughter free;
And this is the mantyll and this the ring
You gaf me of yore as a love-tokenyng."
The knight kissed his daughter hende
Oftimes, and to the bisschope wende:
And he undid the mariage strate,
And weddid Sir Guroun alsgate [174]
To Le Frain, his leman so fair and hend.
With them Le Codre away did wend,
And sone was spousyd with game and gle,
To a gentle knight of that countré.
Thus ends the lay of tho maidens bright,
Le Frain and Le Codre y-hight.]

---

[174] instead

Emare

Jhesu þat ys kyng in trone
As þou shope boþe sonne & mone
And all þat shalle dele & dyghte
Now lene vs grace such dedus to done
In þy blys þat we may wone
Men calle hyt heuen lyghte
And þy modur mary heuyn qwene
Bere our arunde so bytwene
That semely ys of syght
To þy sone þat ys so fre
In heuen wyth hym þat we may be
That lord ys most of myght
Menstrelles þat walken fer & wyde
Her & þer in euery a syde
In mony a dyuerse londe
Sholde at her bygynnyng
Speke of þat ryghtwes kyng
That made both see & sonde
Who so wyll a stounde dwelle
Of mykyll myrght y may yow telle
And mornyng þer a monge
Of a lady fayr & fre
Her name was called Emare
As I here synge in songe
Her fadyr was an Emperour
Of castell & of ryche towre
Syr Artyus was hys nome
He hadde boþe hallys & bowrys
Frythes fayr forestes wyth flowrys
So gret a lord was none
Weddedde he had a lady
That was both fayr & semely
Whyte as whales bone
Dame Erayne hette þe Emperes
She was full of loue & godnesse
So curtays lady was none
Syr Artyus was þe best manne
In þe worlde þat lyuede þanne
Both hardy and þer to wyght
He was curtays in all þyng
Boþe to olde & to yynge
And well kowth dele & dyght
He hadde but on chylde in hys lyue
Begeten on hys weddedde wyfe
And þat was fayr and bryght
For soþe as y may telle þe
They called þat chyld Emare
That semely was of syght
When she was of her modur born
She was þe fayrest creature borne
That yn þe lond was þoo
The Emperes þat fayr ladye
Fro her lord gan she dye
Or hyt kowþe speke or goo
The chyld þat was fayr & gent
To a lady was hyt sente
That men kalled Abro
She thawghth hyt curtesye & thewe
Golde & sylke for to sewe
Amonge maydenes moo
Abro tawghte þys mayden small
Nortur þat men useden in sale
Whyle she was in her bowre
She was curtays in all thynge
Boþe to olde & to yynge
And whythe as lylye flowre
Of her hondes she was slye
All her loued þat her sye
Wyth menske & mychyl honour
At þe meydenes leue we
And at þe lady fayr & fre
And speke we of þe Emperour
The Emperour of gentyll blode
Was a curteys lorde & a gode
In all maner of thynge
Aftur when hys wyf was dede
And ledde hys lyf yn weddewede
And myche louede playnge
Sone aftur yn a whyle
The ryche kynge of Cesyle
To þe Emperour gan wende

Emaré

Jhesu, that ys kyng in trone,[1]
As thou shoope [2] both sonne and mone,
And alle that shall dele and dyghte,[3]
Now lene [4] us grace such deds to done,
In thy blys that we may wone,
Men calle hyt heven-lyghte.
And thy moder, Mary, hevyn-qwene,
Bere our arunde [5] so bytwene,
That semely ys of syght,
To thy sone that ys so fre,
In heven wyth hym that we may be,
That lord ys most of myght.

Menstrelles that walken fer and wyde,
Her and ther in every a syde [6]
In mony a dyverse londe,
Sholde, at her bygynnyng,
Speke of that ryghtwes Kyng
That made both see and sonde.[7]
Whoso wyll a stounde [8] dwelle,
Of mykylle myrth [9] Y may you telle,
And mornyng ther amonge; [10]

---

[1] on throne [2] shaped [3] dispense and rule [4] lend, grant
[5] errand, prayer [6] by-way [7] sea and shore [8] time, while
[9] ms. *myright* [10] sadness intermingled

Of a lady fayr and fre,
Her name was called Emaré,
As I here synge in songe.

Her fadyr was an emperour,
Of castell and of ryche towre,
Syr Artyus was hys nome;
He hadde bothe hallys and bowrys,
Frythes [11] fayr, forestes wyth flowrys:
So gret a lord was none.
Weddedde he had a lady
That was both fayr and semely,
Whyte as whales bone;
Dame Erayne hette [12] that emperes;
She was full of love and goodnesse;
So curtays lady was none.

Syr Artyus was the best manne
In the worlde that lyvede thanne,
Bothe hardy and therto wyght;
He was curtays in all thyng
Bothe to olde and to yynge,
And well kowth [13] dele and dyght.
He hadde but on chyld in hys lyve,
Begeten on hys weddedde wyfe,
And that was fayr and bryght;
For sothe, as Y may telle the,
They called that chyld Emaré,
That semely was of syght.

When she was of her moder born,
She was the fayrest creature borne
That yn the lond was thoo; [14]

---

[11] fields [12] was named [13] knew how to [14] then

The emperes, that fayr ladye,
Fro her lord gan she dye,
Or hyt kowthe speke or goo.[15]
The chyld, that was fayr and gent,
To a lady was hyt sente
That men kalled Abro;
She tawght [16] hyt curtesye and thewe,[17]
Golde and sylke for to sewe
Amonge maydenes moo.[18]

Abro tawghte thys mayden small
Nortur [19] that men useden in sale,[20]
Whyle she was in her bowre.
She was curtays in all thynge,
Both to olde and to yynge,
And whyte [21] as lylye flowre.
Of her hondes she was slye; [22]
All her [23] loved that her sye,
Wyth menske [24] and mychyl honour.
At [25] the meydene leve we,
And at the lady fayr and fre,
And speke we of the emperour.

The emperour, of gentyll blode,
Was a curteys lorde and a gode,
In all maner of thynge;
Aftur, when hys wyf was dede,
A [26] ledde hys lyf yn weddewede,[27]
And myche loved playnge.

---

[15] before the child could talk or walk [16] ms. *thawʒth*
[17] good behavior [18] more, other [19] good manners
[20] hall [21] ms. *whythe* [22] skillful [23] ms. *he*
[24] dignity [25] of
[26] he; ms. *And*
[27] as widower

Sone aftur, yn a whyle,
The ryche kynge of Cesyle [28]
To the emperour gan wende;
A ryche present wyth hym he browght,
A cloth that was wordylye [29] wroght;
He wellcomed hym as the hende.[30]

Syr Tergaunte, that nobyll knyght,[31]
He presented the emperour ryght—
And sette hym on hys kne—
Wyth that cloth rychyly dyght,
Full of stones ther hyt was pyght,[32]
As thykke as hyt myght be;
Off topaze and rubyes
And other stones of myche prys
That semely wer to se,
Of crapowtes and nakette [33]
As thykke ar they sette,
For sothe, as Y say the.

The cloth was dysplayed sone;
The emperour lokede therupone
And myght hyt not se;
For glysteryng of the ryche ston
Redy syght had he non,
And sayde, "How may thys be?"
The emperour sayde on hygh,
"Sertes, thys ys a fayry,[34]
Or ellys a vanyté!" [35]
The King of Cysyle answered than,
"So ryche a jwell ys ther non
In all Crystyanté."

---

[28] Sicily [29] worthily [30] courteous, noble
[31] ms. *kny3t hy3te*, the last word blurred and apparently intended for cancellation [32] studded [33] toadstones and agate
[34] magical trick [35] optical illusion

The Amerayle dowghter of hethennes[36]
Made thys cloth, wythouten lees,
And wrowghte hyt all wyth pride;
And purtreyed hyt[37] wyth gret honour,
Wyth ryche gold and asowr,[38]
And stones on ylke a syde;
And, as the story telles in honde,
The stones that yn thys cloth stonde,
Sowghte they were full wyde.
Seven wynter hyt was yn makynge
Or[39] hyt was browght to endynge —
In herte ys not to hyde.

In that on[40] korner made was
Ydoyne and Amadas,
Wyth love that was so trewe;
For[41] they loveden hem wyth honour,
Portrayed they wer wyth trewe-love flour,[42]
Of stones bryght of hewe:
Wyth carbunkull and safere,[43]
Kassydonys[44] and onyx so clere,
Sette in golde newe;
Deamondes and rubyes,
And other stones of mychyll pryse;
And menstrellys wyth her glewe.[45]

---

[36] the daughter of the Emir of heathendom
[37] portrayed upon it people and scenes from well known stories
[38] azure
[39] before
[40] one
[41] because
[42] an herb whose four leaves resemble a love knot
[43] sapphire [44] chalcedony, a blue or blue-gray quartz
[45] glee; ms. *gle*; possibly this line is a corruption or the inept use of a formula to fill out a line; more likely the poet implies that there were minstrels portrayed in the scene depicted as well as the two lovers

In that other corner was dyght
Trystram and Isowde so bryght,
That semely wer to se;
And for they loved hem ryght,
As fulle of stones ar they dyght,
As thykke as they may be:
Of topase and of rubyes,
And other stones of myche pryse,
That semely wer to se;
Wyth crapawtes and nakette,
Thykke of stones ar they sette,
For sothe, as Y say the.

In the thrydde korner, wyth gret honour,
Was Florys and Dam Blawncheflour,
As love was hem betwene;
For [46] they loved wyth honour,
Purtrayed they wer wyth trewe-love flour,
Wyth stones bryght and shene; [47]
Ther wer knyghtes and senatowres,[48]
Emerawdes of gret vertues,
To wyte, wythouten wene:
Deamoundes and koralle,
Perydotes [49] and crystall,
And gode garnettes bytwene.

In the fowrthe korner was oon [50]
Of Babylone the Sowdan sonne,[51]
The Amerayles dowghtyr hym by;
For hys sake the cloth was wrowght—
She loved hym in hert and thowght,
As testymoyeth thys storye.

---

[46] because [47] good, glistening
[48] *i.e.* in the scene depicted of the two lovers were also knights and nobles; see note to l. 132 [49] a yellow-green chrysolite
[50] one; *i.e.* a portraiture [51] the son of the Sultan of Babylon

The fayr mayden her byforn
Was portrayed an unykorn,
Wyth hys horn so hye;
Flowres and bryddes [52] on ylke a syde,
Wyth stones that wer sowght wyde,
Stuffed wyth ymagerye.[53]

When the cloth to ende was wrowght,
To the Sowdan sone hyt was browght,
That semely was of syght.
"My fadyr was a nobyll man;
Of the Sowdan he hyt wan
Wyth maystrye and wyth myght.[54]
For gret love he gaf hyt me;
I brynge hyt the in specyalté;
Thys cloth ys rychely dyght."
He gaf hyt the emperour;
He receyved hyt wyth gret honour
And thonkede hym fayr and ryght.

The Kyng of Cesyle dwelled ther
As long as hys wyll wer,
Wyth the emperour for to play;
And when he wolde wende,
He toke hys leve at the hende,[55]
And wente forth on hys way.
Now remeveth thys nobyll kyng;
The emperour after hys dowghter hadde longyng
To speke wyth that may; [56]
Messengeres forth he sent
Aftyr the mayde fayr and gent,
That was bryght as someres day.

[52] birds [53] figures
[54] ms. *myʒth* [55] took leave of that courteous one
[56] maiden

Messengeres dyghte hem in hye,[57]
Wyth myche myrthe and melodye;
Forth gon they fare
Both by stretes and by stye [58]
After that fayr lady,
Was godely unther gare.[59]
Her norysse,[60] that hyghte Abro,
Wyth her she goth forth also,
And wer sette in a chare.[61]
To the emperour gan they [62] go;
He come ageyn hem a myle or two;
A fayr metyng was there.

The mayden, whyte as lylye flour,
Lyghte ageyn her fadyr, the emperour;
Two knyghtes gan her lede.
Her fadyr, that was of gret renowne,
That of golde wered the crowne,
Lyghte of hys stede.
When they wer bothe on her fete,
He klypped her and kyssed her swete,
And bothe on fote they yede.[63]
They wer glad and made good chere;
To the palys they yede in fere,[64]
In romans as we rede.

Then the lordes that wer grete,
They wesh and seten down [65] to mete,
And folk hem served swythe.[66]
The mayden, that was of sembelant swete,
Byfore her owene fadur sete,
The fayrest wommon on lyfe,

---

[57] made themselves ready in haste [58] path, by-way
[59] who was goodly under gown [60] nurse [61] carriage
[62] ms. *þe* [63] went [64] together [65] ms. *don*
[66] right away; ms. *swyde*

That [67] all hys hert and all hys thowght [68]
Her to love was ybrowght; [69]
He byhelde her ofte sythe.[70]
So he was anamored hys dowghter [71] tyll
Wyth her he thowght [72] to worche hys wyll,
And wedde her to hys wyfe.

And when the metewhyle [73] was don,
Into hys chamber he wente son,
And called hys counseyle nere;
He bad they shulde sone go and come,
And gete leve of the Pope of Rome
To wedde that mayden clere.
Messengeres forth they went—
They durste not breke hys commandement—
And erles wyth hem yn fere.
They wente to the courte of Rome,
And browght the Popus bullus [74] sone
To wedde hys dowghter dere.

Then was the emperour gladde and blythe,
And lette shape a robe swythe [75]
Of that cloth of golde;
And when hyt was don her upon,
She semed non erthely wommon
That marked was of molde.[76]
Then seyde the emperour so fre,
"Dowghtyr, Y woll wedde the,
Thow art so fresh to beholde."

---

[67] so that [68] ms. *þowȝth* [69] ms. *yn browght*
[70] many times [71] ms. *þowȝter* [72] ms. *þowȝth*
[73] mealtime [74] the pope's bills, dispensation
[75] had a robe made quickly
[76] *i.e.* she seemed to show no signs of being of the common clay of earthly woman

Then sayde that worthy under wede,[77]
"Nay, syr, God of heven hyt forbede
That ever do so we shulde.

Yyf hyt so be-tydde that ye me wedde,
And we shulde play togeder in bedde,
Bothe we were forlorne!
The worde shulde sprynge fer and wyde;
In all the world, on every syde,
The worde shulde be borne.
Ye ben a lorde of gret pryce;
Lorde, lette never suche sorow aryce;
Take God you beforne! [78]
That my fader shulde wedde me,
God forbede that Y hyt so se,[79]
That wered the crowne of thorne!" [80]

The emperour was ryght wrothe,
And swore many a gret othe
That deed shulde she be;
He lette make a nobull boot,[81]
And dede [82] her theryn, God wote,
In the robe of nobull ble.[83]
She moste have wyth her no spendyng,[84]
Nother mete ne drynke;
But shate [85] her ynto the se.
Now the lady dwelled thore
Wythowte anker or ore,
And that was gret pyté!

---

[77] that worthy one in dress; ms. *wordy unþer*
[78] be guided by God [79] may God forbid that I agree to it
[80] ms. *þhorne* [81] boat
[82] put [83] color
[84] money [85] cast

There come a wynd, Y understonde,[86]
And blewe the boot fro the londe;
Of her they lost the syghte.
The emperour hym bethowght
That he hadde all myswrowght,[87]
And was a sory knyghte.
And as he stode yn studyynge,
He fell down in a sowenynge;
To the yrthe was he dyght.
Gret lordes stode therby,
And toke up [88] the emperour hastyly,
And conforted hym fayr and ryght.

When he of sownyng kovered [89] was,
Sore he wepte and sayde, "Alas
For my dowghter [90] dere!
Alas that Y was made man,
Wrecched kaytyf [91] that I hyt am!"
The teres ronne by hys lere.[92]
"I wrowght ageyn Goddes lay [93]
To her that was so trewe of fay;
Alas, why ner [94] she here?"
The teres lasshed out of hys yyen; [95]
The grete lordes that hyt syyen [96]
Wepte and made yll chere.

There was nother olde ny yynge
That kowde [97] stynte of wepynge
For that comely under kelle.[98]

---

[86] ms. *unþerstonde* [87] ms. *myswrowht* [88] ms. *un*
[89] recovered [90] ms. *dowhter*
[91] caitiff, base man [92] cheeks, face
[93] law [94] n'were, is not
[95] eyes [96] saw [97] ms. *kowþe*
[98] that comely one under hood, or hair-net; ms. *unþer*

Into shypys faste gan they thrynge[99]
For to seke that mayden yynge,
That was so fayr of flesh and fell.[100]
They her sowght overall yn the see,
And myghte not fynde that lady fre;
Ageyn[101] they come full snell.[102]
At the emperour now leve we,
And of the lady yn the see
I shall begynne to tell.

The lady fleted[103] forth alone;
To God of Heven she made her mone,
And to Hys Modyr also.
She was dryven wyth wynde and rayn,
Wyth stronge stormes her agayn,
Of the water so blo.[104]
As Y have herd menstrelles syng yn sawe,[105]
Hows ny lond myght[106] she none knowe;
Aferd she was to go.
She was so dryven fro wawe to wawe,[107]
She hyd her hede and lay full lowe;
For watyr she was full woo.

Now thys lady dwelled thore
A good seven-nyght[108] and more,
As hyt was Goddys wylle;
Wyth care-full herte, and sykyng[109] sore,
Such sorow was here yarked yore,[110]
And ever lay she stylle.
She was dryven ynto a lond
Thorow the grace of Goddes sond,[111]
That all thyng may fulfylle;

---

[99] throng [100] skin, complexion [101] back [102] soon
[103] floated [104] blown, rough [105] tale [106] ms. *myȝth*
[107] wave to wave [108] ms. *nyȝth* [109] sighing
[110] ordained long ago [111] mercy

She was on the see so hard bestadde,
For hunger and thurste almost madde;
Woo worth wederes [112] yll!

She was dryven into a lond
That hyght Galys,[113] Y understond,
That was a fayr countré;
The kynges steward dwelled ther bysyde,
In a kastell of mykyll pryde;
Syr Kadore hyght he.
Every day wolde he go,
And take wyth hym a sqwyer or two,
And play hym by the see.
On a tyme [114] he toke the eyr [115]
Wyth two knyghtes gode and fayr;
The wedur was lythe of le.[116]

A boot he fond by the brym,[117]
And a glysteryng thyng theryn;
Therof they hadde ferly.[118]
They went forth on the sond
To the boot, Y understonde,
And fond theryn that lady.
She hadde so longe meteles be
That hym thowght [119] gret dele to se;
She was yn poynt to dye.[120]
The askede her what was her name;
She chaunged hyt ther anon,
And sayde she hette Egaré.[121]

---

[112] weathers [113] was named Galicia; ms. *hyȝth*
[114] one time [115] air
[116] still and pleasant [117] water's edge
[118] wonder [119] ms. *þowht*
[120] at the point of death; ms. *poyn*
[121] *i.e.* "the outcast"

Syr Kadore hadde gret pyté;
He toke up the lady of the see,
And home gan he lede;
She hadde so longe meteles be
That she was wax [122] lene as a tre,
That worthy under [123] wede.
Into hys castell when she came,
Into a chawmbyr they her nam,[124]
And fayr they gan her fede
Wyth all delycyus mete and drynke
That they myght [125] hem on thynke,
That was yn that stede.[126]

When that lady, fayr of face,
Wyth mete and drynk kevered [127] was,
And had colour agayne,
She tawghte hem to sew and marke [128]
All maner of sylkyn [129] werke;
Of her they wer full fayne.
She was curteys yn all thyng,
Bothe to olde and to yynge,
I say yow for certeyne;
She kowde [130] werke all maner thyng
That fell to emperour or to kyng,
Erle, barown, or swayne.

Syr Kadore lette make a feste
That was fayr and honeste,
Wyth hys lorde, the kynge;

---

[122] become, grown [123] ms. *wordy unþer* [124] took
[125] ms. *myȝth* [126] place [127] recovered
[128] probably embroider, but possibly paint
[129] ms. *sylky*, but a final letter has been erased
[130] ms. *kowȝthe*

Ther was myche menstralsé,
Trommpus, tabours, and sawtré,[131]
Bothe harpe and fydyllyng.
The lady, that was gentyll and small,
In kurtull[132] alone served yn hall
Byfore that nobull kyng;
The cloth upon her shone so bryght,[133]
When she was theryn ydyght,[134]
She semed non erdly[135] thyng.

The kyng loked her upon,
So fayr a lady he sygh[136] never non;
Hys herte she hadde yn wolde;[137]
He was so anamered of that syght[138]
Of the mete non he myght,[139]
But faste gan her beholde.
She was so fayr and gent
The kynges love on her was lent,
In tale as hyt ys tolde.
And when the metewhyle was don
Into the chamber he wente son,
And called hys barouns bolde.

Fyrst he called[140] Syr Kadore,
And other knyghtes that ther wore
Hastely come hym tyll;[141]
Dukes and erles, wyse of lore,
Hastely come the kyng before,
And askede what was hys wylle.

---

[131] trumpets, drums, and psaltery (zither-like instruments)
[132] kirtle [133] ms. *bryȝth*
[134] ms. *ydyȝth* [135] earthly [136] saw
[137] power [138] ms. *syȝth* [139] might eat; ms. *myȝth*
[140] ms. *calle* [141] came to him

Then spakke the ryche yn ray,[142]
To Syr Kadore gan he say
Wordes fayre and stylle:
"Syr, whenns [143] ys that lovely may,[144]
That yn the halle served thys day?
Tell me, yyf hyt be thy wylle."

Then sayde Syr Kadore, Y understonde,[145]
"Hyt ys an erles dowghter [146] of ferre londe,
That semely ys to sene.
I sente after her, certeynlye,
To teche my chylderen curtesye,
In chambur wyth hem to bene.
She ys the konnyngest wommon,
I trowe, that be yn Crystendom,
Of werk that Y have sene."
Then sayde that ryche ray,[147]
"I wyll have that fayr may,
And wedde her to my quene."

The nobull kyng, verament,[148]
Aftyr hys modyr he sent,
To wyte what she wolde say.
They browght forth hastely
That fayr mayde, Egarye;
She was bryght [149] as someres day.
The cloth on her shon so bryght
When she was theryn dyght,
And herself a gentell may,
The olde quene sayde anon,
"I sawe never wommon
Halvendell [150] so gay."

---

[142] striped cloth, or array (*i.e.* the richly attired one)
[143] whence [144] maid [145] ms. *unþerstonde* [146] ms. *þowȝter*
[147] *rei,* king [148] truly [149] ms. *bryȝth* [150] half a part

The olde qwene spakke wordes unhende,[151]
And sayde, "Sone, thys ys a fende[152]
In thys worthy[153] wede!
As thou lovest my blessynge,
Make thou never thys weddynge;
Cryst hyt the[154] forbede!"
Then spakke the ryche ray,
"Modyr, Y wylle have thys may!"
And forth gan her lede.
The olde qwene, for certayne,
Turnede wyth ire hom agayne,
And wolde not be at that dede.

The kyng wedded that lady bryght;
Grete purvyance ther was dyght,[155]
In that semely sale.[156]
Grete lordes wer served aryght,
Duke, erle, baron, and knyght,[157]
Both of grete and smale.
Myche folke, forsothe, ther was,
And therto an huge prese,[158]
As hyt ys tolde yn tale.
Ther was all maner thyng
That fell to[159] a kynges weddyng,
And mony a ryche menstralle.

When the mangery[160] was done,
Grete lordes departed sone,
That semely were to se.
The kynge belafte wyth the qwene—
Moch love was hem betwene,
And also game and gle.

---

[151] unkind, discourteous [152] fiend, other-world creature
[153] ms. *wordy* [154] ms. *de* [155] made; ms. *dyȝth*
[156] hall [157] ms. *knyȝth* [158] crowd
[159] belonged to, was appropriate to [160] wedding feast

She was curteys and swete;
Such a lady herde Y never of yete;
They loved both wyth herte fre.
The lady, that was both meke and mylde,
Conceyved, and wente wyth chylde,
As God wolde hyt sholde be.

The kyng of France yn that tyme
Was besette wyth many a Sarezyne,
And cumbered all in tene; [161]
And sente after the kyng of Galys
And other lordys of myche prys,
That semely were to sene.
The kyng of Galys, in that tyde,
Gadered [162] men on every syde,
In armour bryght and shene;
Then sayde the kyng to Syr Kadore
And other lordes that ther wore,
"Take good hede to my qwene!"

The kyng of Fraunce spared none,
But sent for hem everych one,
Both kyng, knyght,[163] and clerke.
The steward,[164] bylafte at home
To kepe the qwene whyte as fome,
He come not at that werke.[165]
She wente wyth chylde yn palace [166]
As longe as Goddes wylle was,
That semely under serke; [167]
Tyll [168] ther was of her body
A fayr chyld borne, and a godelé;
Hadde a dowbyll kynges marke.[169]

---

[161] encumbered in distress [162] gathered [163] ms. *knyȝth*
[164] ms. *stward* [165] *i.e.* that war [166] ms. *place*
[167] that seemly one under gown; ms. *unþer*
[168] ms. *Thyll* [169] birthmark of royalty

They hyt crystened wyth grete honour,
And called hym Segramour;
Frely[170] was that fode.[171]
Then the steward, Syr Kadore,
A nobull letter made he thore,
And wrowghte hyt all wyth gode;
He wrowghte hyt yn hyghynge,[172]
And sente hyt to hys lorde, the kynge,
That gentyll was of blode.
The messenger forth gan wende,
And wyth the kynges moder gan lende,[173]
And ynto the castell he yode.[174]

He was resseyved rychely,
And she hym askede hastyly
How the qwene hadde spedde.[175]
"Madame, there ys of her yborne
A fayr man-chylde, Y tell you beforne,
And she lyth in her bedde."
She gaf hym for that tydynge
A robe and fowrty shylynge,
And rychely hym cladde;
She made hym dronke of ale and wyne,
And when she sawe that hyt was tyme,
To[176] chambur she wolde hym lede.

And when he[177] was on slepe browght,
The qwene, that was of wykked thowght,
To[178] chambur gan she wende;
Hys letter she toke hym fro;
In a fyre she brente[179] hyt tho;[180]
Of werkes[181] she was unhende.

---

[170] gentle, noble [171] child [172] haste [173] stop, tarry
[174] went [175] fared [176] ms. *Tho* [177] ms. *she*
[178] ms. *Tho* [179] burnt [180] ms. *do* [181] doings

Another letter she made wyth evyll,
And sayde the qwene had born a devyll;
Durste no mon come her hende;[182]
Thre heddes hadde he there —
A lyon, a dragon, and a beere —
A fowll, feltred fende.[183]

On the morn, when hyt was day,
The messenger wente on hys way
Both by stye and strete
(In trewe[184] story, as Y say),
Tyll he come thereas the kynge lay,
And speke wordes swete.
He toke the kyng the letter in honde,
And he[185] hyt redde, Y understonde:[186]
The teres downe gan he lete.
And as he stode yn redyng,
Downe he fell yn sowenyng;
For sorow hys herte gan blede.

Grete lordes that stode hym by
Toke up the kyng hastely;
In herte he was full woo.
Sore he grette,[187] and sayde, "Alas
That Y ever man born was!
That hyt ever shullde be so![188]
Alas, that Y was made a kynge,
And sygh[189] wedded the fayrest thyng
That on erthe myght go!
That ever Jhesu hymself wolde sende
Such a fowle, lothly fende
To come bytwene us too!"[190]

---

[182] near [183] a foul, matty-haired fiend [184] ms. *trwe*
[185] the king [186] ms. *unþerstonde* [187] grieved
[188] ms. *so shullde be* [189] then (usually *sythe* or *sythen*)
[190] *i.e.* to be born of us two

When he sawe hyt myght no better be,
Another letter then made he,
And seled hyt wyth hys sele;
He commanded yn all thynge
To kepe well that lady yynge
Tyll she hadde her hele; [191]
Bothe gode men and ylle
To serve her at her wylle,
Bothe yn wo and wele.
He [192] toke thys letter of hys honde,
And rode thorow the same londe,
576 By the kynges modur castell.

And then he dwelled ther all nyght;
He was resseyved and rychely dyght,
And wyste of no treson.
He made hym well at ese, and fyne,[193]
Bothe of brede, ale, and wyne,
And that berafte hym hys reson.
When he was on slepe browght,
The false qwene hys letter sowght;
Into the fyre she kaste hyt downe.
Another letter she lette make:
That men sholde the lady take,
588 And lede her out of towne.

And putte her ynto the see
In that robe of ryche ble,
The lytyll chylde her wyth;
And lette her have no spendyng
For no mete ny for drynke,
But lede her out of that kyth.[194]

---

[191] health [192] the messenger
[193] finally; probably meant to be *a-fyne,* as in l. 913
[194] country; ms. *kygh*

"Upon payn [195] of chylde and wyfe,
And also upon your owene lyfe,
Let her have no gryth!" [196]
The messenger knew no gyle,
But rode hom mony a myle,
By forest and by fryth.[197]

And when the messenger come home,
The steward toke the letter sone,
And bygan to rede.
Sore he syght [198] and sayde, "Alas!
Sertes thys ys a fowle case,
And a delfull [199] dede."
And as he stode yn redynge,
He fell downe yn swonynge;
For sorow hys hert gan blede;
Ther was nother olde ny yynge
That myght forbere of wepynge
For that worthy under [200] wede.

The lady herde grete dele [201] yn hall;
On the steward gan she calle,
And sayde, "What may thys be?
Yyf anythyng be amys,
Tell me what that hyt ys,
And lette [202] not for me."
Then sayde the steward, verament,
"Lo, her,[203] a letter my lord hath sente,
And therfore woo ys me!"
She toke the letter and bygan to rede;
Then fonde she wryten all the dede,
How she moste ynto the see.

---

[195] upon penalty of losing [196] protection; ms. *gryght*
[197] field; ms. *fryght* [198] sighed [199] doleful, sad; ms. *defull*
[200] ms. *unþer* [201] dole, lamenting [202] stop [203] here

"Be stylle, syr," sayde the qwene,
"Lette syche mornynge bene;
For me have thou no kare.
Loke thou be not shente,[204]
But do my lordes commaundement;
God forbede thou spare.
For he weddede so porely,
On me, a sympull lady,
He ys ashamed sore.
Grete well my lord fro me,
So gentyll of blode yn Cristyanté [205]
Gete he never more!" [206]

Then was ther sorow and myche woo
When the lady to shype shulde go;
They wepte and wronge her honde.[207]
The lady, that was meke and mylde,
In her arme she bar her chylde,
And toke leve of the londe.
When she wente ynto the see
In that robe of ryche ble,
Men sowened [208] on the sonde;
Sore they wepte and sayde, "Alas!
Certys, thys ys a wykked kase!
Wo worth dedes wronge!"

The lady and the lytyll chylde
Fleted forth on the water wylde
Wyth full hard happes.[209]
Her surkote [210] that was large and wyde
Therwyth her vysage she gan hyde

---

[204] injured, disgraced [205] ms. *blolde yn cistyante*
[206] in all of Christendom he will not get another of such noble blood [207] ms. *hondes* [208] swooned [209] sore hardships
[210] outer coat

Wyth the hynder lappes.[211]
She was aferde of the see,
And layde her gruf[212] upon a tre,[213]
The chylde to her pappes.
The wawes, that were grete and strong,
On the bote faste they donge[214]
Wyth mony unsemely rappes.

And when the chyld gan to wepe,
Wyth sory herte she songe hyt aslepe,
And putte the pappe in hys mowth,
And sayde, "Myght[215] Y ones gete lond,
Of the water that ys so stronge,
By northe or by sowthe,
Wele owth[216] Y to warye[217] the, see;
I have myche shame yn the!"
And ever she lay and growth.[218]
Then she made her prayer
To Jhesu and Hys moder dere
In all that she kowthe.

Now thys lady dwelled thore
A full sevene nyght and more
As hyt was Goddys wylle;
Wyth karefull herte, and sykyng sore,
Such sorow was her yarked yore,[219]
And she lay full stylle.
She was dryven toward Rome
Thorow the grace of God yn trone,[220]
That all thyng may fulfylle;
On the see she was so harde bestadde,

---

[211] probably the large collars of her coat; ms. *hynþer*
[212] flat, face down
[213] possibly the seat of the boat, but probably the keel — the hewn log running the length of the bottom of the boat [214] struck
[215] ms. *myȝth* [216] ought [217] curse [218] grieved; ms. *growht*
[219] ordained her long ago [220] on throne

For hunger and thurste allmost madde;
Wo worth chawnses [221] ylle!

A marchaunte dwelled yn that cyté,
A ryche mon of golde and fee,
Jurdan was hys name.
Every [222] day wolde he
Go to playe hym by the see,
The eyer for to tane.[223]
He wente forth yn that tyde,
Walkynge by the see syde,[224]
All hymselfe alone.
A bote he fonde by the brymme,
And a fayr lady therynne,
That was ryght wo-bygone.

The cloth on her shon so bryght,[225]
He was aferde of that syght,
For glysteryng of that wede;
And yn hys herte he thowght [226] ryght
That she was non erthyly [227] wyght;
He sawe never non such [228] yn leede.[229]
He sayde, "What hette ye,[230] fayr lady?"
"Lord," she sayde, "Y hette Egarye,
That lye her yn drede."
Up he toke that fayr ladye,
And the yonge chylde her by,
And hom he gan hem lede.

When he come to hys byggynge,[231]
He welcomed fayr that lady yynge
That was fayr and bryght;

---

[221] chances, fortunes [222] ms. *Eevery* [223] to take the air
[224] ms. *syþe* [225] ms. *bryȝth* [226] ms. *þowȝth* [227] ms. *erdyly*
[228] ms. *shuch* [229] among people [230] what is your name?
[231] home

And badde hys wyf yn all thynge
Mete and drynke for to brynge
To the lady ryght:
"What that she wyll crave,
And her mowth wyll hyt have,
Loke hyt be redy dyght.[232]
She hath so longe meteles be
That me thynketh grette pyté;
Conforte her yyf thou myght."

Now the lady dwelles ther,
Wyth alle mete that gode were
She hadde at her wylle;
She was curteys yn all thyng,
Bothe to olde and to yynge;
Her loved bothe gode and ylle.[233]
The chylde bygan for to thryfe;
He wax the fayrest chyld on lyfe,
Whyte as flour on hylle;
And she sewed[234] sylke-werk yn bour,
And tawghte her sone nortowre;[235]
But evyr she mornede stylle.

When the chylde was seven yer olde,
He was bothe wyse and bolde,
And wele made of flesh and bone;
He was worthy under[236] wede,
And ryght well kowde prike[237] a stede;
So curteys a chylde was none.
All men lovede Segramowre,
Bothe yn halle and yn bowre,
Whersoever he gan gone.

[232] provided [233] both high and low
[234] ms. *shewed*, but the *h* seems intended for erasure
[235] nurture, courtesy [236] ms. *unþer* [237] could ride; ms. *ꝁowþe*

Leve we at the lady, clere of vyce,[238]
And speke of the kyng of Galys,
Fro the sege when he come home.

Now the sege broken ys,
The kyng come home to Galys
Wyth mykyll myrthe and pride.
Dukes and erles of ryche asyce,[239]
Barones and knyghtes of mykylle pryse
Come rydynge be hys syde.
Syr Kadore,[240] hys steward thanne,
Ageyn hym rode wyth mony a man,
As faste as he myght ryde;
He tolde the kyng aventowres[241]
Of hys halles and hys bowres
And of hys londys wyde.

The king sayde, "By Goddys name,
Syr Kadore, thou art to blame
For thy fyrst tellynge!
Thow sholdest fyrst have tolde me
Of my lady, Egaré,
I love most of all thyng!"
Then was the stewardes herte wo,
And sayde, "Lorde, why sayst thou so?
Art not thou a trewe kynge?
Lo, her, the letter ye sente me,
Yowr owene self the sothe may se;
I have don your byddynge."

The kyng toke the letter to rede,
And when he sawe that ylke[242] dede,
He wax all pale and wanne.

[238] visage, face [239] assize, estate [240] ms. *kodore*
[241] adventures, happenings [242] same

Sore he grette and sayde, "Alas,
That ever born Y was,
Or ever was made manne!
Syr Kadore, so mot Y the,[243]
Thys letter come never fro me,
I telle the her anone!"
Bothe they wepte and gaf hem ylle;
"Alas," he sayde, "saf Goddys wylle!"[244]
And both they[245] sowened then.

Grete lordes stode by
And toke up the kyng hastyly,
Of hem was gret pyté;
And when they both kevered were,
The kyng toke[246] hym the letter there
Of[247] the heddys thre.
"A, lord," he[248] sayde, "be Goddes grace,
I sawe never thys letter yn place![249]
Alas! how may thys be?"
After the messenger ther they sente;
The kyng askede what way he went;
"Lord,[250] be your modur fre."

"Alas!" then sayde the kynge,[251]
"Whether my moder were so unhende
To make thys treson?
By my krowne, she shall be brent,
Wythowten any other jugement;
That thenketh me best reson!"

---

[243] as I may prosper
[244] saf = save; the sense seems to be "Alas, though it is God's will"
[245] ms. *þe* [246] gave [247] which told of [248] Kadore
[249] anywhere [250] ms. *Lor*
[251] both meter and rhyme suggest a word missing here, but the ms. gives no clue

Grete lordes toke [252] hem betwene
That they wolde exyle the qwene,
And berefe her hyr renowne;
Thus they exiled the false qwene,
And berafte her hyr lyflode [253] clean,
Castell, towre, and towne.

When she was fled over the see-fome,
The nobull kyng dwelled at hom
Wyth full hevy chere;
Wyth karefull hert and drury mone,[254]
Sykynges made he many on [255]
For Egarye the clere.
And when he sawe the childeren play,
He wepte and sayde, "Wellawey,
For my sone so dere!"
Such lyf he lyved mony a day,
That no mon hym stynte [256] may,
Fully seven yere;

Tyll a thowght yn hys herte come
How hys lady, whyte as fome,
Was drowned for hys sake.
"Thorow the grace of God yn trone,
I wolle to the pope of Rome,
My penans for to take!"
He lette ordeyne shypus fele,[257]
And fylled hem full of worldes wele,[258]
Hys men mery wyth to make;

[252] undertook, decided [253] livelihood, property
[254] sorrowful moan
[255] many a one
[256] hinder, stop [257] many
[258] world's wealth; ms. *wordes*

Dolys he lette dyght and dele,[259]
For to wynnen hym sowles hele;[260]
To the shyp he toke the gate.[261]

Shypmen, that wer so mykyll of price,
Dyght her takull on ryche acyse,[262]
That was fayr and fre;
They drowgh up sayl and leyd out ore;
The wynde stode as her lust wore;[263]
The wethur was lythe on le.
They sayled over the salt fome
Thorow the grace of God yn trone,
That most ys of powsté;[264]
To that cyté when they[265] come,
At the burgeys hous hys yn he nome[266]
Theras woned[267] Emarye.

Emaré called her[268] sone
Hastely to here come,
Wythoute ony lettynge,[269]
And sayde, "My dere sone so fre,
Do a lyttull aftur me,[270]
And thou shalt[271] have my blessynge.
Tomorowe thou shall serve yn halle
In a kurtyll of ryche palle,[272]
Byfore thys nobull kyng;
Loke, sone, so curtays thou be
That no mon fynde chalange to the
In no manere thynge.

---

[259] he ordained and distributed alms; ms. *dyȝth*
[260] healing, salvation [261] took his way
[262] dressed their tackle in a noble manner [263] as was their wish
[264] power [265] ms. *þe* [266] he took his inn, lodging
[267] dwelled [268] ms. *he* [269] delay
[270] as I say [271] ms. *shat* [272] finely woven cloth

When the kyng ys served of spycerye,[273]
Knele thou downe hastelye,
And take hys hond yn thyn;
And when thou hast so done,
Take the kuppe of golde, sone,
And serve hym of the wyne.
And what that he speketh to the,
Cum anon and tell me,
On Goddes blessyng and myne!"
The chylde wente ynto the hall
Among the lordes grete and small,
That lufsumme were under lyne.[274]

Then the lordes, that were grete,
Wysh [275] and wente to her mete;
Menstrelles browght yn the kowrs; [276]
The chylde hem served so curteysly,
All hym loved that hym sy,[277]
And spake hym gret honowres.
Then sayde all that loked hym upon,
So curteys a chyld sawe they never non
In halle ny yn bowres.
The kynge sayde to hym yn game,
"Swete sone, what ys thy name?"
"Lorde," he sayde, "Y hyght [278] Segramowres."

Then that nobull kyng
Toke up [279] a grete sykynge,
For hys sone hyght so;

---

[273] dessert, the sweet course
[274] handsome under linen; ms. *unþer*
[275] washed
[276] *i.e.* sang and played as the course was being brought in; ms. *Mentrelles*
[277] saw [278] ms. *hyȝth* [279] began

Certys, wythowten lesynge,
The teres out of hys yen gan wryng—
In herte he was full woo.
Neverthelese, he lette be,
And loked on the chylde so fre,
And mykell he loved hym thoo.[280]
The kyng sayde to the burgeys anon,
"Swete syr, ys thys thy sone?"
The burgeys sayde, "Yoo."[281]

Then the lordes, that were grete,
Whesshen[282] ageyn aftyr mete,
And then come spycerye.
The chyld that was of chere swete,
On hys kne downe he sete,[283]
And served hym curteyslye.
The kynge called the burgeys hym tyll,
And seyde, "Syr, yf hyt be thy wyll,
Gyf me thys lytyll body!
I shall hym make lorde of town and towre,
Of hye halles and of bowre;
I love hym specyally."

When he had served the kyng at wylle,
Fayr he wente hys modyr tyll,
And tellys her how hyt ys.
"Soone, when he shall to chamber wende,
Take hys hond at the grete ende,[284]
For he ys thy fadur, ywysse.

---

[280] then [281] yes [282] washed
[283] kneeled
[284] the meaning seems obscure; possibly what is intended is the hall, or stairway, leading from the central part of the building to the sleeping chambers, the "great end" being that end nearest the central rooms

And byd hym come speke wyth Emaré,
That changed her name to Egaré
In the londe of Galys."
The chylde wente ageyn to halle,
Amonge the grete lordes alle,
And served on ryche asyse.[285]

When they wer well at ese, afyne,
Bothe of brede, ale, and wyne,
They rose up, more and myn.[286]
When the kyng shulde to chamber wende,
He toke hys hond at the grete ende,
And fayre he helpe hym yn,
And sayde, "Syr, yf your wylle be,
Take me your honde and go wyth me,
For Y am of yowr kynne.
Ye shulle come speke wyth Emaré,
That chaunged her nome to Egaré,
That berys the whyte chynne."

The kyng yn herte was full woo
When he herd mynge[287] tho
Of her that was hys qwene,
And sayde, "Sone, why sayst thou so?
Wherto umbraydest[288] thou me of my wo?
That may never bene!"
Nevertheles, wyth hym he wente;
Ageyn hem come the lady gent,
In the robe bryght and shene.
He toke her yn hys armes two;
For joye they sowened, both to,
Such love was hem bytwene.

[285] manner [286] less [287] mention [288] why upbraid

A joyfull metyng was ther thore
Of that lady, goodly under gore,[289]
Frely in armes to folde.
Lorde! Gladde was Syr Kadore
And other lordes that ther wore,
Semely to beholde,
Of the lady that was [290] put yn the see,
Thorow grace of God in Trinité,
That was kevered [291] of cares colde.
Leve we at the lady, whyte as flour,
And speke we of her fadur, the emperour,
That fyrste thys tale of ytolde.

The emperour, her fadyr, then
Was [292] woxen an olde man,
And thowght on hys synne—
Of hys dowghtyr, [293] Emaré,
That was putte ynto the see,
That was so bryght of skynne.
He thowght that he wolde go,
For hys penance, to the pope tho,
And heven for to wynne.
Messengeres he sente forth sone,
And they come to the kowrt of Rome
To take her lordes inne.[294]

Emaré prayde her lord, the kyng,
"Syr, abyde that lordys komyng,
That ys so fayr and fre.
And, swete syr, yn all thyng
Aqweynte you wyth that lordynge;
Hyt ys worshyp to the."

---

[289] goodly in gown; ms. *unþer* [290] ms. *wat* [291] recovered
[292] ms. *Wax* [293] ms. *þowȝtyr*
[294] to arrange for their lord's lodging

The kyng of Galys seyde than
"So grete a lord ys ther non
In all Crystyanté."
"Now, swete syr, whatever betyde,
Agayn that grete lord ye ryde,
And all thy knyghtys wyth the."

Emaré tawghte [295] her sone yynge,
Ageyn the emperour komynge,
How that he sholde done:
"Swete sone, yn all thyng
By redy wyth my lord the kyng,
And be my swete sone.
When the emperour kysseth thy fadur so fre,
Loke yyf he wyll kysse the;
Abowe the to hym, sone,
And bydde hym come speke wyth Emaré,
That was putte ynto the see;
Hymself gaf the dome." [296]

Now kometh the emperour of pryse;
Ageyn hym rode the kyng of Galys,
Wyth full mykull pryde.
The chyld was worthy under [297] wede;
A [298] satte upon a nobyll stede,
By hys fadyr syde.
And when he mette the emperour,
He valed [299] hys hode wyth gret honour,
And kyssed hym yn that tyde;
And other lordys of gret valowre,
They also kessed Segramowre;
In herte ys not to hyde.

---

[295] ms. *thawȝte* [296] judgment [297] ms. *unþer* [298] he
[299] took off, let down

The emperours hert anamered gretlye
Of the chylde that rode hym by
Wyth so lovely chere.
Segramowre, he stayde [300] hys stede;
Hys owene fadur toke good hede,
And other lordys that ther were.
The chylde spake to the emperour,
And sayde, "Lord, for thyn honour,
My worde that thou wyll here:
Ye shull come speke wyth Emaré,
That changede her name to Egaré,
That was thy dowghter [301] dere.

Syr, and ye wyll go wyth me,
I shall the brynge wyth that lady fre,
That ys lovesom on to loke."
The emperour wax all pale,
And sayde, "Sone, why umbraydest me of bale,[302]
And [303] thou may se no bote?" [304]
Neverthelesse, wyth hym he wente;
Ageyn hym come that lady gent,
Walkynge on her fote.
And the emperour alyghte tho,
And toke her yn hys armes two,
And clypte and kyssed her sote.[305]

Ther was a joyfull metynge
Of the emperour and of the kynge,
And also of Emaré;

---

[300] ms. *sayde* [301] ms. *þowȝþer* [302] sorrow [303] if
[304] remedy, cure; in the ms. the order of the first sestet of this stanza (11. 1009-11, 1012-14) is reversed; the inverted order given here is more natural, especially in view of the word "nevertheless" beginning the next sestet
[305] held and kissed her sweetly

And so ther was of Syr Segramour,[306]
That aftyr was emperour;
A full gode man was he.
A grette feste ther was holde
Of erles and barones bolde,
As testymonyeth[307] thys story.
Thys ys on of Brytayne layes,
That was used by olde dayes,[308]
1032 Men callys "Playn d'Egarye." [309]

Jheso, that settes yn Thy trone,
So graunte us wyth The to wone [310]
In thy perpetuall glory! Amen.

Explicit Emaré

---

306 ms. *egramour* 307 testifies

308 that used to be told in olden days

309 ms. *playn þe garye*; the meaning seems clear (the "complaint of Egaré"), though the scribe appears to be imitating a French form of the title

310 ms. *wene*

God lete neuyr no yonge man haue no false oppynyon
ffor he was tratyrously slayn and borne in a gode houre
To the blys of heuyn god hath hym brought And sett hym on hys ryght honde
I prey to god that he so do euery gode man of thys londe
Lythe and lystenyth gentylmen that haue herde thys songe to ende
I prey to god at oure laste day to heuyn that we may wende Amen

Here foloweth the Erle of Tolous

534

34)

Jhesu cryste yn trynyte
Only god & persons thre
Graunt vs wele to spede
And gyf vs grace so to do
That we may come thy blys vnto
On rode as thou can vs bede
Leue lordys y schall you telle
Of a tale some tyme befelle
Farre yn vnkowthe londe lede
How a lady had grete myschefe
And how sche couyrd of hur grefe
I pray yow take hede
Some tyme ther was in Almayn
An Emperrour of moche mayn
Syr Dyoclysyan he hyght
He was a bolde man & a stowte
All crystendome of hym had dowte
So stronge he was in fyght
He dysheryted many a man
And falsely ther londys wan
Wyth maystry and wyth myght
Tyll hyt befell vpon a day
A warre wakenyd as y yow say
Betwene hym and a knyght
The Erle of Tollous syr Barnard
The emperrour wyth hym was harde
And gretly was hys foo
He had reft owte of hys honde
Thre .C. poundys worth be yere of londe
Therfore hys herte was woo

He was an hardy man and a stronge
And sawe the emperour dyd hym wronge
And other men also
He ordeyned hym for batayle
In to the emperours londe saunsfayle
And there he began to brenne & sloo
Thys emperour had a wyfe
The fayrest oon that euyr bare lyfe
Saue mary mekyll of myght
And therto gode in all thynge
Of almesdede and gode berynge
Be day and eke be nyght
Of hur body sche was trewe
As euyr was lady that men knewe
And therto moost bryght
To the emperour sche can say
My dere lorde y you pray
Delyuyr the erle hys ryght
Dere lady he seyde lete that bee
That day schalt thou neuyr see
Yf y may ryde on ryght
That he schall haue hys londe agayne
Fyrste schall y breke hys brayne
Os y am trewe knyght
He warryth faste in my londe
I schall be redy at hys honde
Wythyn thys .xv. nyght
He sende abowte euery whare
That all men schulde make them yare
Agayne the Erle to fyght
He lete crye in euery syde

The Erle of Tolous

Jhesu Cryste yn Trynyté,
Oonly God and persons thre,
Graunt us wele to spede; [1]
And gyf us grace so to do
That we may come Thy blys unto,
On rode [2] as Thou can blede.
Leve [3] lordys, Y schall you telle
Of a tale sometyme befelle
Farre yn unkowthe lede: [4]
How a lady had grete myschefe,[5]
And how sche covyrd [6] of hur grefe;
Y pray you take hede.

Sometyme ther was in Almayn [7]
An emperrour of moche mayn;
Syr Dyaclysyon he hyght.[8]
He was a bolde man and a stowte;
All Crystendome of hym had dowte,[9]
So stronge he was in fyght.
He dysheryted [10] many a man,
And falsely ther londys wan
Wyth maystry and wyth myght,

---

[1] prosper [2] cross [3] dear [4] a strange land [5] trouble
[6] recovered [7] Germany [8] was named [9] fear, awe
[10] disinherited

Tyll hyt befelle upon a day
A warre wakenyd,[11] as Y yow say,
Betwene hym and a knyght.

The Erle of Tollous, Syr Barnard,
The emperrour wyth hym was harde,
And gretely was hys foo;
He had rafte owt of hys honde
Thre hundryd poundys worth be yere of londe;
Therfore hys herte was woo.
He was an hardy man and a stronge,
And sawe the emperour dyd hym wronge,
And other men also;
He ordeyned [12] hym for batayle
Into the emperours lond, saunsfayle,[13]
And there he began to brenne and sloo.[14]

Thys emperour had a wyfe,
The fayrest oon that evyr bare lyfe
Save Mary, mekyll of myght,
And therto gode in all thynge
Of almesdede [15] and gode berynge
Be day and eke be nyght.
Of hyr body sche was trewe
As evyr was lady that men knewe,
And therto moost bryght; [16]
To the emperour sche can say,
"My dere lorde, Y you pray,
Delyvyr the erle hys ryght."

"Dame," he seyde, "let that bee!
That day schalt thou nevyr see—
Yf Y may ryde on ryght [17] —

---

[11] began [12] prepared [13] without fail [14] burn and slay
[15] charity [16] fair, beautiful [17] aright, upright

That he schall have hys londe agayne;
Fyrste [18] schall Y breke hys brayne,
Os Y am trewe knyght.
He warryth faste in my londe;
I schall be redy at hys honde
Wythyn thys fourtenyght!"
He sente abowte everywhare
That all men schulde make them yare [19]
Agayne the erle to fyght.

He let crye in every syde
Thorow hys londe, ferre and wyde,
Bothe in felde and towne:
All that myght wepon bere —
Sworde, alablast,[20] schylde, or spere —
They schoulde be redy bowne.[21]
The erle on hys syde also,
Wyth forty thousand and moo,
Wyth spere and schylde browne:
A day of batayle there was sett;
In felde when they togedur mett,
Was crakydd many a crowne.

The emperour had bataylys [22] sevyn;
He spake to them wyth sterne stevyn,[23]
And sayde, "So mote Y thryve,[24]
Be ye now redy for to fyght;
Go ye and bete them downe ryght,
And leveth non on lyve!
Loke that none raunsomyd bee,
Nothyr for golde, ne for fee,
But sle them wyth swerde and knyfe!"

---

[18] rather [19] ready [20] cross-bow [21] prepared
[22] battalions [23] voice, words
[24] as I hope to thrive, prosper; ms. *he*

For all hys boste, he faylyd yyt;
The erle manly hym mett
Wyth strokys goode and ryfe.[25]

They reryd batayle on every syde;
Boldely [26] togethyr can they ryde
Wyth schylde and many a spere;
They leyde on faste, as they were wode,
Wyth swerdys and axes that were gode —
Full hedeous hit was to here.
There were schyldys and schaftys schakydd,[27]
Hedys thorogh helmys crakydd,
And hawberkys [28] all totere; [29]
The erle hymselfe an axe drowe,
An hundryd men that day he slowe,
So wyght [30] he was in were.

Many a stede there stekyd [31] was;
Many a bolde baron in that place
Lay burland [32] yn hys own blode;
So moche blode there was spylte
That the felde was ovyr-hylte,[33]
As hyt were a flode.
Many a wyfe may sytt and wepe
That was wonte softe to slepe,
And now can [34] they no gode;
Many a body and many a hevyd,[35]
Many a doghty knyght there was levyd,[36]
That was wylde and wode.

---

[25] many [26] ms. *bodely* [27] shattered
[28] breast-armor, mail [29] torn to pieces
[30] strong, fierce [31] pierced
[32] weltering, writhing [33] overflowed
[34] know [35] head
[36] left

The Erle of Tollous wan the felde;
The emperour stode and behelde;
Wele faste can he flee
To a castell there besyde —
Fayne he was hys hedd to hyde —
And wyth hym erlys thre.
No moo, forsothe, scapyd [37] away,
But they were slayn and takyn that day;
Hyt myght non othyr bee.
The erle tyll nyght folowed the chase,
And sythen [38] he thanked God of Hys grace,
That syttyth in Trynyté.

There was slayne in that batayle
Syxty thousand, wythowte fayle,
On the emperours syde;
There was takyn thre hundryd and fyfty
Of grete lordys, sekyrly,[39]
Wyth woundys grymly wyde.
On the erlys syde ther were slayne
But twenty, sothely to sayne,
So boldely they can abyde.
Soche grace God hym sende
That false quarell cometh to evell ende,
For oght that may betyde.

Now the emperour ys full woo;
He hath loste men and londe also;
Sore then syghed hee.
He sware be Hym that dyed on rode,
Mete nor drynke schulde do hym no gode
Or [40] he vengedd [41] bee.

[37] escaped [38] then [39] surely, truly
[40] until [41] avenged

The emperes seyde, "Gode Lorde,
Hyt ys better ye be acorde,[42]
Be oght that Y can see;
Hyt ys grete parell,[43] sothe to telle,
To be agayne the ryght quarell,
Be God, thus thynketh me!"

"Dame," seyde the emperoure,
"Y have a grete dyshonoure;
Therfore myn herte ys woo!
My lordys be takyn, and some dede;
Therfore carefull ys my rede; [44]
Sorowe nye wyll me sloo!"
Then seyde Dame Beulybon,
"Syr, Y rede, be Seynt John,
Of warre that ye hoo! [45]
Ye have the wronge and he the ryght,
And that ye may see in syght
Be thys and other moo."

The emperour was evyll payde —
Hyt was sothe the lady sayde —
Therfore hym lykyd ylle;
He wente awey and syghed sore;
Oon worde spake he no more,
But helde hym wonder stylle.
Leve we now the emperour in thoght —
Game ne gle lyked hym noght,
So gretly can he grylle; [46]
And to the erle turne we agayn,
That thanked God wyth all hys mayn,
That grace had sende hym tylle.[47]

---

[42] accorded [43] peril
[44] my heart is full of care [45] stop
[46] sorrow, complain [47] to

The erle, Barnard of Tollous,
Had fele [48] men chyvalrous
Takyn to hys preson;
Moche gode of them he hadd;
Y cannot telle, so God me gladd,[49]
So grete was ther raunsome.
Among them had he oon
Was grettest of them everychon,[50]
A lorde of many a towne —
Syr Trylabas of Turky;
The emperour hym lovyd sekurly,
A man of grete renowne.

So hyt befelle upon a day
The erle and he went to play [51]
Be a rever syde;
The erle seyde to Trylabas,
"Telle me, syr, for Goddys grace,
Of a thyng that spryngyth wyde [52] —
That youre emperour hath a wyfe,
The fayrest woman that ys on lyfe
Of hewe and eke of hyde.[53]
Y swere by boke and by belle,
Yf sche be so feyre as men telle,
Mekyll may be hys pryde."

Then sayde that lord, anon ryght,
"Be the ordre Y bere of knyght,
The sothe Y schall telle the:
To seeke the worlde, more and lesse,
Bothe Crystendome and hethynnesse,
Ther ys none so bryght of blee!

---

[48] many [49] as God gives me joy
[50] everyone, all [51] *i.e.* to take a walk
[52] a thing that is much talked about [53] of color and complexion

Whyte as snowe ys hur coloure;
Hur rudde [54] ys radder then the rose flower
Yn syght who may hur see.
All men that evyr God wroght
Myght not thynke, nor caste in thoght,[55]
A fayrer for to bee!"

Then seyde the erle, "Be Goddys [56] grace,
Thys worde in mornyng me mas [57] —
Thou seyest sche ys so bryght.
Thy raunsom here Y the forgeve;
My helpe, my love, whyll Y leve,
Therto my trowthe Y plyght —
So that thou wylt brynge me
Yn safegarde for to bee,
Of hur to have a syght —
An hundryd pownde wyth grete honoure
To bye the horses and ryche armoure,
Os Y am trewe knyght!"

Than answeryd Syr Trylabas,
"Yn that covenaunt, in thys place,
My trowthe Y plyght thee:
Y schall holde thy forward gode
To brynge the, wyth mylde mode,[58]
In syght hur for to see;
And therto wyll Y kepe counsayle,[59]
And nevyr more, wythowte fayle,
Agayne [60] yow to bee.
Y schall be trewe, be Goddys ore,
To lose myn own lyfe therfore:
Hardely tryste to mee."

---

[54] complexion [55] imagine
[56] ms. *godds* [57] makes, puts
[58] manner [59] secret [60] against

The erle answeryd wyth wordys hende,[61]
"Y tryste to the as to my frende,
Wythowte any stryfe.
Anon that we [62] were buskyd yare,[63]
On owre jurney for to fare
For to see that wyfe.
Y swere be God and Seynt Andrewe,
Yf hyt be so Y fynde the trewe,
Ryches schall be to the ryfe."
They lettyd [64] nothyr for wynde nor wedur,
But forthe they wente, bothe togedur,
Wythowte any stryfe.

These knyghtes nevyr stynte nor blanne [65]
Tyll to the cyté that they wan [66]
There the emperes was ynne.
The erle hymselfe, for more drede,
Cladd hym in armytes wede [67] —
Thogh he were of ryche kynne —
For he wolde not knowen bee;
He dwellyd there dayes three,
And rested hym in hys ynne.
The knyght bethoght hym on a day
The gode erle to betray —
Falsely he can begynne.

Anone he wente in a rese [68]
To chaumbur, to the emperes,
And sett hym on hys knee.

---

[61] courteous
[62] *we* is written lightly between this and the previous line and marked by a carat for insertion; the hand seems later than that of the scribe and may be a previous editor's. Whatever the case, both sense and meter require the word [63] readied quickly
[64] delayed [65] stopped nor paused [66] came
[67] hermit's clothes [68] ruse

He seyde, "Be Hym that harowed helle,
He kepe yow fro all parelle [69]
Yf that Hys wylle bee;
Madam," he seyde, "be Jhesus,
Y have the Erle of Tollous —
Oure moost enemye ys hee!"
"Yn what maner," the lady can say,
Ys he comyn, Y the pray;
Anone, telle thou me."

"Madam, Y was yn hys preson;
He hath forgevyn me my raunsom,
Be God full of myght;
And all ys for the love of the.
The sothe ys he longyth yow to see,
Madam, onys [70] in syght.
An hundred pownde Y have to mede,[71]
And armour for a nobull stede.
Forsothe, Y have hym hyght [72]
That he schall see yow at hys fylle
Ryght at hys owne wylle:
Therto my trowthe Y plyght.

Lady, he ys to us a foo;
Therfore Y rede [73] that we hym sloo:
He hath done us grete grylle." [74]
The lady seyde, "So mut Y goo,[75]
Thy soule ys loste yf thou do so;
Thy trowthe thou schalt fulfylle.
Sythe [76] he forgaf the thy raunsom,
And lowsydd [77] the owt of preson,
Do away thy wyckyd wylle!

---

[69] peril [70] once [71] for reward
[72] told, promised [73] advise [74] damage, grief
[75] as I hope to prosper [76] since [77] released

Hit were agaynst curtesye
For to do hym vylanye
That trustyth the untyll.[78]

To-morne, when they rynge the mas-belle,
Brynge hym into my chapelle,
And thynke thou on no false slowthe.[79]
There schall he see me at hys wylle,
Thy covenaunt to fulfylle:
Y rede the, holde thy trowthe.
Certys yf thou hym begyle,
Thy soule ys in grete peryle
Syn[80] thou haste made hym othe.
Certys hyt were a traytory[81]
For to wayte[82] hym velany;
Me thynkyth hyt were rowthe."[83]

The knyght to the erle wente;
Yn herte he helde hym foule schente[84]
For hys wyckyd thoght.
He seyde, "Syr, so mote Y the,[85]
To-morne thou schalt my lady see;
Therfore dysmay the noght.
When ye here the mas-belle,
Y schall the[86] brynge to the chapelle;
Thedur sche schall be broght.
Be the oryall-syde[87] stonde thou stylle,
Then schalt thou see hur at thy wylle,
That ys so worthyly wroght."

---

[78] these three lines are missing from the ms. and are supplied from A^1 [79] ms. *sloythe*, possibly *sleythe*; murder
[80] since [81] traitorous act
[82] do, pay [83] a pity
[84] shamed [85] as I hope to prosper
[86] ms. *hur* [87] a recess, probably at the entrance of the chapel

The erle sayde, "Y holde the trewe,
And that schall the nevyr rewe,[88]
As farre forthe as Y may."
Yn hys herte he waxe gladd:
"Fylle the wyne," wyghtly [89] he badd,
"Thys goyth to my pay!" [90]
There he restyd that nyght;
On the morne he can hym dyght [91]
Yn armytes array.
When they ronge to the masse,
To the chapell conne they passe
To see that lady gay.

They had stonden but a whyle —
The mowntaunse of halfe a myle [92] —
Then came that lady free.
Two erlys hur ladd;
Wondur rychely sche was cladd
In golde and ryche perré.[93]
Whan the erle sawe hur in syght,
Hym thoght sche was as bryght
As blossome on the tree;
Of all the syghtys that evyr he sye,
Raysyd nevyr none hys herte so hye,
Sche was so bryght of blee.[94]

Sche stode stylle in that place,
And schewed opynly hur face
For love of that knyght.
He behelde ynly [95] hur face;
He sware there, be Goddys grace,

[88] regret
[89] quickly, heartily [90] goes to my liking [91] dress
[92] *i.e.* no longer than it would take to ride half a mile [93] jewelry
[94] countenance [95] eagerly

He sawe nevyr none so bryght.
Hur eyen were gray as any glas;
Mowthe and nose schapen was
At all maner ryght;
Fro the forhedd to the too
Bettur schapen myght non goo,
Nor none semelyer yn syght.

Twyse sche turnyd hur abowte
Betwene the erlys that were stowte
For the erle schulde hur see;
When sche spake wyth mylde stevyn,[96]
Sche semyd an aungell of hevyn,
So feyre sche was of blee.
Hur syde longe, hur myddyll small,
Schouldurs, armes, therwythall,[97]
Fayrer myght non be;
Hur hondys whyte as whallys bonne,
Wyth fyngurs longe and ryngys upon,
Hur nayles bryght of blee.

Satisfying bodily need for man

When he had beholden hur welle,
The lady wente to hur chapell,
Masse for to here.
The erle stode on that odur syde;
Hys eyen fro hur myght he not hyde,
So lovely sche was of chere.
He seyde, "Lorde God, full of myght,
Leve Y were [98] so worthy a knyght
That Y myght be hur fere,[99]
And that sche no husbonde hadd!
All the golde that evyr God made
To me were not so dere!"

---

[96] voice [97] and all else
[98] *i.e.* how I wish I were . . . [99] companion

When the masse come to ende,
The lady that was feyre and hende,
To the chaumbur can sche fare;
The erle syghed and was full woo
Owt of hys syght when sche schulde goo;
Hys mornyng was the mare.[100]
The erle seyde, "So God me save,
Of hur almes Y[101] wolde crave,
Yf hur wylle ware;
Myght Y but[102] gete of that free[103]
Eche a day hur to see,
Hyt wolde covyr[104] me of my care."

The erle knelyd down anon ryght,
And askyd gode for God Allmight,[105]
That dyed on the tree;
The emperes callyd a knyght,
"Forty floranse[106] that ben bryght,
Anone brynge thou me."
To that armyte sche hyt payde;
Of on hyr fyngyr[107] a rynge sche layde
Amonge the golde so free.
He thankyd hur ofte, as Y yow say;
To the chaumbyr wente that lady gay,
There hur was leveste[108] to bee.

The erle wente home to hys ynnys,
And grete joye he begynnys
When he founde the rynge;

[100] more [101] ms. *he*
[102] ms. *not* [103] that lovely one
[104] recover [105] asked alms in the name of God Almighty
[106] florins, coins [107] off one of her fingers
[108] there she most wished

Yn hys herte he waxe blythe,
And kyssyd hyt fele sythe,[109]
And seyde, "My dere derlynge,
On thy fyngyr thys was;
Wele [110] ys me Y have thy grace,
Of the to have thys rynge!
Yf evyr Y gete grace of the, Queen,
That any love betwene us bene,
Thys may be oure tokenyng!"

The erle, al so soone os hyt was day,
Toke hys leve and wente hys way
Home to hys cuntré;
Syr Trylabas he thanked faste:
"Of thys dede thou done me haste,
Well qwyt [111] schall hyt bee!"
They kyssyd togedur as gode frende;
Syr Trylabas home can wende —
There evell mote he thee! [112]
A traytory he thoght to doo
Yf he myght come thertoo,[113]
So schrewde in herte was hee.

Anon he callyd two knyghtys,
Hardy men at all syghtys —
Bothe were of hys kynne:
"Syrs," he seyde, "wythowt fayle,
Yf ye wyl do be my counsayle,
Grete worschyp schulde ye wynne.
Knowe ye the Erle of Tollous?
Moche harme he hath done us;
Hys boste Y rede we blynne.[114]

---

[109] many times [110] joyful [111] repaid [112] may evil betide him!
[113] if he might find a means [114] I advise we stop

Yf ye wyll do aftur my redd,[115]
Thys day he schall be dedd,
So God save me fro synne!"

That oon knyght, Kaunters, that odur, Kayme,
Falser men myght no man rayme,[116]
Certys, then were thoo;
Syr Trylabas was the thrydde;
Hyt was no mystur [117] them to bydd
Aftur the erle to goo.
At a brygge they hym mett;
Wyth harde strokes they hym besett,
As men that were hys foo.
The erle was a man of mayn;
Faste he faght them agayne,
And soone he slew twoo.

The thrydd fledd and blewe owt [118] faste;
The erle ovyrtoke hym at the laste;
Hys hedd he clofe in three.
The cuntrey [119] gedyrd abowte hym faste,
And aftur hym yorne [120] they chaste —
An hundred there men myght see.
The erle of them was agaste;
At the laste fro them he paste;
Fayne he was to flee.
Fro them he wente into a waste;[121]
To reste hym there he toke hys caste;[122]
A wery man was hee.

All the nyght in that foreste
The gentyll erle toke hys reste;
He had non odur woon.[123]

---

[115] advice [116] accuse [117] need [118] panted [119] people
[120] eagerly [121] desert [122] chance
[123] no other wish; ms. *no nodur*

When hyt dawed,[124] he rose up soone,
And thankyd God that syttyth in trone[125]
That he had scapyd hys foon.[126]
That day he travaylyd many a myle —
And ofte he was in grete parylle[127]
Be the way os he can gone —
Tyll he come to fayre[128] castell,
There hym was levyst to dwelle,
Was made of lyme and stone.

Of hys comyng hys men were gladd;
"Be ye mery, my men," he badd,
"For nothyng ye spare!
The emperour, wythowte lees,
Y trowe wyll let us be in pees,
And warre on us no mare."
Thus dwellyd the erle in that place
Wyth game, myrthe, and grete solase,
Ryght os hym levyst ware.
Let we now the erle alloon,
And speke we of Dame Beulyboon —
How sche was caste in care.

The emperour lovyd hys wyfe
Al so moche os hys own lyfe,
And more yf he myght;
He chose two knyghtys that were hym dere,
Whedur that he were ferre or nere,
To kepe hur day and nyght.
That oon hys love on hur caste;
So dud the todur[129] at the laste:
Sche was feyre and bryght.

---

[124] dawned [125] on throne
[126] foes [127] peril
[128] the article *a* precedes *fayre* in the ms. but is struck through
[129] the other

Nothyr of othyr wyste ryght noght,[130]
So derne [131] love on them wroght;
To dethe they were nere dyght.

So hyt befelle upon a day
That oon can to that othyr say,
"Syr, al so muste Y thee,[132]
Me thynkyth thou fadyste all away
Os man that ys clongyn in clay,[133]
So pale waxeth thy blee." [134]
Then seyde that other, "Y make avowe,
Ryght so me thynketh fareste thou,
Whysoevyr hyt bee;
Telle me thy cawse why hyt ys,
And Y schall telle the myn, ywys;
My trouthe Y plyght to thee."

"Y graunte," he seyde, "wythowt fayle,
But loke hyt be trewe counsayle." [135]
Therto hys trowthe he plyght.
He seyde, "My lady, the emperes,
For love of hur Y am in grete dystresse;
To dethe hyt wyll me dyght."
Then seyde that othyr, "Certenly,
Wythowte drede, so fare Y
For that lady bryght;
Syn owre love ys on hur sett,
How myght owre bale beste be bett? [136]
Canst thou rede on ryght?"

---

[130] neither knew of the other's feelings
[131] secretly [132] as I hope to prosper
[133] *i.e.* one who has gone to the grave
[134] complexion
[135] *i.e.* kept secret
[136] how may our grief be cured?

Then seyde that othyr, "Be Seynt John,
Bettur counsayle can Y noon,
Methynkyth, then ys thys:
Y rede that oon of us twoo
Prevely to hyr goo
And pray hur of hur blys.
Y myselfe wylle go hyr tylle;
Yn case Y may gete hur wylle,
Of myrthe schalt thou not mys:
Thou schalt take us wyth the dede;[137]
Leste thou us wrye,[138] sche wyll drede,
And graunte the thy wylle, ywys."

Thus they were at oon assent;[139]
Thys false thefe[140] forthe wente
To wytt[141] the ladyes wylle.
Yn chaumbyr he founde hyr so free;
He sett hym downe on hys knee
Hys purpose to fulfylle.
Than spake that lady free,
"Syr, Y see now well be the,
Thou haste not all thy wylle;
On thy sekenes now Y see —
Telle me now thy prevyté,
Why thou mornyst so stylle."

"Lady," he seyde, "that durste Y noght
For all the gode[142] that evyr was wroght
Be grete God invysybylle;
But on a book yf ye wyll swere
That ye schull not me dyskere,[143]
Then were hyt possybyll."

[137] in the act [138] that you will betray us [139] agreed
[140] villain [141] know, learn [142] goods, riches
[143] discover, reveal

Then seyd the lady, "How may that bee
That thou darste not tryste to mee?
Hyt ys full orybylle! [144]
Here my trowthe to the Y plyght:
Y schall heyle the [145] day and nyght,
Al so trewe as boke or belle!"

"Lady, in yow ys all my tryste;
Inwardely [146] Y wolde ye wyste
What payne Y suffur you fore;
Y drowpe, Y dare, [147] nyght and day;
My wele,[148] my wytt, ys all away,
But ye leve [149] on my lore.[150]
Y have yow lovyd many a day,
But to yow durste Y nevyr say:
My mornyng ys the more.
But ye do aftur my rede,
Certenly Y am but dede;
Of my lyfe ys no store." [151]

Than answeryd that lovely lyfe,
"Syr, wele thou wottyst Y am a wyfe;
My lorde ys emperoure.
He chase the for a trewe knyght,
To kepe me bothe day and nyght
Undur thy socowre.[152]
To do that dede yf Y assente,
Y were worthy to be brente,[153]
And broght in grete doloure.

---

144 horrible 145 keep your secret
146 earnestly 147 grieve, waste away
148 health 149 believe
150 words 151 worth
152 protection 153 burnt

Thou art a traytour in thy sawe,[154]
Worthy to be hanged and todrawe,[155]
Be Mary, that swete floure!"

"A, Madam," seyde the knyght,
"For the love of God Almyght,
Hereon take no hede!
Yn me ye may full wele tryste ay;
Y dud nothyng but yow to affray,[156]
Al so God me spede!
Thynke, Madam: your trowthe ys plyght
To holde counsayle bothe day and nyght,
Fully, wythowte drede;
Y aske mercy, for Goddys ore;
Hereof yf Y carpe[157] more,
Let drawe me wyth a stede!"

The lady seyde, "Y the forgeve;
Al so longe os Y leve
Counsayle schall hyt bee.
Loke thou be a trewe man
In all thyng that thou can
To my lorde so free."
"Yys, Lady, ellys dyd Y wronge,
For Y have servyd hym longe,
And wele he hath qwytt[158] mee."
Hereof spake he no mare,
But to hys felowe can he fare;
There evyll must they the![159]

---

[154] words, saying; *i.e.* in what you propose [155] drawn
[156] arouse, frighten; it is tempting to emend to *assay, i.e.* "what I did was only to test, or prove, your virtue"; A^1 gives: "Of this matter I have you tolde, / It was to prove your woman hode"
[157] speak [158] repaid
[159] may evil betake them!

Thus to hys felowe ys he gon,
And he hym frayned [160] anon:
"Syr, how haste thou spedd?"
"Ryght noght," seyde that othyr;
"Syth Y was borne, lefe brothyr,
Was Y nevyr so adredd!
Certys, hyt ys a boteles bale [161]
To hur to touche soche a tale,[162]
At borde or at bedde!"
Then sayde that odur, "Thy wytt ys thynne;
Y myselfe schall hur wynne;
Y lay my hedd to wedde!"[163]

Thus hyt passyd ovyr, os Y yow say,
Tyl aftur, on the thrydde day,
Thys knyght hym bethoght:
"Certys, spede os Y may,
My ladyes wylle, that ys so gay,
Hyt schall be thorowly soght."
When he sawe hur in beste mode,
Sore syghyng to hur he yode,
Of lyfe os he ne roght; [164]
"Lady," he seyde, "wythowte fayle,
But ye helpe me wyth yowre counsayle,
Yn bale [165] am Y broght."

Sche answeryd full curtesly,
"My counsayle schall be redy;
Telle me how hyt ys.
When Y wott [166] worde and ende,
Yf my counsayle may hyt mende,
Hyt schall, so have Y blysse."

---

[160] questioned [161] a useless quest
[162] to advance any such proposal [163] *i.e.* I'll bet my head on it!
[164] as though he cared nothing for life [165] sorrow [166] know

"Lady," he seyde, "Y undurstonde;
Ye muste holde up yowre honde
To holde counsayle, ywys."
"Yys," seyde the lady free,
"Thereto [167] my trouthe here to the,
And ellys Y dudd amys."

"Madam," he seyde, "now Y am in tryste;
All my lyfe thogh ye wyste,
Ye wolde me not dyskever;
For yow Y am in so grete thoght,
Yn moche bale Y am broght,
Wythowte othe, Y swere.
And ye may full wele see
How pale Y am of blee —
Y dye nere for dere! [168]
Dere Lady, graunt me youre love,
For the love of God that sytteth above,
That stongen was wyth a spere."

"Syr," sche seyde, "ys that youre wylle?
Yf hyt were myne, then dyd Y ylle!
What woman holdyst thou me?
Yn thy kepeyng Y have ben;
What haste thou herde be me, or sene,
That touchyth to any velanye,
That thou in herte art so bolde
Os Y were a hore or a scolde?
Nay, that schall nevyr bee!
Had Y not hyght [169] to holde counsayle,
Thou schouldest be honged, wythowt fayle,
Upon a galowe tree!"

---

[167] "I pledge" is understood
[168] grief [169] promised

The knyght was nevyr so sore aferde
Syth he was borne into myddyll-erd,[170]
Certys, os he was thoo;
"Mercy," he seyde, "gode Madam,
Wele Y wott Y am to blame;
Therfore myn herte ys woo.
Lady, let me not be spylte;[171]
Y aske mercy of my gylte,
On lyve[172] ye let me goo!"
The lady seyde, "Y graunte wele;
Hyt schall be counseyle, every dele,
But do no more soo."

Now the knyght forthe yede,[173]
And seyde, "Felowe, Y may not spede;
What ys thy beste redd?[174]
Yf sche telle my lorde of thys,
We be but dedd, so have Y blys;
Wyth hym be we not fedd.[175]
Womans tonge ys evell to tryste;
Certys, and[176] my lorde hyt wyste,
Etyn were all owre bredd.[177]
Felow, so mote Y ryde or goo,
Or sche wayte[178] us wyth that woo,
Hurselfe schall be dedd!"

"How myght that be?" that othur sayde.
"Yn herte Y wolde be wele payde
Myght we do that dede."
"Yys, syr," he seyde, "so have Y roo,[179]
Y schall brynge hur wele thertoo,
Therof have thou no drede!

[170] on this earth [171] ruined, punished [172] alive [173] went
[174] advice [175] we shall be exiled [176] if
[177] we should be put to death [178] before she burdens [179] health

Or hyt passe dayes three,
In mekyll sorowe schall sche bee;
Thus Y schall qwyte hur hur mede!"[180]
Now are they bothe at oon assente
In sorow to brynge that lady gente —
The devell mote them spede!

Sone hyt drowe toward nyght;
To soper they can them dyght,
The emperes and they all.
The two knyghtys grete japys[181] made
For to make the lady glade,
That was bothe gentyll and small.
When the soper-tyme was done,
To the chaumbyr they went soone;
Knyghtys cladd in palle,[182]
They daunsed and revelyd os they noght dredd,
To brynge the lady to hur bedde —
There foule muste them falle![183]

That oon thefe callyd a knyght
That was carver to that lady bryght,
An erleys sone was he;
He was a feyre chylde[184] and a bolde,
Twenty wyntur he was oolde;
In londe was none so free:
"Syr, wylt thou do os we the say?
And we schall ordeygne us a play
That my lady may see;
Thou schalt make hur to lagh soo,
Thogh sche were gretly thy foo,
Thy frende schulde sche bee."

---

[180] pay her her reward [181] japes, jests; ms. *yapys*
[182] fine clothes [183] may evil befall them!
[184] a young knight or nobleman

The chylde answeryd anon ryght,
"Be the ordur Y bere of knyght,
Therof wolde Y be fayne,
And hyt wolde my lady plese,
Thogh hyt wolde me dysese,[185]
To renne yn wynde and rayne."
"Syr, make the nakyd save thy breke,[186]
And behynde the yondur curtayn thou crepe,
And do os Y schall sayne;
Then schalt thou see a joly play."
"Y graunte," thys yonge knyght can say,
"Be God and Seynte Jermayne!"

Thys chylde thoght on no ylle:
Of he caste hys clothys stylle,
And behynde the curtayne he went.
They seyde to hym, "What so befalle,
Come not owt tyll we the calle."
And he seyde, "Syrs, Y assente."
They revelyd forthe a grete whyle;
No man wyste of ther gyle
Save they two, veramente.[187]
They voyded the chaumber sone anon;
The chylde they lafte syttyng alone,
And that lady gente.

Thys lady lay in bedd on slepe;
Of treson toke sche no kepe,[188]
For thereof wyste sche noght.
Thys chylde had wonder evyr among
Why these knyghtys were so longe;
He was in many a thoght:

---

[185] harm [186] breeches
[187] truly [188] had no suspicion

"Lorde, mercy; how may thys bee?
Y trowe they have forgeton me
That me hedur broght.
Yf Y them calle, sche wyll be adredd,
My lady lyeth here on hur bedd,
Be Hym that all hath wroght!"

Thus he sate stylle as any stone;
He durste not store [189] nor make no mone [190]
To make the lady afryght.
Thes false men — ay worthe them woo! —
To ther [191] chaumber can they goo,
And armyd them full ryght;
Lordys owte of bedd can they calle,
And badd arme them, grete and smalle:
"Anone that ye were dyght,
And helpe to take a false traytour
That wyth my lady in hur bowre
Hath playde hym all thys nyght!"

Sone they were armyd everychone,
And wyth these traytours can they gone,
The lordys that there wore;
To the emperes chaumber they cam ryght
Wyth swerdys and wyth torchys [192] bryght
Brennyng [193] them before.
Behynde the curtayne they wente;
The yonge knyght, verrament,
Nakyd founde they thore.
That oon thefe wyth a swerde of were
Thorow the body he can hym bere,
That worde spak he no more.

[189] stir, move [190] sound, cry [191] ms. *hur*
[192] ms. *wyth torchys and wyth swerdys* [193] burning

The lady woke and was afryght
Whan sche sawe the grete lyght
Before hur beddys syde;
Sche seyde, "Benedycyte!
Syrs, what men be yee?"
And wonder lowde sche cryedd.
Hur enemyes mysansweryd thore:
"We are here, thou false hore;
Thy dedys we have aspyedd!
Thou haste betrayed my lorde!
Thou schalt have wonduryng in thys worde:[194]
Thy loos[195] schall sprynge wyde!"

The lady seyde, "Be Seynte John!
Hore was Y nevyr none,
Nor nevyr thoght to be!"
"Thou lyest!" they seyde, "Thy love ys lorne!"[196]
The corse[197] they leyde hur beforne:
"Lo, here ys thy lemman[198] free;
Thus we have for the hym hytt;
Thy horedam schall be wele qwytte;[199]
Fro us schalt thou not flee!"
They bonde the lady wondyr faste,
And in a depe preson hur caste:
Grete dele[200] hyt was to see.

Leve we now thys lady in care,
And to hur lorde wyll we fare,
That ferre was hur froo;
On a nyght, wythowt lette,[201]
In hys slepe a swevyn[202] he mett —
The story telleth us soo:

---

[194] wandering in this world; *i.e.* exile [195] reputation
[196] exposed [197] corpse, body [198] paramour [199] punished
[200] dole, sorrow [201] lie [202] dream

Hym thoght ther come two wylde berys,
And hys wyfe all toterys,[203]
And rofe [204] hur body in twoo.
Hymselfe was a wytty [205] man,
And be that dreme he hopyd [206] than
Hys lady was in woo.

Erly [207] when the day was clere,
He bad hys men all in fere [208]
To buske [209] and make them yare [210]
Samer-horsys [211] he lete go before,
And charyettys stuffud wyth store,[212]
Wele twelve myle and mare.
He hopud [213] wele in hys herte
That hys wyfe was not in querte; [214]
Hys herte therfore was in care.
He styntyd not [215] tyll he was dyght,
Wyth erlys, barons, and many a knyght;
Homeward can they fare.

Nyght ne day, nevyr they blanne [216]
Tyll to that cyté they came
There the lady was ynne;
Wythowt the cyté lordys them kepyd—
For wo in herte many oon wepyd;
There teerys myght they not blynne.
They supposyd wele yf he hyt wyste
That hys wyfe had soche a bryste,[217]
Hys joye wolde be full thynne.

---

[203] tore all to pieces [204] broke
[205] intelligent [206] realized
[207] ms. *ȝerly* [208] all together
[209] hurry [210] ready
[211] pack-horses (Old French *sommiers*)
[212] small carts loaded with gear [213] knew, realized [214] safety
[215] wasted no time [216] stopped [217] harm

They ladden stedys to the stabyll,
And the lorde into the halle
To worschyp hym wyth wynne.

Anon to the chaumbur wendyth he;
He longyd hys feyre lady to see,
That was so swete a wyght.
He callys them that schoulde hur kepe:
"Where ys my wyfe? Ys sche on slepe?
How fareth that byrde [218] bryght?"
The two traytours answeryd anon,
"Yf ye wyste how sche had done,
To dethe sche schulde be dyght;
Forsothe, Lord, this is no nay:
Whyle that ye were furthe away,
We toke a man with her at nyght." [219]

"A devyll!" he seyde. "How soo
To dethe that sche ys worthy to go?
Telle me in what manere."
"Syr," he [220] he seyde, "be Goddys ore,
The yonge knyght, Syr Antore,
That was hur kervere,
Be that lady he hath layne,
And therfore we have hym slayne;
We founde them in fere.
Sche ys in preson, verrament;
The lawe wyll [221] that sche be brente,
Be God that boght us dere!"

---

[218] lady

[219] these three lines are omitted in the ms. and are supplied from A^1

[220] other editors emend to *they*; but the sense seems to be that while both traitors make the accusation, only one goes on to explain the circumstances; see ll. 871-73 below [221] requires

"Allas!" seyde the emperoure.
"Hath sche done me thys dyshonoure,
And Y lovyd hur so wele?
Y wende for all thys worldys gode
That sche wolde not have turned hur mode; [222]
My joye begynnyth to kele!" [223]
He hente [224] a knyfe wyth all hys mayn;
Had not a knyght ben,[225] he had hym slayn,
And that traytour have broght owt of heele.[226]
For bale hys armes abrode he bredd,[227]
And fell in swowne upon hys bedd:
There myght men see grete dele!

On the morne, be oon assente
On hur they sett a perlyament,
Be all the comyn rede; [228]
They myght not fynde in ther counsayle
Be no lawe, wythowt fayle,
To save hur fro the dede.[229]
Then bespake an olde knyght:
"Y have wondur, be Goddys myght,
That Syr Antore thus was bestedd! [230]
In chaumbyr thogh he [231] naked were,
They let hym gyf none answere,
But slowe hym, be my hede!

Ther was nevyr man, sekurly,[232]
That be hur founde any velany
Save they two, Y dar wele say.

---

[222] been untrue [223] cool; ms. *kelee*
[224] caught up [225] had it not been for a knight
[226] brought out of health, *i.e.* killed [227] raised
[228] they appointed a jury according to custom, or law
[229] to exonerate her [230] set upon
[231] ms. *þey* [232] surely

Be some hatered hyt may be;
Therfore doyth aftur me,
For my love, Y yow pray.
No mo wyll preve [233] hyt but they twoo;
Therfore we may not save hur fro woo—
Forsothe, os Y yow say—
In hyr quarell, but we myght fynde
A man that were gode of kynde,
That durste fyght agayn them tway."

All they assentyd to the sawe; [234]
They thoght he spake reson and lawe.
Then answeryd the kyng wyth crowne:
"Fayre fall the for thyn avyse!"
He callyd knyghtys of nobyll pryce,
And badd them be redy bowne [235]
For to crye thorow all the londe,
Bothe be see and be sonde,[236]
Yf they fynde mowne [237]
A man that ys so moche of myght
That for that lady dar take the fyght:
"He schall have hys wareson!" [238]

Messangerys, Y undurstonde,
Cryed throw all the londe
In many a ryche cyté:
"Yf any man durste prove hys myght
In trewe quarell for to fyght,
Wele avaunsed schulde he bee!"
The Erle of Tullous harde thys telle [239]—
What anger [240] the lady befelle;
Therof he thoght grete pyté.

---

[233] prove, testify [234] opinion [235] prepared
[236] by sea and land [237] might
[238] reward; what is being suggested, of course, is a trial by combat
[239] heard tell of this [240] misfortune

Yf he wyste that sche had ryght,
He wolde aventure hys lyfe to fyght
For that lady free.

For hur he morned nyght and day,
And to hymselfe can he say
He wolde aventure hys lyfe:
"Yf Y may wytt that sche be trewe,
They that have hur accused schull rewe,
But they stynte of ther stryfe!" [241]
The erle seyde, "Be Seynte John,
Ynto Almayn wyll Y goon,
Where Y have fomen [242] ryfe;
I prey to God, full of myght,
That Y have trewe quarell to fyght,
Owt of wo to wynne that wyfe!"

He rode on huntyng on a day;
A marchand [243] mett he be the way,
And asked hym of whens he was.
"Lorde," he seyde, "of Almayn."
Anon the erle can hym frayne [244]
Of that ylke [245] case:
"Wherefore ys yowre emperes
Put in so grete dystresse?
Telle me, for Goddys grace.
Ys sche gylté, so mote thou the?"
"Nay, be Hym that dyed on tree,
That schope man aftur Hys face!" [246]

Then seyde the erle, wythowte lette,
"When ys the day sett
Brente that sche schulde bee?"

---

[241] unless they withdraw their accusation [242] foes
[243] merchant [244] question
[245] same, forementioned [246] created man in His own image

The marchande seyde, "Sekyrlyke,
Evyn thys day thre wyke,[247]
And therfore wo ys mee!"
The erle seyde, "Y schall the telle:
Gode horsys Y have to selle,
And stedys two or thre;
Certys, myght Y selle them yare,
Thedur wyth the wolde Y fare
That syght for to see."

The marchand seyd wordys hende,
"Into the londe yf ye wyll wende,
Hyt wolde be for yowre prowe;[248]
There may ye selle them at your wylle."
Anon the erle seyde hym tylle,
"Syr, herkyn me nowe;
Thys jurney wylt thou wyth me dwelle,
Twenty pownde Y schall the telle[249]
To mede,[250] Y make a vowe."
The marchand grauntyd anon;
The erle seyde, "Be Seynt John,
Thy wylle Y alowe!"[251]

The erle tolde hym in that tyde
Where he schulde hym abyde,
And homeward wente hee;
He busked hym that no man wyste,
For mekyll on hym[252] was hys tryste;
He seyde, "Syr, go wyth mee."
Wyth them they toke stedys sevyn,
Ther were no fayrer[253] undyr hevyn
That any man myght see.

---

[247] three weeks from this day [248] gain
[249] count, pay [250] reward [251] I am glad of your consent
[252] the merchant [253] ms. *fayre*

Into Almayn they can ryde;
As a coresur [254] of mekyll pryde
He semyd for to bee.

The marchand was a trewe gyde;
The erle and he togedur can ryde
Tyll they came to that place.
A myle besyde the castell
There the emperour can dwell,
A ryche abbey ther was;
Of the abbot leve they gatt
To sojorne and make ther horsys fatt.
That was a nobyll cas:
The abbot was the ladyes eme; [255]
For hur he was in grete wandreme,[256]
And moche mornyng he mase.[257]

So hyt befelle upon a day
To churche the erle toke the way
A masse for to here.
He was a feyre man and an hye; [258]
Whan the abbot hym sye,
He seyde, "Syr, come nere;
Syr, when the masse ys done,
Y pray yow ete wyth me at noone,
Yf youre wylle were."
The erle grauntyd all wyth game; [259]
Afore mete they wysche all same,[260]
And to mete they wente in fere.

Aftur mete, as Y yow say,
Into an orchard they toke the way,
The abbot and the knyght;

---

[254] horse dealer [255] uncle [256] sorrow, anguish
[257] makes [258] tall [259] willingly [260] washed together

The abbot seyde, and syghed sare,
"Certys, Syr, Y leve in care
For a lady bryght;
Sche ys accusyd — my herte ys woo —
Therfore sche·schall to dethe goo,
All agayne the ryght.
But sche have helpe, verramente,
In fyre sche schall be brente
Thys day sevenyght."

The erle seyde, "So have Y blysse,
Of hyr me thynkyth grete rewthe [261] hyt ys,
Trewe yf that sche bee."
The abbot seyde, "Be Seynte Poule,
For hur Y dar ley [262] my soule
That nevyr gylté was sche.
Soche workys nevyr sche wroght,
Neythyr in dede, nor in thoght,
Save a rynge so free
To the Erle of Tullous sche gaf hyt wyth wynne [263]
Yn ese [264] of hym, and for no synne:
In schryfte [265] thus tolde sche me."

The erle sayde, "Syth hyt ys soo,
Cryste wreke [266] hur of hur woo,
That boght hur wyth Hys bloode!
Wolde ye sekyr [267] me, wythowt fayle,
For to holde trewe counsayle,
Hyt myght be for yowre gode."
The abbot seyde be bokes fele
And be hys professyon that he wolde hele,[268]
And ellys he were wode.

---

[261] wrong [262] bet [263] gladly [264] aid, comfort
[265] confession [266] avenge [267] assure [268] hold secret

"Y am he that sche gaf the rynge
For to be oure tokenynge;
Now heyle hyt, for the rode!

Y am comyn, lefe syr,
To take the batayle for hyr —
There to stonde wyth ryght.
But fyrste myselfe Y wole hur schryve;
And yf Y fynde hur clene of lyve,
Then wyll my herte be lyght.
Let dyght me in monkys wede;[269]
To that place that men schulde hyr lede
To dethe to be dyght,
When Y have schrevyn hyr, wythowt fayle,
For hur Y wyll take batayle,
As Y am trewe knyght."

The abbot was nevyr so gladd;
Nere for joye he waxe madd;
The erle can he kysse.
They made meré and slewe care;[270]
All that sevenyght he dwellyd thare
Yn myrthe, wythowt mysse.[271]
That day that the lady schulde be brent
The erle wyth the abbot wente
In monkys wede, ywys;
To the emperour he knelyd blyve,[272]
That he myght that lady schryve;
Anon resceyved he ys.

---

[269] monk's clothes
[270] abandoned grief
[271] misstatement, lie
[272] quickly

He examyned hur, wyttyrly,[273]
As hyt seythe in [274] the story;
Sche was wythowte gylte.
Sche seyde, "Be Hym that dyed on tree,
Trespas was nevyr none in me
Wherefore Y schulde be spylte [275]
Save oonys,[276] wythowte lesynge:
To the Erle of Tollous Y gave a rynge;
Assoyle [277] me yf thou wylte.
But thus my destanye ys comyn to ende,
That in thys fyre Y muste be brende:
1080 There Goddys wylle be fulfyllyd!"

The erle assoyled hur wyth hys honde,
And sythen pertely [278] he can up stonde
And seyde, "Lordyngys, pese!
Ye that have accused thys lady gente,
Ye be worthy to be brente!"
That oon knyght made a rees: [279]
"Thou, carle [280] Monke, wyth all thy gynne,[281]
Thowe youre abbot be of hur kynne,
Hur sorowe schalt thou not cees!
Ryght so thou woldyst sayne
Thowe all youre covent [282] had be hyr layn,
1092 So are ye lythyr and lees!" [283]

The erle answeryd wyth wordys free:
"Syr, that oon Y trowe thou bee
Thys lady accused has;

273 truly
274 this word is written above the ms. line in what looks to be a later hand; a carat below marks it for insertion 275 destroyed
276 once 277 absolve 278 then boldly
279 arose 280 churl
281 tricks 282 convent, monastery
283 wicked and liars

Thowe we be men of relygyon,
Thou schalt do us but reson,
For all the fare thou mas.
Y prove on hur thou sayst not ryght—
Lo, here my glove! Wyth the to fyght
Y undyrtake thys case.
Os false men Y schall yow kenne,[284]
Yn redd fyre for to brenne—
Therto God gyf me grace!"

All that stoden in that place
Thankyd God of Hys grace,
Wythowte any fayle.
The two knyghtys were full wrothe;
He schulde be dedd, they swere grete othe,
But hyt myght not avayle.[285]
The erle wente there besyde,
And armyd hym wyth mekyll pryde
Hys enemyes to assayle.
Manly when they togedur mett
They hewe thorow helme and basenet,[286]
And martyrd many a mayle.[287]

They redyn togedur, wythowt lakk,
That hys oon spere on hym brakk;
That othyr faylyd thoo.
Thys erle smote hym wyth hys spere;
Thorow the body he can hym bere—
To grounde can hym goo.
That sawe that odyr and faste can flee;
The erle ovyrtoke hym undyr a tre,
And wroght hym mekyll woo.

---

[284] reveal, make known [285] it was of no use
[286] a cap, probably of mail, worn inside the helmet
[287] hacked apart many a chain of mail-coat

There thys traytour can hym yylde
Os recreaunt[288] yn the fylde:
He myght not fle hym froo.

Before the emperour they wente,
And ther he made hym, verrament,
To telle for the noonys;[289]
He seyde, "We thoght hur to spylle
For sche wolde not do oure wylle,
That worthy ys in wonnys."[290]
The erle answeryd hym then:
"Therfore, traytours, ye schall brenne
Yn thys fyre, bothe at onys!"
The erle anon them[291] hente,
And in the fyre he them brente—
Flesche, felle,[292] and boonys.

When they were brent, bothe two,
The erle prevely can goo
To that ryche abbaye;
Wyth joye and processyon
They fett[293] the lady into the towne,
Wyth myrthe, os Y telle may.
The emperoure was full gladd,
"Fette me the monke," anon he badd;
"Why went he so awaye?
A byschoperyke Y wyll hym geve,
My helpe, my love, whyll Y leve,
Be God that owyth[294] thys day!"

The abbot knelyd on hys knee,
And seyde, "Lorde, gone ys hee
To hys owne londe.

---

[288] defeated, and thus a false accuser
[289] for the nonce, *i.e.* at that time [290] living [291] ms. *hym*
[292] skin [293] brought [294] owns

He dwellyth wyth the pope of Rome;
He wyll be glad of hys come,[295]
Y do yow to undurstonde."
"Syr," quod the emperoure,
"To me hyt were a dyshonoure;
Soche wordes Y rede thou wonde;[296]
Anone yn haste that Y hym see,
Or thou schalt nevyr have gode of me,
And therto here myn hand!"[297]

"Lorde," he seyde, "sythe hyt ys soo,
Aftur hym that Y muste goo,
Ye muste make me sewrté[298] —
Yn case he have byn youre foo —
Ye schall not do hym no woo;
And then, al so mote Y thee,
Aftur hym Y wyll wynde,
So that ye wyll be hys frende,
Yf youre wylle bee."
"Yys," seyde the emperoure, "full fayne;
All my kynne thogh he had slayne,
He ys welcome to me."

Then spake the abbot wordys free:
"Lorde, Y tryste now on thee
Ye wyll do os ye sey;
Hyt ys Syr Barnard of Tollous,
A nobyll knyght and a chyvalrous,
That hath done thys jurney."
"Now certys," seyde the emperoure,
"To me hyt ys grete dyshonoure;[299]
Anon syr, Y the pray

[295] coming [296] turn from, stop [297] *i.e.* I take a vow
[298] assurance
[299] *i.e.* that it had to be my foe who revealed the treachery of my own knights

Aftur hym that thou wende;
We schall kysse and be gode frende,
Be God that owyth thys day!"

The abbot seyde, "Y assente."
Aftur the erle anon he wente,
And seyde, "Syr, go wyth mee;
My lorde and ye, be Seynt John,
Schull be made bothe at oon,[300]
Goode frendys for to bee."
Therof the erle was full fayne;
The emperoure came hym agayne,[301]
And sayde, "My frende so free,
My wrath here Y the forgeve;
My helpe, my love, whyll Y leve,
Be Hym that dyed on tree!"

Togedur lovely can they kysse —
Therof all men had grete blysse,
The romaunse tellyth soo —
He made hym steward of hys londe,
And sesyd [302] agayne into hys honde
That he had rafte hym froo.
The emperoure levyd but yerys thre;
Be alexion [303] of the lordys free
The erle toke they thoo;
They made hym ther emperoure,
For he was styffe yn stoure [304]
To fyght agayne hys foo.

He weddyd that lady to hys wyfe;
Wyth joye and myrthe they ladd ther lyfe
Twenty yere and three.

---

[300] reconciled [301] came forth to meet him
[302] ceded, returned [303] election [304] strong in battle

Betwene them had they chyldyr fyftene—
Doghty knyghtys all bedene,[305]
And semely on to see.
Yn Rome thys geste[306] ys cronyculyd, ywys;
A Lay of Bretayne callyd hyt ys,
And evyrmore schall bee.
Jhesu Cryste to hevyn us brynge,
There to have owre wonnynge:
Amen, amen, for charytee!

Here Endyth the Erle of Tollous

[305] every one [306] tale

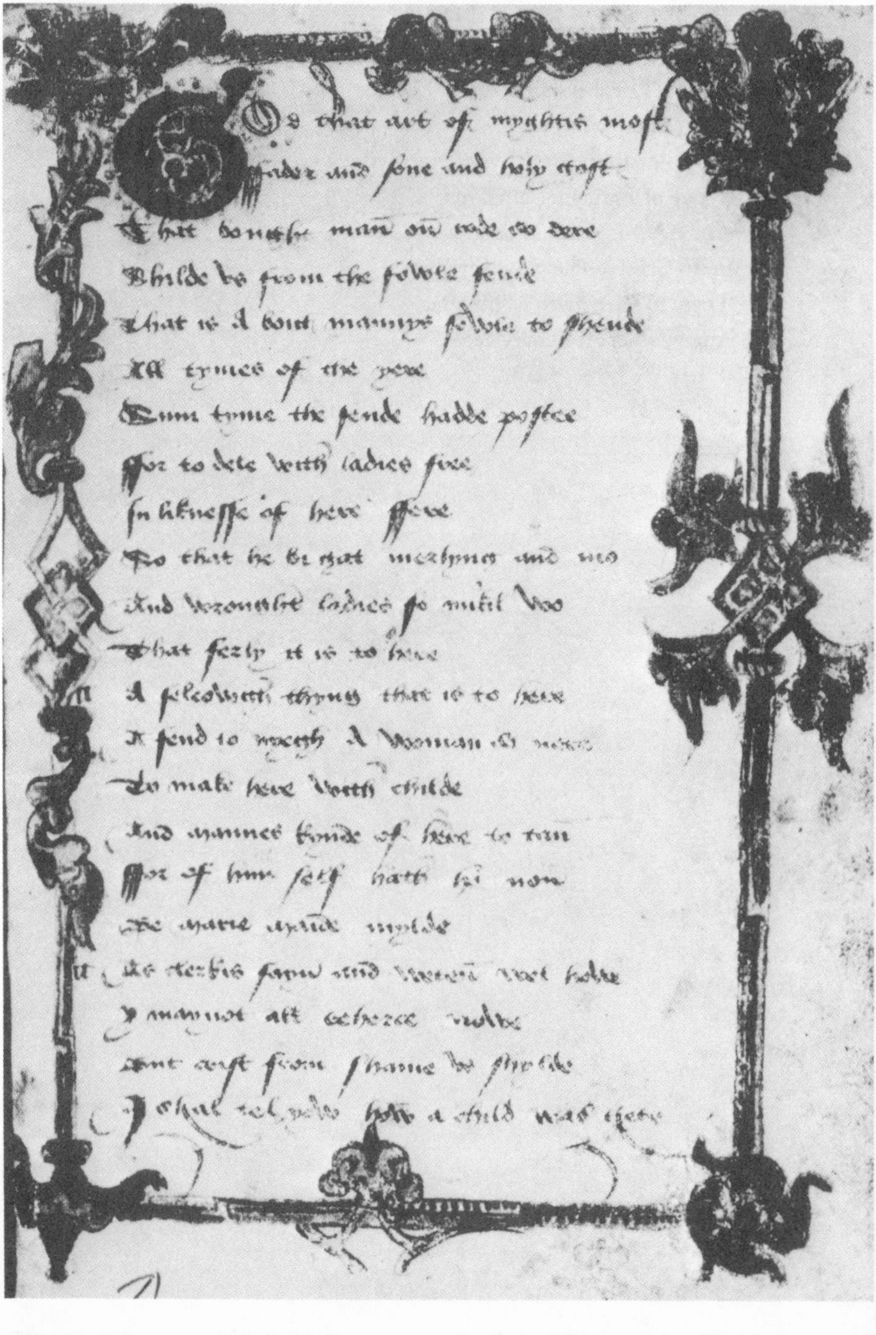

God that art of myghtis most
Fader and sone and holy gost
That bouȝtist man on rode so dere
Shilde us from the fowle fende
That is abowt mannys sowle to shende
All tymes of the yere
Sum tyme the fende hadde postee
For to dele with ladies free
In liknesse of here fere
So that he begat merlyng and mo
And wrouȝht ladies so mikil woo
That ferly it is to here
A selcowth thyng that is to here
A fend to nyeth a woman so nere
To make here with childe
And maunces kynde of here to tan
For of hem self hath thei non
The marie mayde mylde
As clerkis fynd and wreten wel holde
I mannot all sekerle unfolde
But ferst from shame ye shelde
I shal tel yow how a child was there

Sir Gowther

God, that art of myghtis most,
Fader and Sone and Holy Gost,
That bought man on rode [1] so dere,
Shilde us from the fowle fende
That is about mannys sowle to shende [2]
All tymes of the yere!

Sumtyme [3] the fende hadde postee [4]
For to dele with ladies free
In liknesse of here fere,[5]
So that he begat Merlyng and mo,
And wrought ladies so mikil wo
That ferly [6] it is to here.

A selcowgh [7] thyng that is to here,
A fend to nyegh [8] a woman so nere
To make here with childe,
And mannes kynde of here to tan,[9]
For of himself hath he non,[10]
Be Marie, maide mylde!

---

[1] cross [2] destroy [3] once [4] power
[5] human companion, lover, husband [6] wondrous
[7] awesome [8] nigh, approach [9] to take of her (sexually) in the form of a man [10] *i.e.* no form of his own

As clerkis sayn, and weten [11] wel howe,
Y may not all reherce nowe,
But Crist from shame us shyld;
I shal tel yow how a child was gete,
And in what sorow his moder he sett
With his workis [12] so wild.

Of that baron yborn unblithe,
Crist yeve him joy that wulle lythe [13]
Of auntres [14] that befelle:
In the layes [15] of Britanye that was I sowght,
And owt of oon was ybrought
That lovely is to tell.

There was a duk in Ostrych [16]
Weddyd a lady nobil and riche,
She was fayre of flessch and felle; [17]
To the lyly was likened that lady clere;
Here rody [18] was rede as blosmes on brere,
That couteis damysell.

Whan she was weddid, that ladi shene,[19]
Duches she was, withouten wene;
A grete fest gan thei make.
Knyghtes and squyres on the furst day,
On steedes hem gentely to play,
Here shaftes gan thei shake.

On the morowe the lordes gente
Made a riall tournement
For the ladys [20] sake;
The duk wan steedes ten,

---

[11] know
[12] deeds [13] listen [14] adventures
[15] the ms. appears to read *bayes* [16] Austria [17] skin
[18] complexion [19] beautiful [20] ms. *lady is*

And bare downe many dowghti men;
Here shildes gan he crake.

Whan the feste gan to seese,
The worthi duk and ducheese
They levid[21] together with wenne;[22]
Full seven-yere togeder thei were;
He gat no childe, ne none she bere;
Here joy gan wex ful thenne.

As it bifill uppon a day,
To the lady he gan say,
"Now mote[23] we part a-twene,
But ye myght a childe bere
That myght my londes weld and were!"[24]
She wept and myght not blynne.[25]

Than morned the lady clere,
That al falwyd[26] hire faire chere;[27]
For she conceyvid nowght.
She praid to Crist and Marie mylde
Shulde hire grace[28] to have a childe,
In what maner she ne rought.[29]

As she walkyd yn orcheyerde uppon a day
She mett a man in a riche aray;
Of love he here bisowght.
He come in liknesse of here lord free;
Undernethe a chestayne tree
His will with hire he wrought.

---

[21] lived [22] joy
[23] must [24] govern and manage
[25] cease [26] faded
[27] countenance and state of mind [28] *i.e.* give grace
[29] cared

Whan he had his will ydoon,
A fowle fend, he stode uppe soon;
He lokid and hire byhilde,
And said, "Dame, I have gete on the
A childe that yn his yougthe wild shal be
His wepen for to welde."

She blissid hire and from him ran;
Intil [30] hire chamber anon she cam,
That was so strong of belde; [31]
She said to hire lorde so mylde,
"Tonyght Y hope to conceyve a childe
That shall your londes welde.

An angil that was so faire and bright
Told me so this yonder nyght;
I trust to Cristis sonde [32]
That He woll stynt us of owre strife."
In his armys he toke his wife,
That frely was to fonde.

Whan [33] it was even,[34] to bed thei chase,
The riche duk and the duches;
For no man wold thei wonde.[35]
He pleid him with that lady hende;
She was bounde with a fende
Til Crist wold lose hire bonde.

The childe withyn hire was non other
But Marlyngs half brother;
On [36] fende gat hem bothe;
He servid never for other thyng,

---

[30] into [31] so strongly built
[32] mercy, possibly message [33] ms. *what*
[34] evening [35] delay [36] one

But temptid men and women yyng,
To dele with hem, for sothe.

Thus the lady gretid [37] fast
Til she was delivred atte last
Of on that wolde do scathe.[38]
To the church thei gan him bere,
And cristen his name Goughthere,
That afterward wax breme and brathe.[39]

The lord comforted the lady gent,
And after norsis [40] anone he sente,
Of the best in that contree;
Summe were nobill knyghtes wifes;
He sak [41] so sore thei lost here lyfes —
Full sone he hadde slayn three.

The child throfe, and swythe wax; [42]
The duk sent after other sex [43]—
As wetnesse the storie.
Or [44] that the twelve-monthis weren comyn and gon,
Nyen norsys he had ysloon,
Ladies faire and free.

Knightes of that contree gadered hem in same,[45]
And said, "Forsothe, this is no game!" —
To sleyn hire ladies soo;
Thay bad him ordeyne for his sone,
For he myght not have his wone,[46]
Nor non norses moo.

---

[37] became great with child [38] harm
[39] famous and violent [40] nurses
[41] sucked [42] quickly grew
[43] six [44] before
[45] together [46] desire

Than bifill his moder a ferly happe:
On a day she bad him here pappe;[47]
And he arifte[48] hire soo,
He tare the oon side of hir brest;
The lady cried after a prest;
132 Into a chamber she fled him froo.

Than a leche[49] helid uppe the lady sore;
She durst yeve him sowke no more,
That yong childe Gowghtere,
But fedde him uppe with other foode
As moch as him behovid[50]—
138 That dare Y savely[51] swere—

That[52] in oo yere more he wex
Than other childern did in sex.[53]
Him semed wel to ride,[54]
He wax wikked in all withe;[55]
His fader him myght not chastithe,
144 But made him knyght that tyde.

He gaf him his best swerde in honde;
There was no knyghte in all that londe
A dent[56] durst him abyde;
But after, whan his fader was dede,
Carfull[57] was his moder rede;[58]
150 Here sorowe myght no man hide.

Dowrey for him must she have none,
But in castell of lyme and stone

---

[47] suck
[48] ms. *ariȝhte*; I have emended to derive the word from OE *ryven;* thus reft, tore [49] doctor [50] needed [51] safely [52] so that
[53] six [54] it suited him well to ride
[55] ways [56] blow [57] full of care
[58] his mother's mood

Fast from him sho fledde;
She made hire strong and hild hir there;
Hire men myght syng of sorow and care,
156 So strait thai were bestedde.

For where he mett hem bi the way,
"Alas the while," thei myght say,
"That ever his moder him fedde!"
For with his fauchon [59] he wold hem sloo,
Or strik here hors bak a-twoo;
162 Swich parell [60] thei dredde!

Thus was the duk [61] of greet renown;
Men of religion he throug hem down
Where he myght hem mete;
Masse nor mateyns wold he none here,
Ne no prechyng of no frere,
168 Thus dare Y yow behete.[62]

And tho that wold not werk his will,[63]
Erly and late, lowde and still,
Ful sore he wold hem bete;
Huntyng he loved al there best,
In parkes [64] and in wild forest,
174 Where [65] he myght it gete.

As he rode on huntyng uppon a day,
He saw a nonnery bi the highway,
And theder gan he ride;
The prioresse [66] and here covent

---

[59] sword [60] peril [61] *i.e.* Sir Gowther
[62] promise [63] obey his commands
[64] game preserves, usually of noblemen, protected by stringent laws against poachers
[65] wherever [66] ms. *proresse*

With procession agayn him went,[67]
180 Trewly in that tyde.

Thei kneled down oppon here knee,
And said, "Leige lord, welcome be yee!" —
Yn hert is nowght to hide.
He drofe hem home into here churche,
And brend [68] hem uppe: thus gan he werche;
186 His lose [69] sporng ful wide.

Al tho that wold on God belefe,
He was abowte hem to greve
In all that he myght doo.
Maidenes mariagies wold he spill, [70]
And take wyfes agayn here will,
192 And sle here husbondes, too.

He made prestes and clerkes to lepe on cragges,[71]
Monkes and freres to hong on knagges; [72]
Thus wonderly wold he doo.
He brent up hermites on a fere,
And paid wedows the same hire;
198 He wrought hem mochill woo!

A good old erll of that contree,
To the duk than rode hee,
And said, "Sir, whi doest thow so?
Thow comest never of Criste strene;
Thou art sum fendes sone, Y wene;
204 Bi thi werkis it semeth so.

---

[67] went to meet him [68] burned [69] fame
[70] spoil, presumably through rape
[71] *i.e.* from cliffs onto rocky crags below
[72] prongs, or limbs, of trees

Thou doest no good, but ever ill;
Thou art bisibbe [73] the devel of hell!"
Than was Sir Gowghter thro,[74]
And said, "If thou lye on me,
Hanged and todraw shalt thow be
Or that [75] thow fro me go!"

He kept this erll fast in holde,
And to his moderis castel he wold
As fast as he myght [76] ryde.
He said to his moder free,
"Who was my fader? Tell thow me,
Or my swerd shal thorow the glide!"

He set the point to here brest,
And said, "Dame, thow getest non other prest [77]
The sothe if thow hide!"
She said, "Sone, the duke that deyde last,
That is owt of this world past,
He weddid me with pride.

The sothe trewly shal I say:
As Y went in owre orcheyerd uppon a day,
A fend bygatte the thore;
He come in liknesse of my lord so free,
Undernethe a chesten tree."
Tho sythed [78] Sir Gowghter ful sore,

And said, "Shryve the, moder, and do thy best,
For Y will to Rome er that [79] Y rest,
To leve upan other lore." [80]

---

[73] the offspring of, begotten by [74] angered
[75] before; ms. *than* [76] ms. *my* [77] priest [78] sighed
[79] ms. *than* [80] to live by, or believe in, a different teaching

Swych a thought fil uppon him, dowtely,[81]
That ofte he gan to cry, "Mercy!"
To Jhesu, that Marie bore.

Than Sir Gowghter rode him home agayn,
And to the olde erll he gan sayn,
"A trew tale told thow me;
Now wol I to Rome, to that appostell,
To be shreven, and after, asoyled;
Good sir, kepe my castel free."

Thus he left the old erll thare
To kepe his londes, less and mare.
Sir Goughter forth gan glide;
Uppon his fote fast he ranne;
He toke with him hors[82] nor man —
Him was lever to ryn than ryde.

His fauchon [83] he toke with him thoo;
He left that never for wel ne woo,
But hynge that bi his side.
And to the cowrt gan he sech;
Or he myght come to the popis spech,
Ful long he gan abyde.

As sone has he the pope con see,[84]
He kneled down uppon his kne,
And said to him ful sone;
He askid him with high sown [85]
Cryst and absolucion.
The pope him graunted his bone.

---

[81] without doubt; "so strongly" (doughtily) is also possible
[82] ms. *hor* [83] sword
[84] this line is missing in *R* and is supplied from *A*
[85] *i.e.* with great earnestness

"Whens art thow, and of what contré?"
"Duk of Ostrich, sir," said he,
"By trewe [86] God in trone!
That was goten with a fende,
And born of a lady hende:
264 I trowe my good dayes ben done."

"Art thow Crystyn?" said hee.
"Trewly, sir," he saide, "yee;
My name is Gowhter."
"Than," said the pope, "thow art comyn heder;
Or ells,[87] Y most have gon theder,
270 And that ful lothe me were;

For thow hast holy church destroyed."
"Holy fader," he said, "be noght anoyed;
I shall the verely swere
That what penaunce ye me yeve,
I shall do that if Y may leve,
276 And never Crysten man dere." [88]

"Lay down thy fauchon, than, the fro!
Thow shalt be shreven er thow go,
And assoyled er Y blynne." [89]
"Nay, holy fader," said Gowghter,
"This fauchon most Y with me bere;
282 My frendes happely ben ful thynne!"

"Thow shalt walk north and sowthe,
And gete thi mete owt of houndis mouth;
This penaunce shalt thow gynne.[90]

---

[86] ms. *trwe* [87] otherwise
[88] harm [89] *i.e.* before I am finished
[90] do

And speke no word, even ne odde,
Til thow have very wetyng[91] of Godde
Foryevyn be all thy synne."

He kneled byfore the worthy appostell
That solemly gan him assoyle,
With word as Y yow say;
Of all that day mete gat he none
Saufe owt of a houndes mouth a bone,
And forth he went his way.

He trayvayled owt of that cetee
Into another fer contree,
For sothe as I yow say;
He set him down uppon an hill;
An greyhounde brought brede him till
At high none of the day.

Thre dayes there he lay,
And a greyhond every day
A barly lofe him browght;[92]
The fowrethe day him come none;
Up he start and forthe con gon,[93]
And thankid God in thowght.

Bysyde him stode a faire castell;
The emperor of Almayn thereyn gan dwell,
And theder him gothe ful softe;
He set him down withowt the yate,
And durst not goon yn thereate,
Though him were woo yn thowght.

---

[91] token, knowledge [92] ms. *bowght*
[93] this line is missing in *R* and supplied from *A*.

Than waytes blew uppon the wall,[94]
Knyghtes gadered hem into the hall,
They wysshe[95] and went to mete.
Up he rose and yn is goon;
Ussher at the halldore fond he non,
Ne porter at the yate.

He presid blythely thorow the prese,
Even til the hegh bord he chese;
Thereunder he made his sete.
There come the steward with a rod in his honde
To do him thens, thus he wold fond,
And thret him to bete.

"What is that?" said the emperor.
The steward said with grete honowre,
"My lord, it is a man,
The fayrest and the most that ever Y seye—
Come se yowreself that is no lye!"
The emperor till him cam.

But word of him cowde they non gete;
"Lete him sit," said the emperor, "and gete him mete;
Ful litell good he can,[96]
Or that may happe, thorow sum chaunce,
That it is geve him in sum penaunce,"
Thus said the emperore thanne.

Whan the emperor was all servyd
(A knyght had his mete ykervyd),
He sent the domme[97] man part.
He let hit stond and wolde non,

---

[94] watches trumpeted "quarters" on the wall; ms. *that* . . .
[95] washed [96] the sense seems to be: full little is he able to speak
[97] dumb

But a spaynel come rynne with a bone,
And in his mouth he that lart.[98]

The domme man to him he raught,[99]
And that bone to him he cawght;
Thereon fast he tare;
For other sustinaunce he had nowght
But such as he fro houndes cawght;
The more was his care.

The emperor and the emperesse,
Lords and ladies on the deyse,[100]
They satt and him byhilde.
They bed yeve the houndes mete ynowgh;
The domme man with hem gnowh,[101]
There was his best beld.[102]

Thus among houndes he was fedde;
At even to his chamber he was ledde,
And yhelyd [103] under a teld.[104]
And every day he came to hall,
And Hobbe the Fool thei gan hym calle;
To Criste he gan him yelde.

Than hadde the same emperor
A dowghter as white as lilie flowre,
Was, too, so dumme as he;
She wolde have spoke, but she ne myght,
Therefore ful ofte she sighed,
The ladi bright of blee.

---

[98] took, carried [99] reached, drew
[100] dais, raised table [101] gnawed, ate
[102] comfort, protection [103] put, hidden
[104] canopy: apparently a bed, perhaps recessed in a wall, with curtains and canopy

To him she was a ful good frend,
And mete to houndes for his love wold send
Ful ofte and grete plenté.
Ether of hem loved other right,
But to other no word thei speke ne myght:
That was the more peté.

Than in on morow come a masynger
To the emperor with sterne chere,
And said to him ful right:
"Syr, my lord wel greteth the,
That is Sowdan of Percé,[105]
Man most of myght;

And byddeth that thow shuldest him send
Thyn owne dowghter that is so hend,
That he myght hire wedde."
The emperor said, "Y have none but oon,
And she is dumme as eny stone,
The fairest that ever was fedde.

And Y will never, while Y am sownd,
Yeve hire to none hethyn hounde—
Than were my bales bredd![106]
Yet may she sum good halowe[107] seche
Thorow grace of God to have speche."
Agayn[108] the massenger spedde;

And when he told his lord soo,
In that contree was moch woo;
The sowdan cam ful nere.
The emperor was dowghti man under shylde,

---

[105] Persia
[106] *i.e.* that would be the beginning of my woes
[107] holy man, saint [108] back

And mett the sowdan in the field,
For bothe had batayle [109] there.

Sir Gowghter went to chamber smert,[110]
And bysowght God in his hert,
As He had bowght him dere,
To send him bothe armor and shilde
And hors to ride in the fild,
To help his lord yere.[111]

He ne had so sone that ithought,
A col-black stede was him ybrought,
Stode redy withowt the dore,
And armor of the same color.
Up he stert with grete honor;
He was both styf and store.[112]

Shyld on shulder gan he hong,
And cawght a swerd that was larg and long;
He spared nether lesse ne more.
Owt at the castel yates he went;
Al this saw the dumme lady gent
As she stode in hire towre.

The sowdan, that was so sterne and stowte,
Ful fast in the fild he prikyd abowte;
To sembill [113] his men he cast.[114]
By that tyme Sir Gowghter was come there,
And many stowte shildes down he bere,
And laid on wonder fast.

Grete stedes he made to staker,[115]
And knyghts armour all to splatour [116]

---

[109] armies [110] quickly [111] eagerly [112] brave and strong
[113] assemble [114] thought, endeavored [115] stagger
[116] ms. *slatour*; my emendation is entirely conjectural

Whan blode thorow brenyys[117] brast.
Many helmys there he hitt—
Upright myght thei not sitt,
But to the ground he hem cast.

He put the sowdan to flyght—
Sir Gowghter, so moch of myght—
He slow saresines bydene.[118]
He rode home byfore the emperor;
Al this saw the lady in her towre,
That was bothe bright and shene.

He went to his chamber and unarmyd him sone;
His hors and harneys away was done—
He nyst[119] where it bycam.
When the emperor wessh and went to mete,
Undur the hegh bord he made his sete;
Two small raches[120] to him come.

The lady toke twey greyhoundes fyn,
And wyssh here mouthes clene with wyne,
And put a lofe in that one,
And in tho toder flesch full god;[121]
He rawght it fro him with eger mode—
Ful wel was him bygone.

Whan he had made him wel at ese,
He went to chamber and toke his ese
Withyn that worthly wone;[122]
On the morowe agayn come the massynger
Fro the sowdan with sterne chere;
To the emperor is he gone,

---

[117] coats of chain-mail [118] many
[119] ms. *wyst*; *A* gives *ne wyst* [120] dogs
[121] this line is omitted in *R* and is supplied from *A*
[122] dwelling

And said, "Sir, here is my letter;
My lord is come to assay the better;
Yesterday ye slow his men.
He hath asembled in the feld
Of dowghti sarezyns under shild
456 Syxti thowsand and ten.

On the he will avenjed be!"
"Hors and armour, than," said he,
"Hastly had we thenne!"
God sent [123] Sir Gowghter thorow His myght
A blode-rede stede and armour bryght;
462 He folowed thorow frith and fenne.[124]

Both parties have wel araid;
Sir Gowghter, as the story said,
Come ridyng hem betwene;
Grete steedis he made to stomble,
Knyghtes over hors backys to tomble,
468 That hardy were and kene.

He hew asonder bothe helme and shylde,
Feld down here banere in the feld,
That were bothe bryght and shene;
He bet adown the saresyns blak,
And made here backes for to crake;
474 He kede [125] that he was kene.

"Now, dere God," said the emperor,
"Whens [126] com the knyght that is so styf and stowre,
And al araide in rede,
Both hors, armour, and his steede?

---

[123] ms. *send* [124] wood and marsh
[125] showed [126] ms. *when*

A thowsand sarezyns he hath made blede
480 And beten him to dethe,

That heder is come to help me;
And yesterday in blak was he
That stered him in that stede,
Dyscomfytt the sawden and mony a sersyn,[127]
And so he will er he goo hens:
486 His dentis [128] ben hevy as lede."

He behild his fawchon fel,
And saw he beset his stroke well,
And that he wastid none;
The emperor priked into his pres,
A nobill knyght withowten les;
492 He made the sowdan to gon.

Sir Gowghter went to his chamber sone;
His hors and his armour away was done—
He wyst never whare.
The emperor wysshe and went to mete,
And with him other lordes grete
498 That at the bataile were.

Undur the high bord Sir Gowghter him sett;
The lady haght [129] here greyhoundes yfette [130]
Prevely, as nothyng were.
She fed how, the ful sothe to say,
Right as she dyd the first day—
504 For no man wold she spare.

Lordes revelid in the hall;
There daunsid many a lady small

---

[127] this line is missing from *R* and is supplied from *A* [128] blows
[129] commanded [130] brought

With here mynstralsi;
Sir Gowghter went to his bed and lay,
Him lystyd nothyng for to play,
For he was ful weri.

For gret strokes that he had cawght
When he atte bataill fawght
Among the carfull crye.
His thowght was moch uppon his synne—
How he myght his sowle wynne
To blysse above the skye.

Than grette lordes to bedde were bown,
Knyghtes and squyers of grete renown,
In story as it is tolde.
Amorow [131] agayn came the massynger
Fro the sowdan, with sterne chere,
And said, "Sir Emperor, thi joy is cold:

My lord hath sembled a new powere,
And byddeth the send thi dowghter dere;
Or dere [132] hir love shall be sold,
Or he wull hurt the, body and bon,
And alyve leve not on
Of thy burgeys [133] bold!"

"I come to him;" said the emperor,
"I shall do semble a wol strong power
And mete him yf Y may—
Dowghti knyghts, large and long,
Wel y-armyd, ever among,[134]
By high prime of the day,

---

[131] in the morning [132] either dearly . . .
[133] townspeople [134] *i.e.* every one of them

On hors redy with shilde and spere!"
The nobill knyght, Sir Gowghter,
To Jhesu Crist gan he pray
Shuld send him armour tite:
So had he, and a steede mylk white,
540 And rode after in good aray.

Hys twey comyngs the domme lady had seen,[135]
And his thyrdde wendyng, withowten wene;[136]
She prayd for him full radde.[137]
Rode he not with brag nor bost,
Bot preystely pryckyd after the ost;[138]
546 He folowes ever the tradde.[139]

The emperor had the forward,
And Gowghter rode byfore his bard[140]—
Of knyghtes he was odde.[141]
Grete lordis of hethenesse to deth he throng,
And hire baners to the erth he slong;
552 His strokes fil full sadde.

The sowdan bare in sabill blak[142]
Thre lyons, withouten lak,[143]
All of silvur shene;
On was crowned with goules[144] reed,
Another with gold in that stede,
558 The thred with dyvers of grene.

His helme was ful richely fret,[145]
Al with riche charbocles[146] bysett,

---

[135] ms. *seen had* [136] without doubt [137] hard
[138] this line is missing from *R* and is supplied from *A* [139] track
[140] lord [141] *i.e.* in front of, not among, the charging ranks
[142] *i.e.* against a black sable background (the Sultan's banner is the object described) [143] no less [144] jewels seems meant here; in *A* the lions are "rampand" and the first is "Corvon with golys" (gules), where the heraldic device is clearly meant
[145] decorated [146] carbuncles, red stones

And dyamounds bytwene.
His batell [147] was ful well araid,
And his baner ful brode displayed;
Sone after turned to him tene.[148]

For the nobill knyght, Gowghtere,
He bare him so goodely in his gere,
Men nedeth no better to seche;
Al that he with his fawchon hit,
They fil to the grownd and rose not yet
To seke after no leche.[149]

Yet durst he never in anger ne tene
Speke no word, withouten wene,
For dred of Goddes wreche; [150]
And thow him houngerd, he durst not ete
But such as from houndes he myght gete:
He did as the pope gan teche.

Thus did Sir Gowghter, the gentil knyght;
But the emperor, that was so sterne in sight,
Ful smartly he was tanne,[151]
And away with the sowdan he was ledde.
Sir Gowghter rode after and made him leve his wedde,[152]
And smote of his hede thanne.

Thus rescued he his lord, and browght him agayne,[153]
And thankid God, with hert fayne,
That formed both blode and bon.
Right with that come a sarezyn with a spere,

---

[147] army [148] soon after he came to harm
[149] doctor, healer [150] vengeance, wrath
[151] taken
[152] captive (usually one held on pledge of safety, a hostage)
[153] back

Thorow shilde and shulder smote Gowghter:
Tho[154] made the domme lady mone.

For sorow she saw that stowre;[155]
She sowne[156] and fill owt of hir towre,
And brak full negh hir necke;
Two squyres in hire bare,
And thre dais she moved not yare,[157]
As thowh sho had be dede.

The emperor wyssh and went to mete,
And with him other lords grete
That at the batteil hadde ben.
Sir Gowghter was wounded sare;
Into the hall he gan fare:
He myssyd the lady shene.

Among the houndes his mete he wan.
The emperor was a carful[158] man
For his dowghter gent;
Massyngers were sent to Rome
After the pope, and he come sone
To here terement.[159]

Whan cardynales herd this tidyngis,
Thei come to hir beryeng.
Such grace God hath here sent
That she stered hirself and ras
And spake wordes that witti[160] was
To Sir Gowghter, with good entent,

And said, "My Lord of Hevyn greteth the well;
Foryeve ben thi synnes, every dell,[161]

---

[154] then [155] strife, battle [156] swooned [157] at all
[158] sorrowful [159] interment [160] profound, sensible
[161] every part

And graunteth the His blysse;
He byddeth the speke boldely,
To ete and drynk, and make the mery;
Thowe shalt ben on of His!

Fader," she said to the emperor,
"This is the knyght that hath fowghten in stowre
For yow in thre batellis, ywys."
The pope that shroffe Gowghter at Rome,
Byknew him whan he theder come,
And lowly gan him kys:

"Now art thow bycome Godes child;
The dare not dred of thi workys wyld;
Forsothe, I tell it the."
Thorow grace of God and the popis asent [162]
He was made wedde the lady gent,
That curtays was and fre;

She was a lady good and faire,
Of all hir fader lands eyre;
A better may none be.
The pope wold no lenger lend,
But yaf him all his blessyng hend; [163]
To Rome than went he.

Whan the fest was browght to ende,
Sir Gowghter gan to Ostryche wend,
And gaff the old erl all;
Of all his faderis londes he made him eyre,
And made him wedde his moder fayre, [164]
That was bothe gentill and small.

---

[162] ms. *atent* [163] good, noble

[164] the order of these two lines is reversed in the ms., with a marginal *a* and *b* indicating that the latter should come first as here given

Sygthe [165] he bildyd an abbay
And yaf therto rent for ay,[166]
And said, "Be beried here I shall";
And thereyn put monkes blake [167]
To rede and syng for Goddes sake,
And closid it withyn a wall;

For thowh the pope had him yshreve,
And his synnes were foreyeve,
Yet was his hert full sore
That he shuld so wyckedly werch,[168]
To brenne the nonnes in here cherch;
Another abbay made he thore.

There he did make another [169] abbay,
And put theryn monkes gray,[170]
That mykill cowde of lore —
To syng and rede to the worldeys ende
For the nonnes that he brend,
All that Cristen were.

Thus went Sir Gowghter home agayn;
By that tyme he come to Almayn,
His wyfis fader was dede.
Tho was he lord and emperor;
Of all Cristendome he bare the flowre,
Above the sarezyns hede.[171]

What man bad him for Godds sake do,
Trewly he was redy therto,
And stode [172] pouer men in stede;
And mayntayned pouer men in here right,

---

165 then 166 money for its support forever
167 black; Benedictines 168 work, do; ms. *wrech*
169 *i.e.* a second 170 Cistercians 171 in spite of the saracens
172 helped

And halp holy chirche [173]with his myght,
Thus cawght he better rede; [174]

And levid in good lyf many a yere,
Emperor of grete powere,
And wisely gan he wake.[175]
Whan he dayed, forsoth to say,
He was beryed in that abbay
That he first gan make;

There he lyeth in a shryne of gold
And doth maracles, as it is told,
And hatt [176] Seynt Gotlake.
He make blynd men for to se,
Wode [177] men to have here wit, parde,
Crokyd [178] here crucches forsake.

This tale is wreten in parchemen,
In a stori good and fyn,
In the first lay of Britayne;
Now God that is of myghtis [179] most,
Fader and Sone and Holy Gost,
Of owre sowles be fayne!

All that hath herd this talkyng—
Lytill, moche, old, and yyng—
Yblyssyd mote they be;
God yeve hem grace whan they shal ende,
To hevyn blys here sowles wend
With angelys bryght of ble.

Amen, pur charite.
Explicit Vita Sancti.

---

[173] ms. *chiche* [174] thus he took to a better way of life
[175] watch, rule [176] is called [177] mad [178] crippled
[179] ms. *mythes*

Kepe hem wele in þi lyue
That þe lesson wyll rede
And þe wt þe fawlys fede

Kyng Orfewe

Mery tyme is in Aperelle
That mekyll schewys of manys wylle
In feldys and medewys flowrys spryng
In grovys and wodys foules syng
Than wex yong men jolyffe
And þan prowd man and wyffe
The Brytans as þe boke seys
Off diuerse thingys þei made þer leys
Som þei made of harpyngys
And som of oþer diuerse thingys
Som of werre and som off wo
Som of myrthys and joy also
Som of trechery and som off gyle
Som of happes þat felle som whyle
And som be of rybaudry
And many þer ben off fary
Off all þe venturys men here or se
Most off loue for soth þei be
That in þe leys ben iwrought
Ffyrst fond and forth brought
Off auentures þat fell som deys
The Bretonys þerof made þer leys
Off kyngys þat befor us were
When þei myght any wondres here
They lete them wryte as it were do
And þer among is Sir Orfewe
He was for soth a nobull kyng
That most lovyd gle and harpyng
Wele sekyr was euery gode harper
Of hym to haue mekyll honour
Hymself he lernyd forto harpe
And leyd þeron his wyttes scharpe
He lernyd so wele wt outen lees
So gode harper neuer non was
In all þis werld was no man bore
That had kyng Orfew ones be fore
And he myght his harpyng here
Bot he wold wene þat it were
A blysfull note of Paradys
Suche melody þerin is
The kyng jornayed in Tracyens
That is a cyte off grete defence

Kyng Orfew

Mery tyme is in Aperelle
That mekyll schewys of manys wylle;
In feldys and medewys flowrys [1] spryng,
In grenys and wodes foules syng:
Than wex yong men jolyffe,
And than prevyth [2] man and wyffe.
The Brytans, as the boke seys,
Off diverse thingys thei made ther leys —
Som thei made of harpyngys,
And som of other diverse thyngys,
Som of werre and som off wo,
Som of myrthys and joy also,
Som of trechery and som off gyle,[3]
Som of happys that felle somwhyle, [4]
And som be of rybawdry,[5]
And many ther ben off fary.[6]
Off all the venturys men here or se,
Most off luffe, forsoth, thei be,
That in the leys ben iwrought,
Fyrst fond and forth brought.
Off aventours that fell somdeys
The Bretonys therof made ther leys —
Off kyngys that before us were;

---

[1] ms. *flowys* [2] grow amorous [3] guile
[4] events that befell in the past [5] ribaldry
[6] fairies and fairy-land

When thei myght any woundres here,
They lete them wryte as it were do,[7]
And theramong is Syr Orfewo:
He was, forsoth, a nobull kyng,
That most luffyd gle and herpyng—
Wele sekyr [8] was every gode herper
To have off hym [9] mekyll honour.
Hymselve he lernyd for to herpe,
And leyd theron hys wytte so scherpe;
He lernyd so wele, wythouten les,[10]
So gode herper never non was:
In all this werld was no man bore
That had Kyng Orfeo ben before—
And [11] he myght hys herpe here—
Bot he wold wene that it were
A blyssedfull note of paradys,
Suche melody therin is.
  The kyng jorneyd in Tracyens,[12]
That is a cyté off grete defence,[13]
And wyth hym hys quen off price,
That was callyd Dame Meroudys.
A feyrer lady than sche was one
Was never made off flessch ne bone;
Sche was full off lufe and godnes—
Ne may no man telle hyr feyrnes.
  It befelle in the begyning of May,
When foules syng on every sprey,[14]
And blossom spryng on every boughe
(Overall [15] wexyth mery inowhe),
Than the quen, Dame Meroudys,

---

[7] as it had happened [8] certain [9] ms. omits *hym*
[10] without lie [11] if
[12] sojourned, abode in Thrace
[13] well fortified, or of much renown
[14] branch [15] everything

Toke wyth hyr ladys off grete price,
And went in a undryn-tyde [16]
To pley hyr in an horcherd syde.
Than the ladys, all thre,
Sett hem under an hympe tre; [17]
Sche leyd hyr dounne, that comly quen,
And fell on sclepe upon the gren.
The ladys durste hyr nought wake,
Bot lete hyr lyye hyr rest to take;
Sche slepe welle fer after the non,[18]
To [19] the undryn-tyde was gon.
And when that lady gan hyr wake,
Sche cryed and grete noys gan make,
And wrong hyr [20] hondys wyth drery mode,[21]
And crachyd hyr vysage [22] all on blode;
Hyr ryche robys sche all to-rytte,[23]
And was ravysed out of hyr wytte.
  The ladys that stod hyr besyde
Fled and durste not long abyde,
Bot went unto the palys agene,
And told both knyght and sueyn [24]
How that the quen awey wold,[25]
And bad them com hyr to behold.
  Sexty knyghtys, and yit mo,
And also fele [26] ladys therto,
Hastely to the quen thei com,
And in ther armys thei hyr name [27]
And brought hyr to bed in haste,
And kepyd hyr both feyr and faste.
And ever sche began to cryye,
As sche wold up and go hyr weye.
  The kyng come to the chamer, to the quen,

---

[16] morning [17] fruit tree [18] noon [19] until [20] ms. *yr*
[21] anguished mind [22] scratched her face [23] tore to shreds
[24] swain [25] would go [26] many [27] took

And before hym knyghtys tene,
And wepte, and seyd wyth grete pyté,
"My leffe [28] wyff, what ayles the—
Thou that hast be so stylle? [29]
Why cryest thou wonder schylle? [30]
And ever thou hast [31] be meke and myld—
Thou arte becom wode [32] and wyld!
Thy flessch, that was so whyte beforn,[33]
Wyth thi nayles thou hast torn;
Thy lyppes, that was so bryght rede,
Semys as wan as thou wer dede;
And thi fyngyrs, long and smale,
Thei [34] be blody and all pale;
And thi luffsom eyn [35] two
Loke on me as I wer thi fo!
God leman,[36] I cry the mersye;
Thou late be [37] all thys reufull crye,
And telle me, lady, for thi prow,[38]
What thing may the helpe nowe!"[39]
  Sche ley styll at the last
And began to sey full fast,
And thus sche seyd the kyng unto:
"Alas, my lord, Syr Orfeo,
Ever I have lovyd the all my lyfe;
Betwen us was never stryfe,
Never seth [40] we wedyd ware;
Therfor I make full mekyll care.
Bot nowe we must parte [41] atwo:
Do thou the best, [42] for I must go."
"Alas," seyd the kyng, "lost I ame!

---

[28] dear, beloved [29] calm [30] shrilly [31] ms. *ast* [32] mad
[33] ms. *befon* [34] ms. *The* [35] eyes [36] woman, wife
[37] stop [38] as you may prosper
[39] the word is indistinct in the ms. and may or may not be intended to have the final *e*
[40] since [41] ms. *pare* [42] *i.e.* the best you can

Whyder wyll thou go, and to whom?
Wer[43] thou arte, I wol[44] be wyth the,
And wher I ame, thou schall be wyth me!"
"Do wey!" seyd the quen, "that schall not be,
For I schall never the mor se!
I wyll the tell how it is,
And forsoth I wyll not mysse!
As I went thys undyr-tide
To play me be myn orcherd syde,
I felle on slepe all bedene[45]
Under an ympe upon the gren;
My meydens durst me not wake,
Bot lete me lyye and slepe take
Tyll that the tyme overpassyd so
That the undryn was overgo.
When[46] I gan myselve awake,
Ruly[47] chere I gan to make,
For I saw a semely[48] syght:
Towerd me com a gentyll knyght
Wele i-armyd at all ryght,[49]
And bad I schuld up on hygheng,[50]
Com speke wyth hys lord, the kyng.
I ansuerd hym wyth wordys bold—
I seyd I durst not, ne not I wold.
The knyght agen he rode full fast;
Than com ther kyng at the last,
Wyth an hundreth knyghtys, also,
And an hundreth ladys and mo:
All thei rydan on whyte stedys;
Off mylke whyte was all ther wedys.[51]
I saw never, seth I was born,
So feyre creatours herbeforn!

[43] wherever [44] ms. *wold* [45] suddenly [46] ms. *Whe*
[47] rueful [48] fair; ms. appears to read *sembly*
[49] in all respects [50] in haste [51] clothes

The kyng had a crounne on hys hede—
It was no sylver, ne golde rede—
It was all off presyous ston:
Als[52] bryght as any son it schon.
Al so sone as he to me com,
Whether I wold or not, up he me nam,[53]
And made me wyth hym for to ryde
Upon a stede by hys syde.
He brought me to a feyre palas
Wele tyred[54] and rychly in all case;
He schewyd me hys castellys and tourys,
And hys hey[55] haules and boures,
Forestys, ryvers, frutys, and floures;
Hys grete stedys schewyd me ichon,[56]
And sethyn he made me agen to gon
Into the stede wher he me fette.[57]
In that same sted ther he me sete,
And seyd, 'Madam, loke that thou be
Tomorow here under thys tre,
And than schall thou wyth us go
And lyve wyth us evermo so.
Iff that thou make us any lete,[58]
Wherever thou be, thou schall be fete,
And totorn thi lymys all:
Nothyng helpe the ne schall;
And thoff[59] thou be all totorn,
Yit schall thou away wyth us be born.'"
When Kyng Orfeo herd this case,
Than he seyd, "Alas, Alas!"
He askyd rede[60] of many a man,
Bot no man helpe hym ne canne.

---

[52] as [53] took [54] attired, furnished
[55] high, noble [56] every one
[57] to the place he brought me from
[58] if you fail us in any way [59] though [60] advice

"Alas," seyd the kyng, "that I ame wo!
What may I best for my quen do?"
On the morow, when the ondryn cam,
Kyng Orfeo hys armys nam;
Ten hundreth knyghtys he wyth hym toke,
Wele armyd, talle men and stoute.
Wyth hys quen than went he
To the orcherd, under the ympe tre,
And seyd he wold ther abyde
What aventour [61] so betyde:
Lyve and dyye thei wold ichon
Or that [62] the quen schuld from them gon.
Than thei gon batell to make [63]
And sched blode for hys quenys sake.
But among them all, right,
The quen was awey twight,[64]
And wyth the feyry awey i-nome:
Thei [65] ne wyst wer sche was com.
Ther was cry, wepyng, and wo;
The kyng unto hys chamber yede tho,
And oft he knelyd onne the ston,
And made grete [66] sorow for sche was gon,
That ne [67] hys lyve was i-spent:
Bot ther myght be non amendment.
He sent after hys barons,
Knyghtys, squyres off grete renownys;
When thei all com were,
He seyd, "Lordingys,[68] befor you here [69]
I wold orden [70] my hyghe stuerd
To kepe my londys afterwerd,

---

[61] event [62] before [63] made battlements; prepared to do battle
[64] snatched [65] ms. *The* [66] ms. *gre* [67] nigh, nearly
[68] ms. *lodingys*
[69] the lines of this couplet are inverted in the ms., with a marginal *a* and *b* indicating their correct order
[70] ordain

And in my sted be he schalle
To kepe my landys overalle;
When that ye se my lyffe is spent,
Than make you a parlament:
Chese you than a new kyng,
And do your best wyth all my thing.
For now I have my quen lorne,[71]
The best woman that ever was born;
To wyldernes[72] I wyll gon —
For I wyll never woman sene —
And lyve ther in holtys hore[73]
Wyth wyld bestys evermor."
Ther was wepyng in the halle,
And gret sorow among them alle;
Ther was nether olde ne yong
That myght speke a word wyth tong.
They felle on kneys all in fere,[74]
Besought hym iff hys wyll were,
That he schuld not fro them go.
"Do wey!" he seyd, "it schall be so!
All thys kyngdom I forsake!"
A staff to hym he gan take —
He had nether gowne ne hode,
Schert, ne non other gode,
Bot an harpe he toke, algate[75] —
Barefote he went furth at the gate.
Ther was weping and grete crye,
Grete dole, for the maysterye,[76]
When the kyng wythouten crounne
So porely went out off the tounne.
He went thorow wode and hethe,
And into wyldernes he gethe;

---

[71] lost [72] ms. *wylderne* [73] wild woods [74] together
[75] however [76] the very greatest

So fer he went, I sey iwys,[77]
That he wyst not wher he was.
He that sate in boure and halle,
And on hym were the purpull palle,[78]
Now in herd heth he lygheth,[79]
Wyth levys and gress his body hydyth.
He that had knyghtys off pryse,
And before hym knelyd ladys,
He sey not that hys herte lykyth,[80]
Bot wyld bestys that by hym strykyth.[81]
Also he had castells and tourys,
Forestys, ryverse, frutys, and flourys —
Now thoff it be store as frese,[82]
He may not make hys bed in es.[83]
The kyng that had grete plenté
Off mete and drink, wythouten le,
Long he may dyge and wrote[84]
Or he have hys fyll of the rote.
In somour he lyvys be the frute
And berys, that were full suete;
In wynter may he nothing fynd
Bot levys and grasse and of the rynd.[85]
Hys body is away dwyned,[86]
And for grete cold al toschend;[87]
Hys berd was both blake and rowghe,
And to hys gyrdell-sted[88] it drewghe.
He can telle off grete care
That he[89] suffyrd ten wynter and mor;

---

[77] truly [78] wore the fine clothes of royalty
[79] on hard ground he lies; ms. *lyȝet*
[80] saw nothing congenial to him [81] went, ran
[82] though the cold be bitter as freezing
[83] may not find a comfortable bed [84] root, delve
[85] bark of trees [86] dwindled, withered [87] torn, chapped
[88] waist [89] ms. *The*

In a tre that was holow,
Ther was hys haule, evyn and morow.
When the wether was feyre and bryght,
He toke hys herpe anon ryght;
And mydys the wodde he sett hym dounne,
And temperyd [90] hys herpe wyth a mery sounne,
And harpyd after hys awne wylle—
Over all aboute it was full schylle.[91]
The wyld bestys that ther were,
They com aboute hys herpe to here:
The bestys of that forest wyld
Com aboute hym, meke and myld,
To here hys herpyng so fyne,
So mych melody was therine;
When he hys harpyng stynt [92] wylle,
No leng [93] ther abyde thei wylle.
And all the foulys that ther were,
They com aboute hym by bussch and brere.
Than myght he se hym besyde,
In an hote undryn-tide
The king off fary and all hys route [94]
Com ryding hym all aboute
Wyth dynne,[95] cry, and wyth blowyng,
And wyth houndys berkyng—
Bot no dere ne best thei nom; [96]
He wyst not wer thei were becom.
  Other thingys he might se:
A grete hoste com hym bye—
An hundreth knyghtys and mo yit,
Wele armyd at all ryght,
Wyth contynans [97] stoute and fers,
And many spreding baners;

---

[90] tuned, struck [91] loud, shrill [92] stop [93] longer
[94] company [95] noise [96] they took no game
[97] countenances, expressions

Every man a draw suerd had in hond,
Bot he wyst not whether thei wold wend.[98]
Also he myght se everything:
Knyghtys and ladys com daunsing;
Anon he lokyd hym besyde
And say syxty ladys on palferays ryde,
Gentyll and gay as byrd on ryse[99]—
Not a man among them, iwyse,
Bot every lady a faukon bere,
And ryden on huntyng be a ryver.
Off game thei founnd well god haunte—
Suannys, herons, and cormeraunte—
And the faucons forth fleyng,
And the foulys fro the water rysing,
Every facon hys pray slowgh.
  Than sate the Kyng Orfeo and lewgh,[100]
And seyd, "This is gode gam!
Thyder I wyll, be Godys name;
Sych game I was wont for to se!"
  Up he rose and thether went he;
To a ladé he com tho.
He beheld hyr face and body also—
Hym thought that it was in all wyse
Hys awne quen, Dame Meroudys.
He beheld hyr, and sche hym eke,
And never a word to other thei speke;
For the poverté that sche on hym se,
That had ben so rych and hyghe,
The terys ran doune be hyr eyye.
The ladys beheld and that they seyye,[101]
And made hyr awey to ryde:
No lenger myght sche ther abyde.

---

[98] where they were going [99] on the wing
[100] laughed [101] saw

"Alas," seyd Orfeo, "that me is wo!
Why wold not myn hert breke a-two?
Now I may not speke wyth my wyffe;
Al to long lastys my lyffe.
Sche dare not a word wyth me speke;
Alas, why wold not my herte breke?
Alas," seyd the kyng, "that I ne myght
Dyye after thys same syght!
Into what lond thys lady ryde,
Folow[102] I wyll, whatso betyde:
That same wey wyll I streche;
Off my lyve I do not reche!"[103]
He toke a staff as he spake,
And threw an herpe at[104] hys bake;
He sparyd nother stoke[105] ne ston,
He had gode wyll[106] for to gon.
In a roche of stone the ladys ryde;
Orpheo folowyd and not abyde.
When he had therin go
A myle or els two,
He com into a feyre cuntrey
Als bryght as son in somerys dey:
Hyll ne dale was ther non sen;
It was a welle feyre gren.
Orfeo full wele it seye,
A feyre castell, ryall and hyghe;
He beheld the worke full wele:
The overyst worke, above the wall,
Gan schyne as doth the crystalle;
A hundreth tyretys[107] he saw full stout,
So godly thei wer bateyled aboute;
The pylers[108] that com oute off the dyche,
All thei wer of gold full ryche;

[102] ms. *Forow* [103] reckon, care [104] on [105] stalk, tree-stump
[106] *i.e.* such a great desire [107] turrets [108] pillars

The frontys[109] thei wer amelyd[110] all
Wyth all maner dyverse amell;
Therin he saw wyde wonys,[111]
And all wer full of presyos stonys.
  Kyng Orfeo knokyd at the gate;
The porter, was[112] redy therate,
Freyned[113] what he wold do.
He said, "I ame a mynstrell, lo!
To glad thi lord wyth my gle
And[114] it his suete wyll be."
  The porter undyd the gate anon,
And as a mynstrell lete hym gon.
Than lokyd he aboute the walle,
And saw it stond, overalle,
Wyth men that wer thyder brought,
And semyd dede, and wer nought;
Som ther stod wythoutyn hede,
And some armys non hade,
And som ther bodys had wound,
And som onne hors ther armyd[115] sette,
And som wer strangyld at ther mete,
And men that wer no men[116] wyth them ete —
So he saw them stonding ther.
Than saw he men and women in fere[117]
As[118] thei slepyd ther undryn-tide;
He them saw[119] on every syde.
Among them he saw hys wyve,
That he lovyd as hys lyve,
That ley ther under that tre full trew;
Be hyr clothys he hyr knew.

---

[109] facades along the wall [110] enameled
[111] halls, dwellings [112] who was [113] asked [114] if
[115] ms. *armys* [116] *i.e.* eunuchs [117] together [118] as though
[119] the beginning of the line reads *He saw he them saw . . .*, the first two words apparently intended for cancellation, but not so marked

In that castell he saw yit
A tabernakylle [120] wele i-dyght;
And a ryall kyng therin sette,
And hys quen, that was so swete;
Ther crownys and clothys schyn so bryght
That on them loke he ne myght;
A hundryth knyghtys [121] in present
To do the kyngys commandment.
When he had sen all thys thing,
On kneys he fel before the kyng,
And seyd, "Lord, and thi wyll were,
My mynstrallys thou woldyst here."
Than seyd the kyng, "What arte thou,
That hether arte i-come now?
I, nor non that is wyth me,
Never yit sent after the:
Never seth that my reyn began
Fond I never non so herdy man
That hyder durst to us wend
Bot iff I wold after hym send."
"Sir," he seyd, "I trow wele
I ame bot a pore mynstrelle,
And yit it ys the maner off us
For to seke to gret lordys hous,
And thoff we not welcom be,
Yit we behovyth [122] to profer oure gle."
Before the kyng he sette hym doune,[123]
And toke hys herpe, schyll of sown,
And tempered yt, as he wele can;
A blyssedfull note he began.

---

[120] ms. *tabnakylle*; a line through the *b* seems intended to mark the *er* abbreviation, which the meter, of course, requires
[121] ms. *kny3thtys*
[122] it behooves us; ms. *behouyh*
[123] ms. *doue* or *done*

The kyng sate wele styll
To here hys herpe wyth ryght god wyll—
Wele hym lyked to here hys gle;
The ryche quen, so doyd sche.
Men that in the castell wer,
Com hys herpe for to here,
And felle dounne to hys fete,
They thought hys herpe was so suete.
And when he stynt of hys herpyng,
To hym than seyd the ryche kyng,
"Mynstrell, me lykys wele thi gle;
And what thou wyll aske of me,
Largely I wyll the pay—
Speke now and thou may asey." [124]
"Now, Lord, I pray the
That thou wold giff to me
The feyr lady, bryght off ble
That lyyeth [125] under this impe tre."
"Nay," he seyd, "that thought I never!
A foule coupull [126] of you it wer,
For thou arte rowghe and blake,
And sche is wythoutyn lake; [127]
A foule thing it wer, forthey,[128]
To se hyr go in thi company!"
"Lord," he seyd, "thou ryche kyng,
Yit it wer a fouler thing
To here a lesyng [129] of thy mouthe.
That thou me seyst to me nowthe [130]
That I schuld have what I wold;
Bot nedys a kyng word mot hold!" [131]

---

[124] profit [125] ms. *lyȝet*
[126] couple [127] flaw, fault
[128] thus, therefore [129] lie
[130] you said to me just now . . . ; ms. *nouȝe*
[131] a king must needs hold true to his word

The ryche kyng spake wordys than
And seyd, "Thou arte a trew man;
Therfor I grante that it be so.
Thou take hyr be the hond and go;
I wyll that thou be of hyr blyth."
He thankyd hym a hundreth sythe;[132]
He toke hyr by the hond anon,
And fast went forth oute of that wone.
Fast thei hyed out off that palas,
And went ther wey thourow Godys grace;
To wyldernes both forth thei goth,
And passyth over holtys and heth.
So long[133] he hys wey y-nom,
To Trasyens thei wer i-com,
That sometyme was his awne cyté;
Bot no man knew that it was he.
Wyth a pore man he reste that nyght—
Ther he thought to byde aplyght[134]
Unto hym and to hys wyffe
As an harpere off pore lyffe—
And askyd tydingys of that lond,
Who that the kyngdom held in hond.
In that same tym that old man
He told hym all that he can,
And how the quen was twyght awey
Into the lond of fayrey;
And how the kyng exiled yede,[135]
Bot no man wyst into what stede;
And how the stewerd the kyngdom hold,
And many other wonders hym told.
Amorowe, agen the non-tyde,[136]
He made hys quen ther to abyde.

---

[132] times [133] ms. *lo*
[134] pledged; *i.e.* representing himself [135] went
[136] toward noon-time

Forsoth he toke hys herpe anon;
Into the syté he gan gon.
And when he[137] com into the syté,
Many a man com hym to se;
Men and wyves and maydinse bold,
Fast thei com hym to behold.
Also thei seyd, everychon,
How the mosse[138] grew hym upon:
"Hys berd is grewyn to the kne;
Hys body is clong[139] as a tre!"
As the kyng went in the strete,
Wyth hys stewerd he gan mete,
And fell on kneys wyth grete pyté,
And seyd, "Lord, for charyté;
I ame an herper of hethynes;
Helpe me now, Lord, yn thys destres!"
The stewerd seyd, "Cum wyth me hom;
Off my gode thou schall have som;
For my lordys love, Sir Orfeo,
All herpers be welcum me to."
The stewerd and the lordys alle,
Anon thei went into the halle.
The stewerd wessch and went to mete;
The lordys all began to sytte;
Ther wer herpers[140] and trumpers,
And mynstrellys of[141] grete renounys;
Ther was grete myrth in the halle.
Kyng Orfeo sate among them alle,
And lystynd to[142] thei wer styll,
And toke hys herpe and temperde it[143] schyll.
The meryest note he made ther
That every man myght here wyth ere —
All thei lyked wele hys gle;

---

[137] omitted in ms. [138] hair [139] matted [140] ms. *hepers*
[141] ms. & [142] until [143] omitted in ms.

The rych stewerd,[144] so dyd he.
The stewerd the herpe knew full suyth,[145]
And seyd: "Mynstrell, so mote thou thryve,[146]
Wher hadys thou thys herpe and how?
Tell me now, for thi prow!"
"A, Lord! In a morning-tyde
Thorowe a wyld forest I yede;
A man wyth lyons was drawyn smale; [147]
I fond hym lyyeng in a dale:
Etyn he was wyth tethe so scherpe.
By hym I fond thys ryall herpe
Nyghe ten wynters ago."
"Alas," seyd the stewerd, "me is wo!
That was my lord, Sir Orfeo!
Alas," he seyd, "what schall I do
And for my lord that happyd so? [148]
Alas," he seyd, "that me is wo,
That so evyll deth was merkyd,
And so herd grace hym behappyd!"
On swon [149] he fell in the halle.
The lordys com before hym alle,
And toke hym up sone anon,
And comforth hym everychon,
And told hym how thys werld geth: [150]
Ther is no bote [151] of manys deth.
The kyng beheld the stewerd than
And seyd he was a trew man,
And lovyd hym as he aughte to do,
And sterte up and seyd, "Lo,
Syr Stuerd, lystyns now thys thing!

---

[144] ms. *stewe* [145] truly (soothe), or quickly (swithe)
[146] as you may thrive [147] was torn to shreds by a lion
[148] if my lord came to such misfortune
[149] aswoon, fainting
[150] goes [151] help, remedy

Yiff I were [152] Orfeo, the kyng,
Therfor, Stewerd, lystyns to me!
Now thou may the kyng her se;
I have wonyd ten wynters and mor
In wyldernes wyth mekyll sore,
And have wonne my quen awey,
Owte of the land off fary,
And have brought that lady hend [153]
Here unto the tounnes ende;
And oure in [154] was ther i-nome,[155]
And myselve to the courte com
Thus in beger wede [156] full styll
For to asey [157] thi gode wyll.
And for [158] I fond the thus trewe,
Therfor thou schall never it rewe; [159]
For, be my lyve, for lufe or aye,[160]
Thou schall be kyng after my dey.
And if thou have of my deth blyth,
Thow schuld be hangyd al so swyth!" [161]
All the lordys that ther sette,
That was ther kyng, thei underyete; [162]
And wyth that word the stewerd hym knew,
And over the bord [163] anon he threw,
And fell anon dounne to hys fete,
And so dyd all that ther sate.
And all thei seyd wyth a cryeng,
"Welcum, oure Orfew the Kyng!"
Off hys comyng thei wer blyth,
And brought hym to a chamber swyth,
And bathyd hym and schave hys berd,
And tyred [164] hym as a kyng in wede.

---

[152] as if I were (?) [153] noble [154] inn, lodging [155] taken
[156] beggar's clothes [157] assay, test [158] because [159] regret
[160] awe, fear [161] quickly [162] understood
[163] table [164] attired

And sethin wyth grete processyon,
They[165] brought the quen thorow the tounne;
For ther was myrth and melody
Off yche maner mynstralsy.
Ther he was crouned new, iwys;
So was the quen, Dame Meroudys;
And levyd long afterwerd;
And seth[166] was kyng the trew stewerd.
Herpers of Bretayn herd after than[167]
How thys aventour was begon,
And made a ley of grete lykyng,
And callyd it aftyr the kyng
That Orfeo hyght, as men wele wote;
Gode is the ley, suete is the note.
Thus endys here "Orfeo the Kyng";
God grante us all Hys blyssing.
And all that thys wyll here or rede,
God forgyff them ther mysded,
To the blysse of hevyn that thei may com,
And evermor therin to wonne.
And that it may so be,
Prey we all, for charyté.

Explicet Orfew

---

[165] ms. *The* [166] then
[167] what appears to be a single final word in this line is so blurred as to be undecipherable; *after than* is supplied from *A*

The prologe of the ffrankeleyns tale

Thise olde gentil Britouns in hir dayes made
Of diuerse auentures maden layes
Rymeyed in hir firste Briton tonge made
Whiche layes with hir instrumentz they songe
Or elles redden hem for hir plesaunce
And oon of hem haue I in remembraunce
Which I shal seyn with good wyl as I kan
But sires by cause I am a burel man
At my bigynnyng first I yow biseche
Haue me excused of my rude speche
I lerned neuere Rethorik certeyn
Thyng þt I speke it moot be bare and pleyn
I sleep neuere on the Mount of Pernaso
Ne lerned Marcus Tullius Scithero
Colours ne knowe I none with outen drede
But swiche colours as growen in the mede
Or elles swiche as men dye or peynte
Colours of Rethoryk been to queynte
My spirit feeleth noght of swich mateere
But if yow list my tale shul ye heere

Nuce pfer? ffonte labia plui caballino nec in bicipite pnaso me memini sompniasse

Heere bigynneth the ffrankeleyns tale

In Armorik that called is Britayne
Ther was a knyght þt loued and dide his payne
To serue a lady in his beste wise
And many a labour many a greet emprise
He for his lady wroghte er she were wonne
ffor she was oon the faireste vnder sonne
And eek therto comen of so heigh kynrede
That wel vnnethes dorste this knyght for drede
Telle hire his wo his peyne and his distresse
But atte laste she for his worthynesse
And namely for his meke obeysaunce
Hath swich a pitee caught of his penaunce
That pryuely she fil of his accord
To take hym for hir housbonde and hir lord
Of swich lordshipe as men han ouer hir wyues
And for to lede the moore in blisse hir lyues
Of his free wyl he swoor hire as a knyght
That neuere in al his lyf he day ne nyght
Ne sholde vp on hym take no maistrie
Agayn hir wyl ne kithe hire Ialousie

The Franklin's Tale

Thise olde gentil Britouns in hir dayes
Of diverse aventures maden layes,
Rymeyed in hir firste Briton tonge,
Whiche layes with hir instrumentz they songe,
Or elles redden hem for hir plesaunce;
And oon of hem have I in remembraunce:[1]

. . . .

In armorik,[2] that called is Britayne,
Ther was a knyght that loved and dide his payne
To serve a lady in his beste wise;
And many a labour, many a greet emprise,
He for his lady wroghte er she were wonne.
For she was oon[3] the faireste under sonne,
And eek therto comen of so heigh kynrede[4]
That wel unnethes[5] dorste this knyght for drede[6]
Telle hire his wo, his peyne, and his distresse.
But atte last, she for his worthynesse,
And namely for his meke obeysaunce,[7]
Hath swich a pitee caught of his penaunce
That pryvely she fil of[8] his accord
To take hym for hir housbonde and hir lord—

---

[1] the remaining 14 lines of the Franklin's "prologue" are omitted here

[2] Armorica [3] one of [4] lineage [5] hardly [6] awe, fear

[7] obedience, service [8] became

Of swich lordshipe as men han [9] over hir wyves.
And, for to lede the moore in blisse hir lyves,
Of his free wyl he swoor hire as a knyght
That nevere in al his lyf he day ne nyght
Ne sholde upon hym take no maistrie [10]
Agayn hir wyl, ne kithe [11] hire jalousie,
But hire obeye and folwe hir wyl in al
As any lovere to his lady shal,
Save that the name of soveraynetee,[12]
That wolde he have, for shame of [13] his degree.
  She thanked hym, and with ful greet humblesse
She seyde, "Sire, sith of your gentillesse [14]
Ye profre me to have so large [15] a reyne,
Ne wolde nevere God bitwixe us tweyne,
As in my gilt, were outher werre or stryf: [16]
Sire, I wol be youre humble, trewe wyf,
Have heer my trouthe, til that myn herte breste." [17]
Thus been they bothe in quiete and in reste.
  For o thyng, sires, saufly dar I seye,
That freendes everych oother moot [18] obeye
If they wol longe holden compaignye:
Love wol nat been constreyned by maistrye;
Whan maistrie comth, the god of love anon
Beteth hise wynges and farewel—he is gon!
Love is a thyng, as any spirit, free;
Wommen, of kynde,[19] desiren libertee,
And nat to ben constreyned as a thral; [20]
And so doon men, if I sooth seyen shal!
Looke! Who that is moost pacient in love,
He is at his avantage [21] all above.

---

[9] have [10] mastery, authority [11] show [12] authority
[13] for the respect due [14] nobility, generosity [15] free
[16] may God never permit strife between us two because of any fault of mine
[17] breaks [18] must [19] by nature [20] servant, slave
[21] ms. *avantate*

Pacience is an heigh vertu, certayn,
For it venquysseth, as thise clerkes seyn,
Thynges that rigour sholde nevere atteyne;
For every word men may nat chide or pleyne.[22]
Lerneth to suffre, or elles, so moot I goon,[23]
Ye shul it lerne wher [24] so ye wole or noon;
For in this world, certein, ther no wight is
That he ne dooth or seith somtyme amys:
Ire, siknesse, or constellacioun,[25]
Wyn, wo, or chaungynge of complexioun,[26]
Causeth ful ofte to doon amys or speken—
On every wrong a man may nat be wreken.[27]
After the tyme moste be temperaunce
To every wight that kan on [28] governaunce.
And therfore hath this wise, worthy knyght,
To lyve in ese suffrance [29] hire behight; [30]
And she to hym ful wisly gan to swere
That nevere sholde ther be defaute in here.
Heere may men seen an humble, wys accord;
Thus hath she take hir servant and hir lord:
Servant in love; and lord in mariage.
Thanne was he bothe in lordshipe and servage.[31]
Servage? Nay, but in lordshipe above,
Sith he hath bothe his lady and his love—
His lady, certes, and his wyf also,
The which that lawe of love acordeth to.
And whan he was in this prosperitee,
Hoom with his wyf he gooth to his contree;
Nat fer fro Pedmark [32] ther his dwellyng was,
Whereas he lyveth in blisse and in solas.

---

[22] complain [23] as I may thrive [24] whether
[25] fate, or one's temperament, as determined by his astrological influences
[26] humor, temperament [27] avenged [28] knows of
[29] sovereignty [30] given [31] servitude
[32] Penmarch, in Brittany

Who koude tell, but [33] he hadde wedded be,
The joye, the ese, and the prosperitee
That is bitwixe an housbonde and his wyf?
A yeer and moore lasted this blisful lyf,
Til that the knyght the [34] which I speke of thus —
That of Kayrrud was cleped Arveragus [35] —
Shoope [36] hym to goon and dwelle a yeer or tweyne
In Engelond, that cleped was eek Briteyne,
To seke in armes worshipe and honour
(For al his lust [37] he sette in swich labour),
And dwelled there two yeer — the book seith thus.
Now wol I stynten [38] of this Arveragus,
And speken I wole of Dorigene, his wyf,
That loveth hire housbonde as hire hertes lyf.
For his absence wepeth she and siketh,[39]
As doon thise noble wyves whan hem liketh;
She moorneth, waketh, wayleth, fasteth, pleyneth;
Desir of his presence hire so destreyneth [40]
That al this wyde world she sette at noght.
Hire freendes, whiche that knewe hir hevy thoght,
Conforten hire in al that ever they may:
They prechen hir, they telle hire nyght and day
That causelees she sleeth hirself, allas!
And every confort possible in this cas
They doon to hire with all hire bisynesse,
Al for to make hire leve hire hevynesse.
By proces, as ye knowen everichoon,
Men may so longe graven [41] in a stoon
Til som figure therinne emprented be;
So longe han they conforted hire til she
Receyved hath by hope and be resoun
The emprentyng of hire consolatioun,

---

[33] unless [34] ms. *of* [35] *i.e.* was named Arveragus of Kayrud
[36] planned, readied [37] joy [38] cease
[39] sighs [40] sorrows [41] engrave, cut into

Thurgh which hire grete sorwe gan aswage:[42]
She may nat alwey duren[43] in swich rage.[44]
And eek Arveragus in al this care
Hath sent hire lettres hoom of his welfare,
And that he wol come hastily agayn,
Or elles hadde this sorwe hir herte slayn.
Hire freendes sawe hir sorwe gan to slake,[45]
And preyde hire on knees, for Goddes sake,
To come and romen[46] hire in compaignye,
Awey to dryve hire derke fantasye.
And finally she graunted that requeste,
For wel she saugh that it was for the beste.
Now stood hire castel faste by the see,
And often with hire freendes walketh shee,
Hire to disporte,[47] upon the bank an heigh,
Whereas she many a shipe and barge seigh[48]
Seillynge hir cours, whereas hem liste go.
But thanne was that a parcel of hire wo,
For to hirself ful ofte, "Allas!" seith she.
"Is ther no shipe of so many as I se
Wol[49] bryngen hom my lord? Thanne were myn herte
All warisshed[50] of hise[51] bittre peynes smerte!"
Another tyme ther wolde she sitte and thynke,
And cast hir eyen dounward fro the brynke;
But whan she saugh the grisly rokkes blake,
For verray feere so wolde hir herte quake
That on hire feet she myghte hire noght sustene.
Thanne wolde she sitte adoun upon the grene,
And pitously into the see biholde,
And seyn right thus with sorweful sikes[52] colde:
"Eterne God, that thurgh thy purveiaunce

[42] assuage, abate [43] endure [44] passion
[45] slacken, diminish [46] walk, stroll [47] amuse
[48] saw [49] that will [50] cured
[51] its [52] sighs

Ledest the world by certein governaunce,
In ydel,[53] as men seyn, Ye no thyng make.
But, Lord, thise grisly, feendly rokkes blake,
That semen rather a foul confusioun
Of werk than any fair creacioun
Of swich a parfit, wys God, and a stable —
Why han Ye wroght this werk unresonable?
For by this werk south, north, ne west, ne eest,
Ther nys yfostred [54] man, ne bryd, ne beest.
It dooth no good, to my wit,[55] but anoyeth;
Se Ye nat, Lord, how mankynde it destroyeth?
An hundred thousand bodyes of mankynde
Han rokkes slayn, al be they nat in mynde,[56]
Which mankynde is so fair part of Thy werk
That Thou it madest lyk to Thyn owene merk.[57]
Thanne semed it Ye hadde a greet chiertee [58]
Toward mankynde; but how thanne may it bee
That Ye swiche meenes make it to destroyen,
Whiche meenes do no good, but evere anoyen?
I woot wel clerkes wol seyn as hem leste
By argumentz that al is for the beste,
Though I kan the causes nat yknowe;
But thilke [59] God that made wynd to blowe,
As kepe my lord! — this [60] my conclusioun.
To clerkes lete [61] I al [62] disputisoun,
But wolde God that alle thise rokkes blake
Were sonken into helle for his sake!
Thise rokkes sleen myn herte for the feere!"
Thus wolde she seyn with many a pitous teere.
  Hire freendes sawe that it was no disport
To romen by the see, but disconfort,
And shopen for to pleyen somwher elles;

---

[53] idleness [54] benefited [55] as I see
[56] though they are not remembered [57] image [58] charity, mercy
[59] that same [60] this is [61] leave [62] ms. *al this*

They leden hire by ryveres and by welles,
And eek in othere places delitables;
They dauncen and they pleyen at ches and tables.[63]
  So on a day, right in the morwe-tyde,[64]
Unto a gardyn that was ther bisyde,
In which that they hadde maad hir ordinaunce [65]
Of vitaille [66] and of oother purveiaunce,[67]
They goon and pleye hem al the longe day.
And this was in the sixte morwe of May,
Which May hadde peynted with his softe shoures
This gardyn ful of leves and of floures;
And craft [68] of mannes hand so curiously [69]
Arrayed hadde this gardyn, trewely,
That nevere was ther gardyn of swich prys [70]
But if it were the verray Paradys.
The odour of floures and the fresshe sighte
Wolde han maked any herte lighte
That evere was born, but if [71] to greet siknesse,
Or to greet sorwe, helde it in distresse.
So ful it was of beautee with plesaunce,
At after-dyner gonne they to daunce,
And synge also, save Dorigen allone,
Which made alwey hir compleint and hir moone,
For she ne saugh hym on the daunce go
That was hir housbonde, and hir love also.
But nathelees, she moste a tyme abyde,
And with good hope lete hir sorwe slyde.[72]
  Upon this daunce, amonges othere men,
Daunced a squier biforn Dorigen
That fressher was and jolyer of array,
As to my doom,[73] than is the monthe of May.
He syngeth, daunceth, passynge [74] any man

---

[63] backgammon [64] morning-time [65] preparations
[66] food [67] provisions [68] skill [69] expertly [70] beauty
[71] unless [72] abate [73] in my judgment [74] surpassing

That is, or was, sith that the world bigan.
Therwith he was, if men sholde him discryve,[75]
Oon of the beste farynge [76] man on lyve:[77]
Yong, strong, right vertuous, and riche, and wys,
And wel biloved, and holden in greet prys.[78]
And shortly, if the sothe I tellen shal,
Unwityng of this Dorigen [79] at al,
This lusty squier, servant to Venus,
Which that ycleped was Aurelius,
Hadde loved hire best of any creature
Two yeer and moore, as was his aventure.
But never dorste he tellen hire his grevaunce;
Withouten coppe he drank al his penaunce.
He was despeyred; no thyng dorste he seye,
Save in his songes somwhat wolde he wreye [80]
His wo, as in a general compleynyng:
He seyde he lovede and was biloved no thyng; [81]
Of swich matere made he manye layes,
Songes, compleintes, roundels, virelayes,
How that he dorste nat his sorwe telle,
But langwissheth as a furye dooth in helle;
And dye he moste, he seyde, as dide Ekko
For Narcisus, that dorste nat telle hir wo.
In oother manere than ye heere me seye
Ne dorste he nat to hire his wo biwreye,[82]
Save that paraventure [83] somtyme at daunces,
Ther yong folk kepen hir observaunces,[84]
It may wel be he looked on hir face
In swich a wise as man that asketh grace;
But nothyng wiste she of his entente.

---

[75] describe [76] handsomest [77] alive [78] esteem
[79] without Dorigen's knowing of this [80] show
[81] not loved in return [82] reveal [83] by chance
[84] where young people gather

Nathelees, it happed er they thennes wente,
Bycause that he was hire neighebour,
And was a man of worshipe and honour,
And hadde [85] yknowen hym of tyme yoore,
They fille in speche; and forthe moore and moore
Unto his [86] purpos drough Aurelius,
And whan he saugh his tyme, he seyde thus:
"Madame," quod he, "by God that this world made,
So [87] that I wiste it myghte youre herte glade,[88]
I wolde that day that youre Arveragus
Wente over the see, that I, Aurelius,
Hadde went ther [89] nevere I sholde have come agayn.
For well I woot my servyce is in vayn;
My gerdon [90] is but brestyng of myn herte.
Madame, reweth [91] upon my peynes smerte,
For with a word ye may me sleen or save;
Heere at youre feet God wolde that I were grave! [92]
I ne have as now no leyser moore to seye;
Have mercy, sweete, or ye wol do me deye!" [93]
She gan to looke upon Aurelius;
"Is this youre wyl," quod she, "and sey ye thus?
Nevere erst," [94] quod she, "ne wiste I what ye mente;
But now, Aurelie, I knowe youre entente.
By thilke God that yaf me soule and lyf,
Ne shal I nevere been untrewe wyf
In word ne werk,[95] as fer as I have wit.
I wol been his to whom that I am knyt; [96]
Taak this for fynal answere as of me." [97]
But after that in pley [98] thus seyde she:
"Aurelie," quod she, "by heighe God above,
Yet wolde I graunte yow to been youre love,

---

[85] and she had [86] ms. *this* [87] if [88] gladden [89] where
[90] reward [91] have pity [92] buried [93] cause me to die
[94] before [95] deed [96] married
[97] as far as I'm concerned [98] jest

Syn I yow se so pitously complayne.
Looke! What day that endelong [99] Britayne
Ye remoeve alle the rokkes, stoon by stoon,
That they ne lette [100] shipe ne boot to goon —
I seye whan ye han maad the coost so clene
Or rokkes that ther nys no stoon ysene,
Than wol I love yow best of any man:
Have heer my trouthe [101] in al that evere I kan!"
  "Is ther noon oother grace in yow?" quod he
  "No, by that Lord," quod she, "that maked me;
For wel I woot that it shal never bityde! [102]
Lat swiche folies out of youre herte slyde!
What deyntee [103] sholde a man han in his lyf,
For to go love another mannes wyf,
That hath hir body whan so that him lyketh?"
  Aurelius ful ofte soore siketh;
Wo was Aurelie whan [104] he this herde,
And with a sorweful herte he thus answerde:
  "Madame," quod he, "this were an impossible! [105]
Thanne moot I dye of sodeyn deth horrible."
And with that word he turned hym anon.
Tho coome hir othere freendes many oon,
And in the aleyes [106] romeden up and doun,
And nothyng wiste of this conclusioun,
But sodeynly bigonne revel newe,
Til that the brighte sonne lost his hewe,
For th'orisonte [107] hath reft the sonne his lyght
(This is as muche to seye as it was nyght!),
And hoom they goon in joye and in solas,
Save oonly wrecche Aurelius, allas!

---

[99] the length of [100] prevent
[101] promise [102] come to pass
[103] dignity, esteem [104] ms. *whan that*
[105] *i.e.* an impossible task [106] pathways
[107] the horizon

He to his hous is goon with sorweful herte.
He seeth he may nat fro his deeth asterte;[108]
Hym semed[109] that he felte his herte colde.
Up to the hevene his handes he gan holde
And on hise knowes[110] bare he sette hym doun,
And in his ravyng seyde his orisoun.[111]
For verray wo out of his wit he breyde;[112]
He nyste what he spak, but thus he seyde
With pitous herte; his pleynt hath he bigonne
Unto the goddes, and first unto the sonne.
He seyde, "Appollo, god and governour
Of every plaunte, herbe, tree, and flour,
That yevest,[113] after thy declinacioun,[114]
To ech of hem his tyme and his sesoun,
As thyn herberwe[115] chaungeth, lowe or heighe—
Lord Phebus, cast thy merciable eighe[116]
On wrecche Aurelie, which am but lorn![117]
Lo, lord! My lady hath my deeth ysworn
Withoute gilt, but[118] thy benignytee
Upon my dedly herte have som pitee;
For wel I woot, lord Phebus, if yow lest,[119]
Ye may me helpen, save[120] me lady, best.
Now voucheth sauf[121] that I may you devyse
How that I may been holpen, and in what wyse:
Youre blisful suster, Lucina the sheene,[122]
That of the see is chief goddesse and queene
(Though Neptunus have deitee in the see,
Yet emperisse aboven hym is she),
Ye knowen wel, lord, that right as hir desir
Is to be quyked[123] and lightned of youre fir,

[108] escape [109] it seemed to him [110] knees [111] prayer
[112] went [113] gives
[114] according to your distance from the earth
[115] place in the sky [116] eye [117] lost [118] unless
[119] if it pleases you [120] except [121] permit
[122] bright [123] given life

For which she folweth you ful bisily,
Right so the see desireth naturelly
To folwen hire, as she that is goddesse
Bothe in the see and ryveres, moore and lesse.
Wherfore, lord Phebus, this is my requeste:
Do this miracle, or do [124] myn herte breste —
That now next at this opposicioun
Which in the signe shal be of the leoun,[125]
As preieth hire so greet a flood to brynge
That fyve fadme at the leeste it oversprynge
The hyeste rokke in Armorik Briteyne;
And lat this flood endure yeres tweyne.
Thanne certes to my lady may I seye,
'Holdeth youre heste; [126] the rokkes been aweye!'
  Lord Phebus, dooth this miracle for me.
Preye hire she go no faster cours than ye —
I seye, preyeth your suster that she go
No faster cours than ye thise yeres two:
Thanne shal she been evene atte fulle alway,
And spryng flood laste bothe nyght and day.
And but she vouche sauf in swich manere
To graunte me my sovereyn lady deere,
Prey hire to synken every rok adoun
Into hir owene dirke [127]regioun
Under the ground, ther Pluto dwelleth inne,
Or nevere mo shal I my lady wynne.
Thy temple in Delphos wol I barefoot seke;
Lord Phebus, se the teeris on my cheke,
And of my peyne have som compassioun!"
And with that word in swowne [128] he fil adoun,

---

[124] cause
[125] when you are next in the zodiacal sign of the Lion and the moon is opposite (in Aquarius)
[126] promise
[127] dark [128] swoon

And longe tyme he lay forth in a traunce.
His brother, which that knew of his penaunce,
Up caughte hym and to bedde he hath hym broght.
Dispeyred in this torment and this thoght,
Lete I this woful creature lye —
Chese he, for me,[129] wheither he wol lyve or dye.
Arveragus, with heele[130] and greet honour,
As he that was of chivalrie the flour,
Is comen home, and othere worthy men:
O blisful artow now, thou Dorigen,
That hast thy lusty housbonde in thyne armes,
The fresshe knyght, the worthy man of armes,
That loveth thee as his owene hertes lyf!
Nothyng list hym to been ymaginatyf[131]
If any wight had spoke, whil he was oute,
To hire of love; he hadde of it no doute.[132]
He noght entendeth to[133] no swich mateere,
But daunceth, justeth, maketh hire good cheere;
And thus in joye and blisse I lete hem dwelle,
And of the sike Aurelius I wol yow telle.
In langour and in torment furyus
Two yeer and moore lay wrecche Aurelyus
Er any foot he myght on erthe gon,
Ne confort in this tyme hadde he noon
Save of his brother, which that was a clerk.
He knew of al this wo and al this werk,
For to noon oother creature, certeyn,
Of this matere he dorste no word seyn.
Under his brest he baar it moore secree[134]
Than evere dide Pamphilus for Galathee.[135]

---

[129] let him choose, as far as I'm concerned
[130] healthy [131] he had no wish whatever to be curious
[132] fear [133] cares about, pays attention to [134] secretly
[135] the reference is to a widely known romance of Chaucer's time, *Pamphilus de Amore*

His brest was hool, withoute for to sene,[136]
But in his herte ay[137] was the arwe[138] kene;
And wel ye knowe that of a sursanure[139]
In surgerye is perilous the cure,
But[140] men myghte touche the arwe, or come therby.
His brother weepe and wayled pryvely
Til atte laste hym fil in remembrance
That whiles he was at Orliens in France,
As yonge clerkes that been lykerous[141]
To reden artes that been curious[142]
Seken in every halke and every herne[143]
Particuler sciences for to lerne—
He remembred that upon a day
At Orliens in studie a book he say[144]
Of magyk natureel,[145] which his felawe,
That was that tyme a bacheler of law[146]—
Al[147] were he ther to lerne another craft—
Hadde prively upon his desk ylaft,
Which book spak muchel of the operaciouns
Touchynge the eighte and twenty mansiouns[148]
That longen[149] to the moone, and swich folye
As in oure dayes is nat worth a flye
(For hooly chirches feith, in oure bileve,
Ne suffreth noon illusioun us to greve[150]).
And whan this book was in his remembraunce,
Anon for joye his herte gan to daunce,
And to hymself he seyde pryvely,
"My brother shall be warisshed[151] hastily,
For I am siker[152] that ther be sciences

---

[136] from all outward appearances [137] always
[138] *i.e.* Cupid's arrow [139] a wound only superficially healed
[140] unless [141] anxious [142] out-of-the-way
[143] every nook and cranny [144] saw
[145] natural magic, as opposed to necromancy [146] law student
[147] although [148] houses, phases [149] belong [150] harm
[151] cured [152] certain

By whiche [153] men make diverse apparences [154]
Swiche as thise subtile tregetours [155] pleye;
For ofte at feestes have I wel herd seye
That tregetours withinne an halle large
Have maad come in a water and a barge,
And in the halle rowen up and doun.
Somtyme hath semed come a grym leoun,
And somtyme floures sprynge as in a mede, [156]
Somtyme a vyne and grapes white and rede,
Somtyme a castel, al of lym [157] and stoon,
And whan hym lyked, voyded [158] it anoon —
Thus semed it to every mannes sighte.
Now, thanne, conclude I thus: that, if I myghte
At Orliens som oold felawe yfynde,
That hadde this moones mansions in mynde,[159]
Or oother magyk natureel above,
He sholde wel make my brother han his love.
For with an apparence a clerk may make,
To mannes sighte, that alle the rokkes blake
Of Britaigne weren yvoyded, everichon,
And shippes by the brynke [160] comen and gon,
And in swich forme enduren a wowke [161] or two.
Thanne were my brother warisshed of his wo;
Thanne most she nedes holden hire biheste,
Or elles he shal shame hire atte leeste."
What [162] sholde I make a lenger tale of this?
Unto his brotheres bed he comen is,
And swich confort [163] he yaf hym for to gon
To Orliens that he upstirte anon,
And on his wey forthward thanne is he fare [164]
In hope for to been lissed [165] of his care.

---

[153] ms. *whce* [154] illusions [155] magicians [156] meadow
[157] lime [158] made it vanish [159] memory, knowledge
[160] shore [161] week [162] why [163] encouragement
[164] gone [165] relieved

Whan they were come almoost to that citee,
But if it were a two furlong or thre,
A yong clerk romynge by himself they mette,
Which that in Latyn thriftily hem grette,[166]
And after that he seyde a wonder thyng:
"I knowe," quod he, "the cause of youre comyng";
And er they ferther any foote wente,
He tolde hem al that was in hire entente.
This Briton clerk hym asked of felawes
The whiche that he had knowe in olde dawes,[167]
And he answerde hym that they dede were,
For which he weep ful ofte many a teere.
Doun of his hors Aurelius lighte anon,
And with this magicien forth is he gon
Hoom to his hous, and maden hem wel at ese;
Hem lakked no vitaille that myghte hem plese.
So wel arrayed hous as ther was oon,
Aurelius in his lyf saugh nevere noon.
He shewed hym, er he wente to sopeer,
Forestes, parkes ful of wilde deer; [168]
Ther saugh he hertes [169] with hir hornes hye,
The gretteste that evere were seyn with eye.
He saugh of hem an hondred slayn with houndes,
And somme with arwes bled of bittre woundes.
He saugh, whan voyded were thise wilde deer,
Thise fauconers [170] upon a fair ryver,
That with hir haukes han the heron slayn.
Tho saugh he knyghtes justyng in a playn,
And after this he dide hym swich plesaunce
That he hym shewed his lady on a daunce,
On which hymself he daunced, as hym thoughte.
And whan this maister that this magyk wroughte

[166] greeted them pleasantly [167] days
[168] animals [169] harts
[170] falconers

Saugh it was tyme, he clapte hise handes two,
And, farewel! al oure revel was ago.[171]
And yet remoeved they nevere out of the hous
Whil they saugh al this sighte merveillous,
But in his studie, theras hise bookes be,
They seten stille, and no wight but they thre.
To hym this maister called his squier,
And seyde hym thus: "Is redy oure soper?
Almoost an houre it is, I undertake,
Sith I yow bad oure soper for to make
Whan that thise worthy men wenten with me
Into my studie, theras my bookes be."
"Sire," quod this squier, "whan it liketh [172] yow,
It is al redy, though ye wol right now."
"Go we thanne soupe," [173] quod he, "as for the beste.
This amorous folk somtyme moote [174] han hir reste."
At after-soper fille they in tretee [175]
What somme [176] sholde this maistres gerdon [177] be
To remoeven alle the rokkes of Britayne
And eek from Gerounde to the mouth of Sayne.[178]
He made it straunge,[179] and swoor, so God hym save,
Lasse than a thousand pound he wolde not have,
Ne gladly for that somme he wolde nat goon.
Aurelius, with blisful herte anoon
Answerde thus: "Fy on a thousand pound!
This wyde world, which that men seye is round,
I wolde it yeve if I were lord of it!
This bargayn is ful dryve,[180] for we be knyt; [181]
Ye shal be payed, trewely by my trouthe.
But looketh now for no necligence or slouthe [182]

---

[171] gone [172] pleases [173] sup [174] must
[175] bargaining [176] sum [177] reward, price
[178] the rivers Gerond and Seine
[179] difficult [180] driven, made
[181] agreed [182] waste of time

Ye tarie us heere no lenger than tomorwe."
"Nay," quod this clerk, "have heer my feith to borwe."[183]
To bedde is goon Aurelius whan hym leste,
And wel ny al that nyght he hadde his reste;
What for his labour and his hope of blisse,
His woful herte of penaunce hadde a lisse.[184]
Upon the morwe, whan that it was day,
To Britaigne took they the righte way —
Aurelius and this magicien bisyde —
And been descended ther they wolde abyde;
And this was — as thise bookes me remembre —
The colde, frosty seson of Decembre.
Phebus wax old and hewed lyk latoun,[185]
That in his hoote declynacioun
Shoon as the burned gold with stremes brighte;
But now in Capricorn adoun he lighte,
Whereas he shoon ful pale, I dar wel seyn.
The bittre frostes, with the sleet and reyn,
Destroyed hath the grene in every yerd.
Janus[186] sit by the fyr, with double berd,[187]
And drynketh of his bugle horn the wyn;
Biforn hym stant brawen[188] of the tusked swyn,
And "Nowel!" crieth every lusty man.
Aurelius, in al that evere he kan,
Dooth to his maister chiere and reverence,
And preyeth hym to doon his diligence
To bryngen hym out of his peynes smerte,
Or with a swerd that he wolde slitte his herte.
This subtil clerk swich routhe[189] had of this man
That nyght and day he spedde hym that[190] he kan

[183] in pledge [184] relief
[185] the sun grew weak and pale (copper-colored) [186] January
[187] *i.e.* double face, looking backward to the old year and forward to the new
[188] meat [189] pity [190] all

To wayten [191] a tyme of his conclusioun —
This is to seye, to maken illusioun
By swich an [192] apparence, or [193] jogelrye [194]
(I ne kan [195] no termes of astrologye),
That she and every wight sholde wene and seye
That of Britaigne the rokkes were aweye,
Or ellis they were sonken under grounde.
So atte laste he hath his tyme yfounde
To maken his japes [196] and his wrecchednesse
Of swich a supersticious cursednesse.
His tables Tolletanes [197] forth he brought,
Ful wel corrected, ne ther lakked nought
(Neither his collect [198] ne hise expanse yeeris,[199]
Ne hise rootes,[200] ne hise othere geeris,
As been his centris,[201] and his argumentz,[202]
And hise proporcioneles convenientz [203])
For hise equacions in every thyng.
And by his eighte speere in his wirkyng,
He knew ful wel how fer Alnath was shove
Fro the heed of thilke fixe Aries above,
That in the ninthe speere considered is: [204]
Ful subtilly he hadde kalkuled [205] al this.
Whan he hadde found his firste mansioun,

[191] discover [192] ms. *a* [193] ms. *of* [194] magic
[195] know [196] tricks
[197] astronomical tables, calculated from the location of the city of Toledo
[198] long-term calculations (20-3000 years)
[199] short-term calculations (1-20 years)
[200] bases for computation
[201] points on the astrolabe denoting fixed star positions
[202] known numbers, or propositions, from which unknowns can be deduced
[203] proportional, or fractional, tables from which to calculate less-than-yearly movements of the stars
[204] calculating from the eighth fixed sphere, he knew how far Alnath, a star in the ninth sphere, had moved from the head of fixed Aries, the true equinoctial point [205] calculated

He knew the remenaunt by proporcioun,
And knew the arisyng of his moone weel,
And in whos face and terme,[206] and everydeel,
And knew ful weel the moones mansioun
Accordaunt to his operacioun,
And knew also hise othere observaunces
For swiche illusiouns and swiche meschaunces[207]
As hethen folk useden[208] in thilke dayes.
For which no lenger maked he delayes,
But thurgh his magik, for a wyke or tweye
It semed that alle the rokkes were aweye.
  Aurelius, which that yet despeired is
Wher[209] he shal han his love or fare amys,
Awaiteth nyght and day on this myracle.
And whan he knew that ther was noon obstacle,
That voyded were thise rokkes, everychon,
Doun to hise maistres feet he fil anon,
And seyde, "I, woful wrecche, Aurelius,
Thanke yow, lord, and lady myn, Venus,
That me han holpen fro my cares colde."
And to the temple his wey forth hath he holde,[210]
Whereas he knew he sholde his lady see.
And whan he saugh his tyme, anon right hee,
With dredful[211] herte and with ful humble cheere,
Salewed[212] hath his sovereyn lady deere:
  "My righte lady," quod this woful man,
"Whom I moost drede and love as I best kan,
And lothest were of al this world displese,
Nere it[213] that I for yow have swich disese[214]
That I moste dyen heere at youre foot anon,

[206] divisions of the zodiacal signs
[207] misdoings [208] practiced
[209] whether [210] held, taken
[211] fearful [212] greeted
[213] were it not [214] pain, suffering

Noght wolde I telle how me is wo bigon.[215]
But certes, outher moste I dye or pleyne;[216]
Ye sle me giltlees for verray peyne.
But of my deeth thogh that ye have no routhe,
Avyseth[217] yow er that ye breke youre trouthe;
Repenteth yow, for thilke God above,
Er ye me sleen bycause that I yow love.
For, madame, wel ye woot what ye han hight[218]—
Nat that I chalange anythyng of right
Of yow, my sovereyn lady, but youre grace—
But in a gardyn yond at swich a place,
Ye woot right wel what ye behighten me,
And in myn hand youre trouthe plighten[219] ye
To love me best—God woot ye seyde so,
Al be[220] that I unworthy be therto.
Madame, I speke it for the honour of yow
Moore than to save myn hertes lyf ryght now;
I have do so as ye comanded me;
And if ye vouche sauf, ye may go see.
Dooth as yow list; have youre biheste[221] in mynde,
For quyk[222] or deed right there ye shal me fynde.
In yow lith al to do me lyve or dye[223]—
But wel I woot the rokkes been aweye!"

He taketh his leve, and she astonied[224] stood;
In al hir face nas a drope of blood;
She wende nevere han come in swich a trappe.
"Allas," quod she, "that evere this sholde happe!
For wende I nevere by possibilitee
That swich a monstre or merveille myghte be;
It is agayns the proces of nature!"

---

[215] how woe-begone I am [216] complain [217] think
[218] promised [219] pledged [220] although [221] promise
[222] alive [223] in you lies all the power to make me live or die
[224] astounded

And hoom she goth, a sorweful creature;
For verray feere unnethe [225] may she go.
She wepeth, wailleth, al a day or two,
And swowneth that it routhe was to see;
But why it was to no wight tolde shee,
For out of towne was goon Arveragus.
But to hirself she spak, and seyde thus,
With face pale and with ful sorweful cheere,
In hire compleynt, as ye shal after heere:
  "Allas," quod she, "on thee, Fortune, I pleyne,
That unwar [226] wrapped hast me in thy cheyne,
For which t'escape woot I no socour [227]
Save oonly deeth or elles [228] dishonour:
Oon of thise two bihoveth me to chese.[229]
But nathelees, yet have I levere to lese [230]
My lif than of my body have a shame,
Or knowe myselven fals,[231] or lese my name; [232]
And with my deth I may be quyt,[233] ywys.
Hath ther nat many a noble wyf er this,
And many a mayde, yslayn hirself, allas,
Rather than with hir body doon trespas?
  Yis, certes! Lo, thise stories beren witnesse:
Whan thritty tirauntz, ful of cursednesse,
Had slayn Phidon in Atthenes at feste,
They comanded his doghtres for t'areste,[234]
And bryngen hem biforn hem in despit,
Al naked, to fulfille hir foul delit.
And in hir fadres blood they made hem daunce
Upon the pavement—God yeve hem myschaunce!
For which thise woful maydens, ful of drede,
Rather than they wolde lese hir maydenhede,
They prively been stirt [235] into a welle,

---

[225] hardly [226] unawares [227] ms. *scour* [228] omitted in ms.
[229] I must needs choose [230] I would rather lose [231] unfaithful
[232] reputation [233] released [234] to be seized [235] have leaped

And dreynte[236] hemselven, as the bookes telle.
They of Mecene[237] leete enquere and seke
Of Lacedomye[238] fifty maydens eke,
On which they wolden doon hir lecherye;
But was ther noon of al that compaignye
That she nas[239] slayn, and with a good entente
Chees rather for to dye than assente
To be oppressed[240] of hir maydenhede.
Why sholde I thanne to dye been in drede?
Lo, eek the tiraunt, Aristoclides,
That loved a mayden heet[241] Stymphalides;
Whan that hir fader slayn was on a nyght,
Unto Dianes temple goth she right,
And hente[242] the ymage in hir handes two,
Fro which ymage wolde she nevere go.
No wight ne myght hir handes of it arace[243]
Til she was slayn right in the selve[244] place.
Now, sith that maydens hadden swich despit
To been defouled with mannes foul delit,
Wel oghte a wyf rather hirselven slee
Than be defouled, as it thynketh me.
What shal I seyn of Hasdrubales wyf,
That at Cartage birafte hirself hir lyf?
For whan she saugh that Romayns wan the toun,
She took hir children alle and skipte[245] adoun
Into the fyr, and chees rather to dye
Than any Romayn dide hire vileynye.
Hath nat Lucresse yslayn hirself, allas,
At Rome, whan she oppressed was
Of Tarquyn, for her thoughte it was a shame
To lyven whan she had lost hir name?
The seven maydens of Melesie[246] also

---

236 drowned 237 Messene 238 Lacedaemonia 239 was not
240 ravished 241 named 242 caught 243 tear away
244 same 245 leaped 246 Miletus

Han slayn hemself for drede and wo,
Rather than folk of Gawle[247] hem sholde oppresse.
Mo than a thousand stories, as I gesse,
Koude I now telle as touchynge this mateere.
Whan Habradate[248] was slayn, his wyf so deere
Hirselven slow,[249] and leet hir blood to glyde
In Habradates woundes depe and wyde,
And seyde, 'My body, at the leeste way,[250]
Ther shal no wight defoulen, if I may!'[251]
What[252] sholde I mo ensamples[253] heerof sayn,
Sith that so manye han hemselven slayn
Wel rather than they wolde defouled be?
I wol conclude that it is bet[254] for me
To sleen myself than been defouled thus.
I wol be trewe unto Arveragus,
Or rather sleen myself in som manere,
As dide Demociones[255] doghter deere
By cause that she wolde nat defouled be.
O, Cedasus![256] It is ful greet pitee
To reden how thy doghtren deyde, allas,
That slowe hemself for swich manere cas!
As greet a pitee was it, or wel more,
The Theban mayden that for Nichanore[257]
Hirselven slow right for swich manere wo.
Another Theban mayden dide right so
For oon of Macidonye[258] hadde hire oppressed;
She with hire deeth hir maydenhede redressed.
What shal I seye of Nicerates wyf,
That for swich cas birafte hirself hir lyf?
How trewe eek was to Alcebiades
His love, that[259] rather for to dyen chees

---

[247] the Galatians [248] Abradates [249] slew
[250] leastwise [251] if I can prevent it [252] why
[253] examples [254] better [255] Demotion's [256] Scedasus
[257] Nicanor [258] Macedonia [259] omitted in ms.

Than for to suffre his body unburyed be.
Lo, which[260] a wyf was Alceste!" quod she;
"What seith Omer[261] of goode Penalopee?
Al Grece knoweth of hire chastitee!
Pardee,[262] of Lacedomya[263] is writen thus:
That whan at Troie was slayn Protheselaus,[264]
No lenger wolde she lyve after his day.
The same of noble Porcia[265] telle I may:
Withoute Brutus koude she nat lyve,
To whom she hadde all hool[266] hir herte yive.[267]
The parfit wyfhod of Arthemesie[268]
Honured is thurgh al the barbarie.[269]
O Teuta, queene! thy wyfly chastitee
To alle wyves may a mirour bee.
The same thyng I seye of Bilyea,[270]
Of Rodogone,[271] and eek Valeria."
  Thus pleyned Dorigene a day or tweye,
Purposynge evere that she wolde deye.
  But nathelees, upon the thridde nyght,
Hoom cam Arveragus, this worthy knyght,
And asked hire why that she weepe so soore.
And she gan wepen ever lenger the moore:
  "Allas," quod she, "that evere I was born!
Thus have I seyd," quod she, "thus have I sworn";
And toold hym al as ye han herd bifore —
It nedeth nat[272] reherce it yow namoore.
  This housbonde, with glad chiere, in freendly wyse
Answerde and seyde as I shal yow devyse:[273]
"Is ther oght elles, Dorigen, but this?"
  "Nay, nay," quod she; "God helpe me so as wys![274]

---

260 what   261 Homer   262 truly   263 Laodamia
264 Protesilaus   265 Portia   266 completely
267 given; ms. *yeve*   268 Artemisia
269 heathendom   270 Bilia   271 Rhodogune
272 there is no need to   273 tell   274 as He is wise

This is to muche, and [275] it were Goddes wille!"
"Ye, wyf," quod he, "lat slepen that [276] is stille;
It may be wel, paraventure,[277] yet today.
Ye shul youre trouthe holden, by my fay! [278]
For God so wisly have mercy upon me,
I hadde wel levere ystiked [279] for to be
For verray love which that I to yow have
But if [280] ye sholde youre trouthe kepe and save;
Trouthe is the hyeste thyng that man may kepe."
But with that word he brast anon to wepe,[281]
And seyde, "I yow forbede, up [282] peyne of [283] deeth,
That nevere whil thee [284] lasteth lyf ne breeth,
To no wight telle thou of this aventure.
As I may best, I wol my wo endure,
Ne make no contenance of hevynesse,
That folk of yow may demen [285] harm, or gesse."
And forth he cleped a squier and a mayde:
"Gooth forth anon with Dorigen," he sayde,
"And bryngeth hire to swich a place anon."
They take hir leve and on hir wey they gon,
But they ne wiste why she thider wente;
He nolde [286] no wight tellen his entente.
Paraventure an heepe [287] of yow, ywis,
Wol holden hym a lewed man [288] in this,
That he wol putte his wyf in jupartie.[289]
Herkneth the tale er ye upon [290] hire crie;
She may have bettre fortune than yow semeth; [291]
And whan that ye han herd the tale, demeth.[292]
This squier which that highte Aurelius,
On Dorigen that was so amorus,

---

[275] if [276] that which [277] perhaps [278] faith [279] stabbed
[280] unless [281] burst into weeping [282] upon
[283] omitted in ms. [284] in you [285] think [286] would not
[287] perhaps many [288] a fool [289] jeopardy
[290] for [291] than you think
[292] judge

Of aventure happed [293] hire to meete
Amydde [294] the toun, right in the quykkest [295] strete,
As she was bown [296] to goon the wey forthright
Toward the gardyn, theras she had hight.[297]
And he was to the gardyn-ward also,
For wel he spyed whan she wolde go
Out of hir hous to any maner place.
But thus they mette, of aventure or grace,[298]
And he saleweth hire with glad entente,
And asked of hire whiderward she wente.
  And she answerde, half as she were mad,
"Unto the gardyn, as myn housbonde bad,[299]
My trouthe for to holde, allas! allas!"
  Aurelius gan wondren on this cas,
And in his herte hadde greet compassioun
Of hire and of hire lamentacioun,
And of Arveragus, the worthy knyght,
That bad hire holden al that she had hight—
So looth hym was his wyf sholde breke hir trouthe.
And in his herte he caughte of this greet routhe,[300]
Considerynge the beste on every syde,
That fro his lust yet were hym levere abyde [301]
Than doon so heigh a cherlyssh wrecchednesse
Agayns franchise [302] and alle gentillesse.
For which, in fewe wordes, seyde he thus:
  "Madame, seyeth to youre lord, Arveragus,
That sith [303] I se his grete gentillesse
To yow, and eek I se wel youre distresse,
That him were levere han shame—and that were [routhe—
Than ye to me sholde breke thus youre trouthe,

---

[293] happed by chance [294] in the middle [295] busiest
[296] bound [297] promised [298] by chance or fortune
[299] commanded [300] pity [301] he would rather refrain
[302] nobility, generosity [303] since

I have wel levere evere to suffre wo
Than I departe[304] the love bitwix yow two.
I yow relesse, madame, into youre hond,
Quyt,[305] every surement[306] and every bond
That ye han maad to me as heerbiforn,
Sith thilke tyme which that ye were born.
My trouthe I plighte, I shal yow never repreve[307]
Of no biheste, and heere I take my leve
As of the trewest and the beste wyf
That evere yet I knew in al my lyf.
But every wyf be war[308] of hire biheeste;
On Dorigene remembreth, atte leeste.
Thus kan a squier doon a gentil dede
As wel as kan a knyghte, withouten drede."[309]
  She thonketh hym upon hir knees al bare,
And hoom unto hir housbonde is she fare,
And tolde hym al as ye han herd me sayd.
And be ye siker,[310] he was so well apayd[311]
That it were inpossible me to wryte;
What[312] shoulde I lenger of this case endyte?[313]
  Arveragus and Dorigen his wyf
In soveryn blisse leden forth hir lyf;
Never eft[314] ne was ther angre hem bitwene.
He cherisseth hire as though she were a queene,
And she was to hym trewe for everemoore.
Of thise two[315] ye gete of me namoore.
  Aurelius, that his cost[316] hath al forlorn,[317]
Curseth the tyme that evere he was born:
"Allas!" quod he, "allas that I bihighte[318]

---

[304] divide [305] discharged
[306] pledge; the abbreviated form in the ms. should give *serement*
[307] reprove [308] wary, careful [309] doubt [310] sure
[311] gratified [312] why [313] tell [314] after, again
[315] omitted in ms. [316] expense [317] lost
[318] promised

Of pured[319] gold a thousand pound of wighte[320]
Unto this philosophre! How shal I do?
I se namoore but that I am fordo![321]
Myn heritage moot I nedes selle,
And been a beggere; heere may I nat dwelle,
And shamen al my kynrede in this place
But[322] I of hym may gete bettre grace.
But nathelees, I wole of hym assaye,[323]
At certeyn dayes, yeer by yeer, to paye,
And thanke hym of his grete curteisye:
My trouthe wol I kepe, I wol nat lye."
With herte soor he gooth unto his cofre[324]
And broghte gold unto this philosophre,
The value of fyve hundred pound, I gesse,
And him besecheth, of his gentillesse,
To graunte hym dayes of the remenaunt;[325]
And seyde, "Maister, I dar wel make avaunt,[326]
I failled nevere of my trouthe as yit;
For sikerly[327] my dette shal be quyt[328]
Towardes yow, howevere that[329] I fare
To go a-begged[330] in my kirtle bare.[331]
But wolde ye vouche sauf, upon seuretee,[332]
Two yeer or thre, for to respiten me,[333]
Than were I wel — for elles moot[334] I selle
Myn heritage. Ther is namoore to telle."
This philosophre sobrely answerde,
And seyde thus whan he thise wordes herde:
"Have I nat holden covenant unto thee?"
"Yes, certes, wel and trewely," quod he.
"Hastow[335] nat had thy lady as thee liketh?"

---

[319] purged, refined [320] weight [321] undone, ruined
[322] unless [323] try [324] chest
[325] a certain time to pay the remainder [326] boast [327] truly
[328] repaid [329] even though [330] a-begging
[331] *i.e.* in shirt-sleeves [332] surety
[333] delay my need to pay this debt [334] must [335] have you

"No, no," quod he, and sorwefully he siketh.[336]
"What was the cause? Tel me if thou kan."
Aurelius his tale anon bigan,
And tolde hym al, as ye han herd bifoore;
It nedeth nat to yow reherce it moore.
He seide Arveragus, of gentillesse,
Hadde levere dye in sorwe and in distresse
Than that his wyf were of hir trouthe fals.
The sorwe of Dorigen he tolde hym als;[337]
How looth hire was to been a wikked wyf,
And that she lever had lost that day hir lyf,
And that hir trouthe she swoor thurgh innocence;
She nevere erst[338] hadde herd speke of apparence.[339]
"That made me han of hire so greet pitee;
And right as frely as he sente hire me,
As frely sente I hire to hym ageyn.
This al and som;[340] ther is namoore to seyn."
This philosophre answerde, "Leeve[341] brother,
Everich[342] of yow dide gentilly til[343] oother.
Thou art a squier and he is a knyght;
But God forbede, for His blisful myght,
But if a clerk koude doon a gentil dede
As wel as any of yow, it is no drede![344]
Sire, I releesse thee thy thousand pound
As[345] thou right now were cropen[346] out of the ground,
Ne nevere er now ne haddest knowen me.
For, sire, I wol nat taken a peny of thee
For al my craft, ne noght for my travaille.
Thou hast ypayed wel for my vitaille:[347]
It is ynogh; and farewel, have good day!"

---

336 sighed 337 also 338 before 339 illusion
340 this is the whole and the part of it
341 dear 342 each 343 to
344 doubt 345 as though
346 had crept 347 food

And took his hors, and forth he goth his way.
  Lordynges, this questioun, thanne, wolde I aske now:
Which was the mooste fre,[348] as thynketh yow?
Now telleth me, er that ye ferther wende.
I kan namoore; my tale is at an ende.

Heere is ended the Frankeleyns Tale.

---

[348] generous, noble

Bibliography

The bibliography given here aims to be full, but by no means absolutely complete. It is arranged as follows:

I. *Bibliographies*: sources for further references.
II. *General Studies*: those items that are especially pertinent to the romances and lays are preceded by an asterisk; otherwise the works listed contain valuable background material.
III. *Collections*: mostly old and now out of print, these are collections of romances and tales; those which include one or more of the lays in this edition are preceded by an asterisk. Collections of ballads and text-book anthologies of Middle English literature are excluded, as are editions and collections of the English romances in modernized versions.
IV. *The Breton Lays*: each of the lays is listed separately in the order of its sequence in this edition; items pertaining to each lay are then arranged under the following headings:
   A. Manuscripts: where more than one manuscript exists, and where more than one was used in preparing the texts of this edition, those drawn upon are preceded by parenthetical italicized letters corresponding to the letters used in footnotes to designate variant readings adopted. The primary manuscript is always listed first and further identified by an asterisk preceding its letter designation.
   B. Separate Editions: these are usually scholarly editions, most of them containing full and valuable information on manuscripts, dates, sources, analogues, etc.
   C. Collections: here are indicated which of the collections of Section III above contain the lay.
   D. Studies: these are miscellaneous studies on various aspects of the lay concerned; though not repeated separately for each lay, item 23 should be consulted for all of them except *Sir Launfal*, and item 54 for those in tail-rhyme stanzas.

I. *Bibliographies*:

1. Billings, Anna H. *A Guide to the Middle English Metrical Romances* (Yale Studies in English, IX; New York, 1900).
2. *Cambridge Bibliography of English Literature* (Cambridge, 1941), I, 151–153.
3. Hibbard (Loomis), Laura. (See item 23 below.)

4. Holmes, U. T. Jr. *A Critical Bibliography of French Literature*; Vol. I, *The Medieval Period* (Syracuse, N. Y., 1952), pp. 79–135.
5. Renwick, W. L., and Orton, H. *The Beginnings of English Literature to Skelton, 1509* (rev. ed., London, 1952), pp. 349–388.
6. Wells, J. E. *A Manual of the Writings in Middle English 1050–1400*, 9 Supplements (New Haven, Conn., 1916–1951).
7. Zesmer, D. M. (Bibliography by S. B. Greenfield), *Guide to English Literature: From* Beowulf *through Chaucer and Medieval Drama* (New York, 1961), pp. 332–336.

II. *General Studies*:

8. Auerbach, Erich. *Mimesis: The Representation of Reality in Western Literature*; tr. W. Trask (Princeton, N.J., 1953; reprinted New York, 1957).
9.*Barrow, S. F. *Medieval Society Romances* (New York, 1924).
10.*Baugh, A. C. "Improvisation in the Middle English Romances," *Proceedings of the American Philosophical Society*, CIII (1959), 418–454.
11.*Bromwich, R. "A Note on the Breton Lays," *Med. AEv.*, XXVI (1957), 36–38.
12.*Chaytor, H. J. *From Script to Print: An Introduction to Medieval Literature* (Cambridge, 1945).
13.*Christensen, P. A. "The Beginnings and Endings of the Middle English Metrical Romances," (dissertation; Stanford University, 1927).
14. Cutts, Edward L. *Scenes and Characters of the Middle Ages* (London, 1930); see esp. pp. 267–310, "The Minstrels of the Middle Ages."
15.*Crosby, Ruth. "Oral Delivery in the Middle Ages," *Speculum*, XI (1936), 88–110.
16.*Donovan, M. J. "The Form and Vogue of the Middle English Breton Lay" (dissertation; Harvard University, 1951).
17.*Dunlap, A. R. "The Vocabulary of the Middle English Romances in Tail-rhyme Stanza," *Delaware Notes,* XIV (1941), 1–43.
18.*Everett, D. "A Characterization of the English Medieval Romances," *Essays and Studies of the English Association*, XV (1929), 98–121.
19. ———. *Essays on Middle English Literature*, ed. Patricia Kean (Oxford, 1955).
20.*French, W. H. *Essays on King Horn* (Ithaca, N.Y., 1940).
21.*Gist, Margaret A. *Love and War in the Middle English Romances* (Philadelphia, 1947).
22.*Griffin, N. E. "Definition of Romance," *PMLA*, XXXVIII (1923), 50–70.
23.*Hibbard (Loomis), Laura A. *Medieval Romance in England: A Study of the Sources and Analogues of the Non-cyclic Metrical Romances* (New York, 1924; reprinted with additional bibliography, 1959).
24.*———. "Chaucer and the Breton Lays of the Auchinleck MS," *SP*, XXXVIII (1941), 18–29; reprinted in item 26 below.
25. ———. "The Auchinleck MS and a Possible London Bookshop of 1330–1340," *PMLA*, LVII (1942), 595–627; reprinted in item 26 below.
26. ———. *Adventures in the Middle Ages: A Memorial Collection of Essays and Studies by Laura Hibbard Loomis* (New York, 1962).
27. Huizinga, J. *The Waning of the Middle Ages* (London, 1924).

28. Jeanroy, A. *Les Origines de la Poésie Lyrique en France au Moyen Age* (Paris, 1904).
29. Jusserand, J. J. *English Wayfaring Life in the Middle Ages* (4th ed.; New York, 1950).
30.*Kane, George. *Middle English Literature: A Critical Study of the Romances, the Religious Lyrics, "Piers Plowman"* (London, 1951); esp. pp. 1–103.
31. Kelly, Amy. *Eleanor of Aquitaine and the Four Kings* (Cambridge, Mass., 1952).
32. Ker, W. P. *Epic and Romance* (London, 1908; reprinted New York, 1958).
33. Lawrence, W. W. *Medieval Story and the Beginnings of the Social Ideals of English-Speaking People* (New York, 1911).
34. Leach, H. G. *Angevin Britain and Scandinavia* (Cambridge, Mass., 1921).
35. Lewis, C. S. *The Allegory of Love* (London, 1938; reprinted New York, 1958).
36.*Loomis, R. S. *Celtic Myth and Arthurian Romance* (New York, 1926).
37.*———. *The Development of Arthurian Romance* (London, 1963).
38. Mott, L. *The System of Courtly Love* (London, 1904).
39.*Nutt, A. *The influence of Celtic upon Mediaeval Romance* (London, 1904).
40.*Owings, M. A. *The Arts in Middle English Romances* (New York, 1952).
41. Painter, Sidney. *French Chivalry* (Baltimore, 1940; reprinted Ithaca, N.Y., 1957, 1961, 1962).
42. Parry, J. J. *The Art of Courtly Love by Andreas Capellanus* (New York, 1941). [A translation with valuable introduction.]
43.*Patch, H. R. *The Other World According to Descriptions in Medieval Literature* (Cambridge, Mass., 1950).
44.*Paton, Lucy A. *Studies in the Fairy Mythology of Arthurian Romance* (New York, 1903; reprinted 1959).
45.*Saintsbury, G. *The Flourishing of Romance and the Rise of Allegory* (New York, 1897).
46.*Schofield, W. H. *English Literature from the Norman Conquest to Chaucer* (New York, 1906); esp. pp. 181–201.
47. ———. *Chivalry in English Literature* (London, 1912).
48.*Smithers, G. V. "Story Patterns in Some Breton Lays," *Med. AEv.*, XXII (1953), 61–92.
49.*Speirs, John. *Medieval English Poetry: The Non-Chaucerian Tradition* (London, 1957); esp. pp. 139–167.
50.*Spence, Lewis. *A Dictionary of Medieval Romance and Romance Writers* (London, 1913; reprinted New York, 1962).
51. Strong, C. "History and Relations of the Tail-Rhyme Strophe in Latin, French, and English," *PMLA*, XXII (1907), 371–417.
52.*Taylor, A. B. *An Introduction to Medieval Romance* (London, 1930).
53. Thompson, S. *Motif-Index of Folk-Literature*, 6 Vols. (Bloomington, Ind., 1955–1958).

54.*Trounce, A. McI. "The English Tail-rhyme Romances," *Med. AEv.*, I (1932), 87–108, 168–182; II (1933), 34–57, 189–198; III (1934), 30–50.

55.*Weston, Jessie L. *From Ritual to Romance* (Cambridge, 1920; reprinted New York, 1957).

56. Wilson, R. M. *Early Middle English Literature* (2nd ed., London, 1951).

III. *Collections*:

57.*Ellis, G. *Specimens of Early English Metrical Romances*, 3 Vols. (London, 1805; revised by Halliwell, 1848). [Synopses of many of the romances with passages, "specimens," given in Middle English.]

58. Ewert, Alfred, ed. *Marie de France: Lais* (Oxford, 1947).

59.*French, W. H. and Hale, C. B. *Middle English Metrical Romances* (New York, 1930).

60.*Hales, J. W. and Furnivall, F. J. *Bishop Percy's Folio Manuscript*, 4 Vols. (London, 1867–1869).

61. Halliwell, J. O. *The Thornton Romances* (Camden Society; London, 1844).

62.*———. *Illustrations of the Fairy Mythology of A Midsummer Night's Dream* (London, 1845).

63.*Hazlitt, W. C. *Early Popular Poetry of Scotland*, 2 Vols (London, 1865).

64.*———. *Fairy Tales, Legends, and Romances* (London, 1875).

65. Loomis, R. S. and Loomis, Laura H. *Medieval Romances* (New York, 1957). [Translations.]

66. Mason, E. *French Medieval Romances from the Lays of Marie de France* (Ev. Lib.; London, 1924). [Translations.]

67.*Ritson, Joseph. *Ancient English Metrical Romances*, 3 Vols. (London, 1802; revised E. Goldsmid, Edinburgh, 1884).

68. Robson, J. *Three Early English Metrical Romances* (Camden Society; London, 1842).

69. Thoms, W. J. *A Collection of Early Prose Romances* (revised ed.; London, 1907).

70.*Utterson, E. V. *Select Pieces of Early Popular Poetry*, 2 Vols. (London, 1817).

71.*Weber, H. *Metrical Romances of the XIII, XIV, and XV Centuries*, 3 Vols. (Edinburgh, 1810).

IV. *The Breton Lays:*

Sir Launfal:

A. Manuscript:

72. British Museum; MS Cotton Caligula A. II.

B. Separate Editions:

73. Bliss, A. J. *Thomas Chestre: Sir Launfal* (London and Edinburgh, 1960). [An excellent edition, with exceptionally full introduction, bibliography, and glossary. An Appendix gives the text of Marie de France's *Lanval* (MS Harley 978) and the Middle English *Landevale* (MS Rawlinson C 86) for comparison with Chestre's version.]

C. Collections:
74. French and Hale (item 59 above).
75. Halliwell (item 62 above).
76. Hazlitt (item 64 above).
77. Ritson (item 67 above).
D. Studies:
78. Bliss, A. J. "The Hero's Name in Middle English Versions of *Lanval*," *Med. AEv.*, XXVII (1958), 80–85.
79. Cross, T. P. "The Celtic Fée in *Launfal*," *Kittredge Anniversary Papers* (Boston, 1913), pp. 377–387.
80. ———. "The Celtic Elements in the Lays of *Lanval* and *Graelent*," *MP*, XII (1915), 585–644.
81. Everett, D. "The Relationship of Chestre's *Launfal* and *Lybeaus Desconus*," *Med. AEv.*, VII (1938), 29–49.
82. Harris, J. "A Note on Thomas Chestre," *MLN*, XLVI (1931), 24–25.
83. Kittredge, G. L. "Launfal," *AJPhil*, X (1889), 1–33.
84. Kolls, A. F. H. *Zur Lanvalsage* (Berlin, 1886).
85. Schofield, W. H. "The Lays of Graelent and Lanval and the Story of Wayland," *PMLA*, XV (1900), 121–180.
86. Stokoe, W. C., Jr. "The Work of the Redactors of *Sir Launfal*, *Richard Coeur de Lion*, and *Sir Degaré*," (dissertation; Cornell University, 1946).
87. ———. "The Sources of *Sir Launfal*: *Lanval* and *Graelent*," *PMLA*, LXIII (1948), 392–404.
Sir Degaré:
A. Manuscripts and Early Prints:
[Six mss. and three early prints survive, more or less complete; only those used in preparing the text of the present edition are here listed.]
88. (**R*) Bodleian Library, Oxford; MS Rawlinson F. 34.
89. (*C*) Cambridge University Library; MS Ff. II. 38 (frag).
90. (*A*) National Library of Scotland; Auçhinleck MS, Advocates' 19. 2. 1.
91. (*P*) Percy Folio MS. (ed. Hales and Furnivall, item 60 above).
92. (*U*) *Syr Degore*, undated 16th c. quarto edition by W. Copland; reprinted by Utterson (item 70 above).
B. Separate Editions:
93. Carr, Muriel B. "*Sire Degarre*: A Middle English Metrical Romance Edited from the MS and Black Letter Texts with Introductory Chapters on the Filiation of Text and Phonology," (dissertation; University of Chicago, 1923).
94. Laing, D. *Sir Degaré* (Abbotsford Club, 1849).
95. Schleich, G. *Sire Degarre* (Heidelburg, 1929).
C. Collections:
96. French and Hale (item 59 above).
97. Utterson (item 70 above).
D. Studies:
98. Faust, C. P. *Sire Degaré: A Study of the Text and Narrative Structure* (Princeton, N.J., 1935).

99. Hibbard (Loomis), Laura A. (items 24–26 above).
100. Newstead, Helene. "The Besieged Ladies in Arthurian Romance," *PMLA*, LXIII (1948), 803–830.
101. Potter, M. A. *Sohrab and Rustem: The Epic Theme of a Combat between Father and Son*, Grimm Library, No. 14 (London, 1902).
102. Slover, C. H. *Sire Degarre: A study of a Mediaeval Hack Writer's Methods*, Texas University Studies in English, No. 11 (Austin, 1931).
103. Stokoe, W. C., Jr. "The Double Problem of *Sir Degaré*," *PMLA*, LXX (1955), 518–534.
104. ———. (item 86 above).

Lay le Freine:

A. Manuscript:
105. National Library of Scotland; Auchinleck MS, Advocates' 19. 2. 1.

B. Separate Editions:
106. Varnhagen, H. "Lai le Freine," *Anglia*, III (1880), 415–423.
107. Wattie, Margaret. *The Middle English Lai le Freine* (Northampton, Mass., 1929).

C. Collections:
108. Weber (item 71 above).

D. Studies:
109. Guillaume, G. "The Prologues of *Lay le Freine* and *Sir Orfeo*," *MLN*, XXXVI (1921), 458–464.
110. Holthausen, F. "*Lay le Freine*, V. 91," *Anglia*, XIII (1890–91), 360.
111. Laurin, A. *Essay on the Language of Lay le Freine* (dissertation; Upsala, 1869).
112. Matzke, J. "The Legend of the Husband with Two Wives," *MP*, V (1907), 211–239.
113. Zupitza, J. "Zum Lay le Freine," *Englische Studien*, X (1886), 41–48.

Emaré:

A. Manuscript:
114. British Museum; MS Cotton Caligula A. II.

B. Separate Editions:
115. Gough, A. B. *Emaré* (Old and Middle English Texts, II, London, New York, and Heidelberg, 1901).
116. Rickert, Edith. *The Romance of Emaré* (EETS ES, No. 99, 1908).

C. Collections:
117. French and Hale (item 59 above).
118. Ritson (item 67 above).

D. Studies:
119. Gough, A. B. *On the Middle English Metrical Romance of Emaré*, (dissertation; Kiel, 1900).
120. ———. "The Constance Saga," *Palaestra*, No. 23 (Berlin, 1902).
121. Holthausen, F. "Zu *Emaré*, V. 49 ff.," *Anglia Beiblatt*, XIII (1902), 46.

122. Isaacs, N. D. "Constance in Fourteenth-Century English," *Neuphilologische Mitteilungen*, LIX (1958), 260–277.

123. Krappe, A. H. "The Offa-Constance Legend," *Anglia*, LXI (1937), 361–369.

124. Rickert, E. "The Old English Offa Saga," *MP*, II (1904–05), 29–76, 321–376.

125. Schlauch, Margaret. *Chaucer's Constance and the Accused Queens* (New York, 1927).

The Erle of Tolous:

A. Manuscripts:

126. (**C*) Cambridge University Library; MS Ff. II. 38.

127. (A^1) Bodleian Library, Oxford; MS Ashmole 45.

128. (A^2) Bodleian Library, Oxford; MS Ashmole 61.

129. Lincoln Cathedral Library; Thornton MS, A. 5. 2.

B. Separate Edition:

130. Lüdtke, G. *The Erle of Tolous* (*Sammlung Englischer Denkmaeler in Kritischer Ausgaben*, III; Berlin, 1881).

C. Collections:

131. French and Hale (item 59 above).

132. Ritson (item 67 above).

D. Studies:

133. Greenlaw, E. A. "The Vows of Baldwin," *PMLA*, XXI (1906), 575–636.

134. Paris, S. "Le Roman du Comte de Toulouse," *Annales du Midi*, XXI (1900), 1–31.

135. Thomas, A. "Le Roman de Goufier de Lastours," *Romania* XXXIV (1905), 55–65.

Sir Gowther:

A. Manuscripts:

136. (**R*) British Museum; MS Royal 17. B. 43.

137. (*A*) National Library of Scotland; MS Advocates' 19. 3. 1.

B. Separate Edition:

138. Breul, K. *Sir Gowther* (Oppeln, 1886).

C. Collection:

139. Utterson (item 70 above).

D. Studies:

140. Crane, R. S. "An Irish Analogue of the Legend of Robert the Devil," *Rom. Rev.*, V (1914), 55–67.

141. Meyer, P. "L'Enfant Voué au Diable," *Romania*, XXXIII (1904), 163–178.

142. Ogle, M. "The Orchard Scene in *Tyordel* and *Sir Gowther*," *Rom. Rev.*, XIII (1922), 37–43.

143. Ravenal, F. L. "*Tyordel* and *Sir Gowther*," *PMLA*, XX (1905), 152–178.

144. Weston, Jessie L. *The Three Days' Tournament* (London, 1902).

Kyng Orphew (*Sir Orfeo*):

A. Manuscripts:

145. (**B*) Bodleian Library, Oxford; MS Ashmole 61.

146. (*A*) National Library of Scotland; Auchinleck MS, Advocates' 19. 2. 1.
147. British Museum; MS Harley 3810.
B. Separate Editions:
148. Bliss, A. J. *Sir Orfeo* (Oxford, 1954). [An excellent edition of all three mss., with full critical apparatus.]
149. Zielke, O. *Sir Orfeo, ein englischen Feenmärchen aus dem Mittelalter* (Breslau, 1880).
C. Collections:
150. French and Hale (item 59 above).
151. Halliwell (item 62 above).
152. Hazlitt (item 63 above).
153. ——— (item 64 above).
154. Ritson (item 67 above).
D. Studies:
155. Carpinelli, F. B. "Sir Orfeo," *Explicator,* XIX (1960), Item 13.
156. Davies, Constance. "Notes on the Sources of 'Sir Orfeo'," *MLR,* XXXI (1936), 354–357.
157. Donovan, M. J. "Herodis in the Auchinleck *Sir Orfeo," Med. AEv.,* XXVII (1958), 162–165.
158. Foulet, L. "The Prologue of *Sir Orfeo," MLN,* XXI (1906), 46–50.
159. Guillaume, G. (item 109 above).
160. Hibbard (Loomis), Laura A. (items 24–26 above).
161. Kittredge, G. L. "Sir Orfeo," *AJPhil,* VII (1886), 176–202.
162. Loomis, R. S. "*Sir Orfeo* and Walter Map's *De Nugis," MLN,* LI (1936), 28–30. *See also* Chap. XXIV of Loomis' *Arthurian Tradition and Chrétien de Troyes* (New York, 1949), pp. 162–168.
163. Marshall, L. E. "Greek Myths in Modern English Poetry," *Studi di filologia moderne,* V (1912), 203–232.
164. Wirl, J. "Orpheus in der Englischen Literatur," *Wiener Beiträge,* XL (1913).

Chaucer's Franklin's Tale:
A. Manuscript:
[Of the eighty-odd more or less complete manuscripts of Chaucer's *Canterbury Tales,* only the one used for the text of this edition is listed here.]
165. Huntington Library, California; MS Ellesmere 26. c. 12.
166. *The Ellesmere Chaucer,* facsimile reproduction, 2 Vols. (Manchester University Press, 1911).
B. and C. Editions and Collections:
[Of the many editions of Chaucer's works, only three recent ones are listed here; Robinson's is still regarded the standard edition.]
167. Baugh, A. C. *Chaucer's Major Poetry* (New York, 1963).
168. Donaldson, E. T. *Chaucer's Poetry: An Anthology for the Modern Reader* (New York, 1958).
169. Robinson, F. N. *The Works of Geoffrey Chaucer,* 2nd. ed. (Boston, 1957).

D. Studies:

170. Archer, J. W. "On Chaucer's Source for 'Arveragus' in the Franklin's Tale," *PMLA*, LXV (1950), 318–322.
171. Dempster, G. and Tatlock, J. S. P. "The Franklin's Tale," *Sources and Analogues of Chaucer's Canterbury Tales*, edd. W. F. Bryan and G. Dempster (Chicago, 1941; reprinted New York, 1958), pp. 377–397.
172. Foulet, L. "Le Prologue du *Franklin's Tale* et les lais Bretons," *Zfr P*, XXX (1906), 698–711.
173. Harrison, B. S. "The Rhetorical Inconsistency of Chaucer's Franklin," *SP*, XXXII (1935), 55–61.
174. Hart, W. M. "The Franklin's Tale," *Haverford Essays: Studies in Modern Literature* (Haverford, Pa., 1909), pp. 185–234.
175. Hibbard (Loomis), Laura A. (items 24–26 above).
176. Holman, C. H. "Courtly Love in the Merchant's and Franklin's Tales," *ELH*, XVIII (1951), 241–252.
177. Lowes, J. L. "*The Franklin's Tale, Teseida*, and the *Filocolo*," *MP*, XV (1918), 689–728.
178. Lumiansky, R. M. "The Character and Performance of Chaucer's Franklin," *UTQ*, XX (1951), 344–356.

ADDENDA TO KING ORPHEUS BIBILOGRAPHY

Allen, Dorena. "Orpheus and Orfeo: The Dead and the Taken," *Med. AEv.*, XXXIII (1963), 102–111.

Hill, D. M. "The Structure of 'Sir Orfeo'," *Med. St.*, XXIII (1961), 136–153.

Mitchell, B. "The Fairy World of Sir Orfeo," *Neophil.*, LVIII (1963), 155–159.

The manuscript was prepared for publication by Ralph Busick. The book was designed by Edgar Frank. The type face used is Linotype Granjon designed by George W. Jones in 1924 and based on a design originally executed by Claude Garamond in the sixteenth century. The display face is Garamont which was designed by Frederic W. Goudy.

The book is printed on Warren's Olde Style Antique and bound in Columbia Mills' Riverside Linen over boards. Manufactured in the United States of America.